From Centralised to Decentralising Global Economic Architecture

Pradumna B. Rana · Xianbai Ji
Editors

From Centralised to Decentralising Global Economic Architecture

The Asian Perspective

palgrave
macmillan

Editors
Pradumna B. Rana
S. Rajaratnam School of International Studies
Nanyang Technological University
Singapore, Singapore

Xianbai Ji
School of International Studies
Renmin University of China
Beijing, China

ISBN 978-981-19-2040-0 ISBN 978-981-19-2041-7 (eBook)
https://doi.org/10.1007/978-981-19-2041-7

Cover illustration: Maram_shutterstock.com

This Palgrave Macmillan imprint is published by the registered company Springer Nature Singapore Pte Ltd.
The registered company address is: 152 Beach Road, #21-01/04 Gateway East, Singapore 189721, Singapore

Foreword

The global economic architecture of the post-World War II period, comprising the international monetary system, the global trading system, and the international economic development framework, was designed by the advanced economies of the West. They also dominated the leadership and decision-making at the IMF, GATT/WTO, and the World Bank with the so-called Washington Consensus providing the intellectual foundation. This system of global economic governance worked well for several decades and brought long-term economic growth and prosperity all over the world.

Presently, however, the balance of economic and financial power is shifting towards the emerging market economies, especially in Asia. These emerging markets have demanded greater voice and representation at the IMF and the World Bank. But the pace of reforms that would grant these economies larger vote and quota shares at these Bretton Woods institutions has been slow. Dissatisfaction with global institutions and great power politics has led emerging markets to establish new regional institutions and to embark on initiatives to provide various types of regional public goods.

With the proliferation of new regional institutions since the 1990s, the centralised global economic architecture has been decentralising and becoming multi-layered with the co-existence of a "senior" global institution and a number of regional institutions catering to contemporary needs.

This book addresses the important question of how the on-going move from centralised multilateralism to decentralising multilateralism has affected global economic governance and the provision of global public goods. A related question is how much global and regional public goods emerging market economies will be able to provide to help maintain financial stability, open trading regimes, and sustainable economic development.

A further question is how the decentralisation process might evolve after the COVID-19 pandemic and what policies should be adopted by the global and regional institutions to manage that process.

The book uses an innovative benefit-risk analysis and concludes that the benefits of decentralisation and creation of new regional institutions have outweighed the risks.

The book concludes that decentralisation of the global economic architecture has, therefore, not led to fragmentation and deterioration of global economic governance, so far.

The book argues that the decentralisation process is expected to continue in the post-pandemic period as new regional institutions are established and they seek to implement relevant policies that should be adopted both by global and regional institutions to manage the decentralisation process.

One of the editors of the book, Pradumna Rana, has many years of experience at the Asian Development Bank. The other, Xianbai Ji, is a faculty member of Renmin University of China and has a PhD in International Political Economy from the S. Rajaratnam School of International Studies (RSIS) in Singapore's Nanyang Technological University. The book grew out of years of academic exchange and joint research by Rana and Jason (as Xianbai is known in Singapore). I commend them for the wonderful work and their continued research collaboration.

Besides policymakers, the book is also a valuable resource for those in academia, think tanks, development institutions, as well as students and interested general readers. It will be a welcome contribution to the growing literature on multilateralism, regionalism, and the provision of global and regional public goods.

As a small city-state, Singapore's survival depends on its economy and its role in the global and regional marketplace. Singapore is, therefore, active in global institutions such as the WTO and IMF. It is fully committed to regional institutions such as ASEAN and APEC. Singapore plays an active role in the newly established mega-FTAs—CPTPP and RCEP—and the high-standard Digital Economy Partnership Agreements signed by the increasingly digitalised economies of the region and beyond.

Singapore keenly follows the evolving relationship between global and regional institutions and its impact on global economic governance and delivery of various global and regional public goods. For example, Singapore is a founding member and the current Chair of the Global Governance Group at the UN in New York. This is an informal grouping of small and medium-sized countries that seeks greater representation/participation in policy dialogues and exchanges, such as the G20 process, for more effective governance of the global economic architecture, particularly the multilateral trading system, inclusive international finance, and a long-term sustainable development framework.

This book provides the relevant backdrop and setting on the external factors and institutions which are important for Singapore's economic diplomacy and policy development. The readers will likely get a fuller appreciation of the challenges facing small states and their economic future.

Ambassador Ong Keng Yong
Executive Deputy Chairman
S. Rajaratnam School
of International Studies
Nanyang Technological University
Singapore, Singapore

Preface

The idea for this book came up from the course on global economic governance that Pradumna B. Rana teaches at the S. Rajaratnam School of International Studies in Singapore. Xianbai Ji (Jason), who has been conducting joint research with Rana for many years, strongly encouraged Rana to go ahead and complete this book project. Also, an earlier book that Rana edited together with his colleagues in 2014, entitled *New Global Economic Architecture: The Asian Perspective*, needed to be updated in a fast-changing world of global economic governance. The central thesis of that book was that the global economic governance architecture was starting to show signs of decentralisation as a host of new regional economic institutions was being established by non-Western emerging economies and led by them. Since the publication of the book, several notable developments attesting to the book's prescient arguments have taken place across international trade, economic development, and monetary dimensions of global economic governance.

In the field of international trade, the Regional Comprehensive Economic Partnership (RCEP) backed jointly by China and the Association of Southeast Asian Nations (ASEAN) has taken effect from January 2022. Overshadowing the European Single Market and the United States-Mexico-Canada Agreement, RCEP is on course to being the world's largest regional free trade bloc. The Comprehensive and Progressive Agreement for Trans-Pacific Partnership (CPTPP) involving eleven countries on the Pacific Rim—which went into force in end 2018 and has attracted membership applications from Britain, China, South Korea, and Thailand. Together with RCEP, the two mega-scale regional trade deal will likely pave the way for the eventual establishment of the Free Trade Area of the Asia-Pacific. In relation to economic development, the Asian Infrastructure Investment Bank (AIIB) based in Beijing opened for business in 2016 and has become a "leaner, cleaner and greener" alternative to the World Bank in Washington, DC. The AIIB has also played an important role in the context of the Belt and Road Initiative personally championed by President Xi Jinping as his foreign policy signature campaign. The BRICS New Development Bank established in 2015 has taken major steps to multilateralise its operation, management, and relevance by admitting new members such as Bangladesh, United Arab Emirates, Uruguay, and Egypt.

In the monetary and financial sector, the Chinese renminbi was added to the International Monetary Fund's special drawing rights "basket" in 2016 and the ascendency of digital currencies, private and central bank-issued, has undoubtedly had implications for the prevailing global monetary order. The fourth and a new pillar of the global economic architecture, the international financial regulation architecture has also gained traction with the increased incidence of financial crises, among others, the Asian Financial Crisis, the Global Financial Crisis, and the Eurozone crisis.

Also, in terms of oversight bodies of global economic governance, a proper division of labour and complementarity must be found between the G20, G7, and specialised international economic institutions.

To do justice to these crucial developments bearing important systematic implications for the future of global economic governance, a new book (in some way as a sequel to the aforementioned book) was called for. We decided to respond by coming up with this edited volume. Three chapters of this volume have been reprinted with kind permission from copyright holders who are herewith acknowledged: John Wiley & Sons for the article "Rise of Complementarity between Global and Regional Financial Institutions: Perspectives from Asia", *Global Policy* 9(2), May 2018; Springer Nature for the article "Promoting regional development bank complementarity: challenges to Asia and lessons from Europe", *Asia Europe Journal* 15(3), September 2017; and World Scientific for the article "The Decentralizing International Trade Architecture: Perspectives from and Role of Asia", *The Singapore Economic Review* 66(1), 2021. Though not making substantial revisions, the contributors have updated the original drafts. Some factual information has been added and errors corrected. We would like to thank all the contributors from Singapore, Beijing, and London for their kind cooperation.

The book project received support from the Centre for Multilateralism Studies of the S. Rajaratnam School of International Studies in Singapore and the International Political Economy of the Global Currency System Platform and the Major Innovation & Planning Interdisciplinary Platform for the "Double-First Class" Initiative of Renmin University of China. We are also grateful for the support and encouragement of Ambassador Ong Keng Yong, Dean Ralf Emmers, Dean Yang Guangbin, Associate Dean Di Dongsheng, and Professor Yang Dong in steering the book project towards successful completion. Thanks are also due to Associate Professor Alan Chong, Dr Guanie Lim, Wang Xueying, Yang Xinxu, Qi Weiqun, and other colleagues in Singapore and Beijing.

In relation to Palgrave Macmillan, a special word of thanks goes to Kumaravel Senbagaraj, Vishal Daryanomel, Ruth Jenner, Chitra Gopalraj, Karnika, and two anonymous proposal reviewers for their kind help, assistance, patience, and above all the professional manner in which they handled our proposal and manuscript publication.

Finally, we are both grateful to our families for their continued support without which this edited volume could not have been prepared.

Singapore, Singapore
Beijing, China
January 2022

Pradumna B. Rana
Xianbai Ji

Contents

1 **Introduction and Overview** 1
Pradumna B. Rana and Xianbai Ji

2 **The Evolution of Global Oversight Institutions: From the Library Group to the Group of Twenty** 27
Xianbai Ji

3 **International Monetary and Economic Development Architecture: Complementarity Between Global and Regional Institutions** 49
Pradumna B. Rana and Ramon Pacheco Pardo

4 **Promoting Development Bank Complementarity in Asia** 87
Xianbai Ji

5 **Reforming the Global Reserve System** 113
Pradumna B. Rana and Elgin Chan

6 **The Evolving International Monetary System: Will Dollar Hegemony Outlive the Digital Revolution?** 131
Xueying Wang, Dongsheng Di, and Ruiling Liu

7 **Managing the Decentralising International Trade Architecture** 161
Pradumna B. Rana, Wai-Mun Chia, and Xianbai Ji

8 **Strengthening the International Financial Regulation Architecture** 197
Pradumna B. Rana

Index 217

Notes on Contributors

Chan Elgin has more than 16 years of experience at investment banks in New York and Hong Kong, where he was most recently Head of Trading, Managing Director, at China Everbright Bank International (CEBI). Before joining CEBI, Elgin was an Executive Director at Mizuho Securities Asia Ltd. Elgin holds a master's in Statistics from Columbia University and a bachelor's in economics (Honours) from Rutgers University, and is currently pursuing a master's in International Political Economy at Nanyang Technological University's S. Rajaratnam School of International Studies.

Chia Wai-Mun is Associate Professor of Economics at the School of Social Sciences, Nanyang Technological University. Her research covers topics in International Macroeconomics and Cost-Benefit Analysis (CBA). She is an associate editor of the Singapore Economic Review and the Treasurer of the Economic Society of Singapore and Singapore Economic Review since 2017. In 2011, she was awarded the National Day Commendation Award for her contributions in teaching and research. She holds a PhD from Nanyang Technological University, a MSc from London School of Economics, and a BSc from University of London, all in economics.

Di Dongsheng is Associate Dean and Professor of International Political Economy/ World Economy at the School of International Studies, Renmin University of China (RUC). He is also Senior Research Fellow at International Monetary Institute (IMI) of the RUC. His research interest covers topics such as the politics and economics of global currency and financial issues, as well as Chinese foreign economic relations. Since obtaining his PhD in 2004 from the RUC, he has published several books, dozens of papers, and hundreds of op-ed articles in both Chinese and English. In 2019, his new book *The Power of Money: Relations among Politics, the Market and the People* was published by China Social Science Press.

Ji Xianbai is Associate Professor and Distinguished Young Scholar at the School of International Studies, Renmin University of China (RUC). He is also Executive Director of the International Political Economy Research Centre, Director of Continuing Education Office, and Research Fellow at the Institute of International Development Studies, all housed at the School. He obtained his doctorate from the S. Rajaratnam School of International Studies, Nanyang Technological University (NTU), Singapore where he was a Nanyang President's Graduate Scholar. His recent book publications include *Mega-regionalism and Great Power Geo-economic Competition* (2021) and *China's Belt and Road Initiative: Impacts on Asia and Policy Agenda* (2020). Prior to RUC, he held research and visiting positions at NTU, The Australian National University, and the European Union Centre in Singapore.

Liu Ruiling is pursuing her master's degree in Economics at the London School of Economics and Political Science (LSE). She obtained her bachelor's degree in International Politics from the Renmin University of China (RUC), with quantitative courses taken at the Columbia University and University of California Los Angeles. She is interested in international political economy, international trade, international finance, political economy of development, government and business, as well as innovation.

Pacheco Pardo Ramon is Professor of International Relations at King's College London and the KF-VUB Korea Chair at the Brussels School of Governance of Vrije Universiteit Brussel. He is also King's Regional Envoy for East and Southeast Asia, helping to shape and implement the university's strategy for the region. Prof Pacheco Pardo is also Adjunct Fellow (Non-Resident) with the Korea Chair at CSIS and Committee Member at CSCAP EU. He has held visiting positions at Korea University, the Lee Kuan Yew School of Public Policy, and Melbourne University.

Prof Pacheco Pardo has been editor of *Millennium: Journal of International Studies* and currently sits in the editorial boards of *East Asia: An International Quarterly*, *EU-China Observer* and *Global Studies Journal*. His publications include the book *North Korea-US Relations from Kim Jong Il to Kim Jong Un*, published in 2019.

Rana Pradumna B. is Senior Fellow at the S. Rajaratnam School of International Studies, Nanyang Technological University (NTU), Singapore. He is International Economist with expertise in the areas of international macroeconomics, trade, and development issues focusing on Asia. He was Senior Director of the Asian Development Bank's Office of Regional Economic Integration which spearheaded ADB's support for Asian economic integration. Prior to that, he held various senior positions at the ADB for many years. He has taught at NTU, National University of Singapore, and the Tribhuvan University, Nepal. He obtained his PhD from Vanderbilt University where he was a Fulbright Scholar and a master's in Economics from Michigan State University and Tribhuvan University where he was a gold medallist. He has written widely in the areas of Asian economic development and integration, financial crises, and economic policy reforms in transition economies. These include 17 authored or edited books, over 25 chapters in books, and over 50 articles in international scholarly journals. His recently co-authored books are *China's Belt and Road Initiative: Impacts on Asia and Policy Agenda*, *Jumpstarting South Asia: Revisiting Economic Reforms and Look East Policies*, *South Asia: Rising to the Challenge of Globalisation*, and *Asia and the Global Economic Crisis: Challenges in a Financially Integrated World*. His recently co-edited books are *Pan-Asian Integration: Linking East and South Asia* and *National Strategies for Regional Integration: South and East Asian Case Studies*. He has written widely in internationally reputed journals such as the *Journal of International Economics, The Review of Economic and Statistics, Journal of Development Economics, World Development, International Trade Journal, Journal of Asian Economics, Singapore Economic Review, East Asian Economic Review, Global Governance, and Global Policy.*

Wang Xueying is PhD Candidate at the School of International Studies, Renmin University of China (RUC). She holds master's degrees from the RUC (World Economy) and Free University of Brussels (European Integration). Her research interest covers international monetary system, unconventional monetary policies, and European integration.

Abbreviations

3G	Global Governance Group
ABMI	Asian Bond Markets Initiative
ACP	Africa, Caribbean and Pacific
ADB	Asian Development Bank
ADF	Asian Development Fund
AFC	Asian Financial Crisis
AFSB	Asian Financial Stability Board
AIIB	Asian Infrastructure Investment Bank
ALA	Asia and Latin America
AMRO	ASEAN+3 Macroeconomic Research Office
APEC	Asia-Pacific Economic Cooperation
APTA	Asia-Pacific Trade Agreement
ASA	ASEAN Swap Arrangement
ASEAN	Association of Southeast Asian Nations
ASEAN+3 RFSN	ASEAN+3 regional financial safety net
AU	African Union
B20	Business20
BCBS	Basel Committee on Banking Supervision
BIC	Bank of International Settlements
BIS	Bank of International Settlements
BRI	Belt and Road Initiative
C20	Civil20
CAFTA	China-ASEAN Free Trade Area
CBDC	Central Bank Digital Currencies
CETA	Comprehensive Economic and Trade Agreement
CGFS	Committee on the Global Financial System

CIPS	Cross-Border Interbank Payment System
CJK	China-Japan-Korea
CMI	Chiang Mai Initiative
CMIM	Chiang Mai Initiative Multilateralisation
COVID-19	Coronavirus pandemic
CPMI	Committee on Payments and Market Infrastructure
CPSS	Committee on Payments and Settlements System
CPTPP	Comprehensive and Progressive Agreement for Trans-Pacific Partnership
CRA	Contingent Reserve Arrangement
CRTA	Committee on Regional Trade Agreements
D10	Democracies Ten
DAC	Development Assistance Committee
DDA	Doha Development Agenda
DSSI	Debt Service Suspension Initiative
EBRD	European Bank for Reconstruction and Development
EC	European Commission
ECB	European Central Bank
ECSC	European Coal and Steel Community
EEC	European Economic Community
EIB	European Investment Bank
EIF	European Investment Fund
ERPD	Economic Review and Policy Dialogue
ESAs	European Supervisory Authorities
ESFS	European System of Financial Supervision
ESM	European Stability Mechanism
EU	European Union
FDI	Foreign Direct Investment
FSAP	Financial Sector Assessment Programme
FSB	Financial Stability Board
FSF	Financial Stability Forum
FTAAP+	expanded Free Trade Area of the Asia-Pacific
G20	Group of Twenty
G7	Group of Seven
G8	Group of Eight
GATT	General Agreement on Tariffs and Trade
GCC	Gulf Cooperation Council
GEA	Global Economic Architecture
GFA	Global Financial Architecture
GFC	Global Financial Crisis
GFSN	Global Financial Safety Net
GRS	Global Reserve System
IAIS	International Association of Insurance Supervisors

IASC	International Accounting Standards Committee
IBRD	International Bank for Reconstruction and Development
ICSID	International Centre for Settlement of Investment Disputes
ICU	International Clearing Union
IDA	International Development Association
IEI	International Economic Institution
IFC	International Finance Corporation
IFI	International Financial Institution
IFRA	International Financial Regulation Architecture
IMF	International Monetary Fund
INGO	International Non-Governmental Organisation
IOSCO	International Organization of Securities Commissions
ISI	Import Substitution Industrialisation
ITO	International Trade Organisation
JEEPA	Japan-EU Economic Partnership Agreement
L20	Labour20
LARF	Latin American Reserve Fund
M2P	Mega-regionalism-to-Plurilateralism
MAP	Mutual Assessment Process
MDB	Multilateral Development Bank
MFN	Most-Favoured-Nation
MIGA	Multilateral Investment Guarantee Agency
MNC	Multi-National Corporation
MOU	Memorandum of Understanding
MSME	Micro, Small- and Medium-Sized Enterprise
NAFTA	North American Free Trade Agreement
NBW	New Bretton Woods
NDB	New Development Bank
NEPAD	New Partnership for Africa's Development
NTM	Non-Tariff Measure
OCR	Ordinary Capital Resources
OECD	Organisation for Economic Co-operation and Development
PA	Plurilateral Trade Agreement
RCEP	Regional Comprehensive Economic Partnership
RMB	Renminbi
RMU	Regional Monetary Unit
ROSC	Review of Standards and Code
RST	Resilience and Sustainability Trust
RTA	Regional Trade Agreement
S20	Science20
SAARC	South Asian Association for Regional Cooperation
SDF	SAARC Development Fund
SDR	Special Drawing Rights

SME	Small and Medium Sized Enterprise
SSB	Standard Setting Body
T20	Think20
TAG	Trade Agreement on Goods
TPP	Trans-Pacific Partnership
TTC	Trade and Technology Council
TTIP	Transatlantic Trade and Investment Partnership
U20	Urban20
US	United States
W20	Women20
WB	World Bank
WFO	World Finance Organisation
WTO	World Trade Organisation
Y20	Youth20

List of Figures

Fig. 3.1	Centralised global financial safety net	56
Fig. 3.2	Decentralising GFSN (global financial safety net)	57
Fig. 3.3	Decentralising economic development architecture	67
Fig. 4.1	Comparison of geographical composition of EIB's and EBRD's cumulative investment, 1991–2014	101
Fig. 6.1	Global share of major currencies	134
Fig. 6.2	Balance sheets of major central banks	137
Fig. 6.3	US current account deficits and inflation rates since 1960	139
Fig. 6.4	Deindustrialisation in the US	142
Fig. 6.5	Correlation between financial crises and dollar index	144
Fig. 6.6	RMB Internationalisation Index	146
Fig. 6.7	Federal debt and interest payments	148
Fig. 6.8	Comparison of US dollar and euro uses as worldwide payment currency	151
Fig. 7.1	Rising popularity of RTAs	163
Fig. 7.2	Pre-WTO centralised international trade architecture	166
Fig. 7.3	The decentralising international trade architecture post-GFC	174
Fig. 7.4	The governance trilemma and two plausible ways to reform the WTO	184
Fig. 8.1	Post-AFC IFRA	202
Fig. 8.2	Post-GFC IFRA	206

List of Tables

Table 3.1	Structured ASEAN+3 RFSN and IMF cooperation	62
Table 3.2	Details on traditional and non-traditional MDBs	69
Table 3.3	Traditional MDBs changing priorities and operations	72
Table 3.4	World Bank and ADB agreements with AIIB and NDB	77
Table 4.1	Comparisons of properties of EIB, EBRD, ADB and AIIB	93
Table 4.2	Selected projects co-financed by AIIB and ADB	106
Table 5.1	SDR Allocations by Level of Development	121
Table 6.1	Volatility in the financial markets of various countries in 2008	141
Table 6.2	GDP and reserve currency shares of major regions, 2020	144
Table 7.1	Rising regionalism in Asia	168

CHAPTER 1

Introduction and Overview

Pradumna B. Rana and Xianbai Ji

Introduction

The contemporary global economic architecture (GEA) traces its origin to the Bretton Woods Conference of 1944, formally known as the United Nations Monetary and Financial Conference, where delegates from 44 allied nations of the West pondered on ways in which the post-war economic, financial and monetary relations and transactions between countries could be governed and regulated (Bordo and Eichengreen 1993; Steil 2013). Participating countries were eager to avoid the destructive trade dynamics, financial imbalances and price instability that led to the outbreaks of the two world wars and the Great Depression of the 1930s (Kindleberger 2013). For purposes of global economic governance

P. B. Rana
S. Rajaratnam School of International Studies, Nanyang Technological University, Singapore, Singapore
e-mail: prana@ntu.edu.sg

X. Ji (✉)
School of International Studies, Renmin University of China, Beijing, China
e-mail: xbji@ruc.edu.cn

P. B. Rana and X. Ji (eds.), *From Centralised to Decentralising Global Economic Architecture*, https://doi.org/10.1007/978-981-19-2041-7_1

and international macroeconomic coordination, a set of global international economic institutions (IEIs) was established at the Bretton Woods Conference.

The IEIs charged with providing global public goods initially included the International Monetary Fund (IMF) and the International Bank for Reconstruction and Development (IBRD). In 1945, the former came into existence with the mandate of ensuring exchange rate stability and prohibiting the manipulation of national currency for trade competitiveness purposes. As its name reveals, the latter institution was founded in 1944 to finance and facilitate the reconstruction of the war-torn European nations (Kapur et al. 1997). At the United Nations Conference on Trade and Employment held in 1947, the General Agreement on Tariffs and Trade (GATT) was negotiated and the creation of an International Trade Organisation (ITO) to operate alongside the IMF and the World Bank was proposed. However, the US Congress refused to give its consent to the ITO, and since 1950 the GATT served as the de facto international agreement to promote and regulate world trade.

This rules-based, institutionally centralised GEA and its pillars, the international monetary architecture or the global financial safety net (GFSN), and the economic development and the international trade architectures, quickly put the world economy devastated by the two wars on the recovery track (Vonyó 2008). Although uneven, the post-war economic booms of the 1950s, 1960s, and early 1970s were seen as among the world's fastest periods of economic growth (Wangwe and Kawamura 2018). This was because the Bretton Woods international monetary system of adjustably pegged exchange rate regimes kept inflation low, produced domestic and international monetary stability and prevented competitive devaluation of national currencies in pursuit of export competitiveness (Bordo 1993). The World Bank (of which the IBRD is a part, see below) also played an important role in the rapid recovery and rebuilding of the European economies and subsequently the newly independent developing countries. In addition to capital provision, thanks to what is referred to as "concentration of talent" (Mallaby 2004) the World Bank also gradually established itself as the centre and source of knowledge and policy advice in areas of economic development. The GATT, though falling short of being a formal institution like the aborted ITO, liberalised trade by slashing tariffs, facilitated industrial development, and brokered rules of transparency and openness. Eight rounds of multilateral negotiating managed to reduce tariffs from approximately 40% average immediately after World War II to less than 10% when GATT was upgraded to the World Trade Organisation (WTO) in 1995. These developments helped the course of globalisation and knitted national economies into an inter-dependent world marketplace.

Overtime, with the proliferation of new regional institutions, this GEA has become progressively decentralised. These new regional institutions include for example regional financial safety nets (RFSNs), regional trade agreements (RTAs) and regional development banks. Decentralisation or multi-layering means the co-existence of "senior" global IEIs with a plethora of newly established regional IEIs in a particular policy area. With the decentralisation of the GEA, global economic governance has become more complicated. What are the factors that are driving the decentralisation process? Has the decentralisation process contributed to or fragmented global economic governance and the provision of transnational public goods? Are the global Bretton Woods institutions and the emerging regional IEIs destined for inter-institutional conflict and confrontation? If no, is there scope for a division of labour between the two based on their comparative advantages and their respective mandates? Alternatively, could "unhealthy " competition between IEIs that might lead to duplication of efforts and a "race to the bottom" in standards be replaced by positive dynamics such as "functional complementarity" and "healthy" competition?

Against this background, the objectives of this edited volume are fourfold: (i) to describe and analyse the establishment of global and regional international economic institutions from the Bretton Woods period to the present; (ii) to discuss the evolution of the global economic architecture, comprising the monetary, economic development, international trade and international financial regulation architectures; (iii) to identify various benefits (namely, "healthy" competition and functional complementarity) and risks (namely "unhealthy" competition) associated with the decentralisation process and assess whether the benefits outweigh the risks; and (iv) to assess how the decentralisation process might evolve in the post-pandemic period and offer recommendations to manage the process. The volume also discusses proposals to reform the international monetary system including the global reserve system with a focus on how to reduce the hegemony of the US dollar. Asia's role in the decentralising GEA is also identified.

The remainder of this chapter is structured as follows. The next section discusses various interpretations and manifestations of the decentralisation process from the global perspective. The section that follows defines the scope of our study. The next section focuses on the theoretical and analytical framework of the present volume, namely the benefit-risk analysis, which is based on the existing global governance literature. Then the chapter summarises the key findings of the various chapters in the volume. Finally, the chapter highlights the role that Asian countries could play in the decentralising GEA.

Different Interpretations of Decentralisation

The historic Bretton Woods Conference gave rise to a centralised GEA with its three pillars. A decentralisation process has been unfolding in the past few decades. Specifically, decentralisation manifests itself in four related ways.

First, while in the past only a handful of countries participated in the process of global economic governance, today the participation in global economic governance has been nearly universal. The number of countries that took part in the Bretton Woods Conference in 1944 was 44. These 44 countries were the original members of the IMF and the World Bank. Now, the IMF's membership embraces 190 countries, with staff drawn from 150 nations. The World Bank is owned and governed by 189 member states,[1] with each country represented on the Board of Governors. The World Bank's staff from over 170 countries work in offices in more than 130 countries. As to GATT, the number of negotiating parties increased from 23 during the Geneva Round of 1947 to 123 in the Uruguay Round of 1986–1994. The WTO now has 164 members plus 25 countries with observer status. While Europe and the United States enjoy a monopoly on the top posts of the IMF and the World Bank, the expansion of membership of the Bretton Woods institutions has helped to reduce the political centrality and policy influence of the Western advanced economies, to some extent, in relation to international economic governance (Luckhurst 2018). Membership in global institutions gives every country regardless of size and development level some say, however small, over the management of the world economy.

[1] Kosovo is a member of the IMF but not a member of the World Bank.

Notably, in the twenty-first century, the appointment of the WTO's director-general was made largely to favour contending candidates from developing countries (with the exception of the Pascal Lamy, a French national, between 2005 and 2013). In a sense, decentralisation of GEA is synonymous with de-Westernisation and the "rise of the rest" in global economic governance (Kahler 2013; Stephen 2017).

Second, within global institutions themselves, decentralisation took the form of expanding the narrowly conceived mandates at Bretton Woods and internal functional diversification in part to assist in the achievement of either shifting institutional objectives or new governance challenges that came up as times changed. This is most evident in regard to the intra-World Bank institutional development (Delivorias 2016). With an initial purpose of helping Europe rebuild after World War II, the IBRD has gradually prioritised worldwide poverty reduction and the promotion of private sector as its key missions. The IBRD's private-sector arm, the International Financial Corporation (IFC), came into being in 1956 with the objective of jumpstarting private-sector-led economic growth in countries. Its concessional loan arm, the International Development Association (IDA), was set up in 1960 to channel loans and grants to the poorest countries of the world. When international investment and the advancement of multinational corporations became new sources of international development, the World Bank, a parental partnership of the IBRD, IDA and the IFC, responded by creating the International Centre for Settlement of Investment Disputes (ICSID) to mediate disagreements and disputes between international investors and host countries. A complement of the ICSID, the Multilateral Investment Guarantee Agency (MIGA) was created in 1988 as the investment insurance affiliate of the World Bank Group. MIGA's mission also evolved from insuring international investment against non-commercial and political risks to leveraging foreign direct investment for economic development in developing countries.

Third, the "central authority" in the global economic architecture once accorded nearly exclusively to Bretton Woods institutions is decentralising and "pluralising" (Gordenker and Weiss 1995) to incorporate non-governmental and subnational policy actors in any given area of global governance (Kahler 2018). The number of international non-governmental organisations (INGOs) built around labour union, humanitarian aid purposes, environmentalist groups, occupational associations, academic communities, religiously affiliated entities, etc. has exploded from 832 in 1951 to 9176 in 2017 (Gotz 2019). The vast number of INGOs shape outcomes of global economic governance through, for example, forging structured or improvised INGO-IEI engagement mechanisms (Ruhlman 2019), providing forum shopping opportunities (Murphy and Kellow 2013), raising domestic and transnational awareness of the stakes of global economic governance in certain policy areas, such as (de)legitimising the decisions of IEIs, bridging local norms and global values (Castells 2005), locking in reforms of the international system (Murazzani 2009), depoliticising global governance, holding IEIs to account, and addressing functional governance deficits.

Last but not the least, the decentralisation of the GEA is marked by the proliferation of regional IEIs in an environment where "senior" global IEIs already exist (Rana 2014). The year 1958 saw the establishment of the first regional development bank, the European Investment Bank. Two waves of MDB-building followed as the United States and the Soviet Union battled for influence in various parts of the world (Engen and Prizzon 2018). Six regional multilateral development banks (MDBs) were created in the 1960s—they were the Central American Bank for Economic Integration (1960[2]), African Development Bank (1963), Asian Development Bank (ADB, 1966), East African Development Bank (1967), Arab Fund for Economic and Social Development (1968) and Caribbean Development Bank (1969). In the 1970s, seven new MDBs were established including the Development Bank of Latin America (1970), International Investment Bank (1970), West African Development Bank (1973), Arab Bank for Economic Development in Africa (1974), Development Bank of the Central African States (1975), Islamic Development Bank (1975) and OPEC Fund for International Development (1976). From 1980s onwards, the enthusiasm for establishing new regional MDBs cooled. A few notable regional MDBs created since then are Trade and Development Bank (1985), European Bank for Reconstruction and Development (1991), Black Sea Trade and Development Bank (1997), ECOWAS Bank for Investment and Development (2003), ECO Trade and Development Bank (2005), Eurasian Development Bank (2006), New Development Bank (NDB, 2014) and the Asian Infrastructure Investment Bank (AIIB, 2015). The majority of new MDBs were created and led by developing countries.

[2] This, as the years below, refers to the year in which treaty was signed. The MDB normally became operative in the following year.

In the field of international trade, regional trade agreements (RTAs) that involve only a subset of WTO members have gained sustained popularity. As of January 2022, a total of 573 physical RTAs had been notified, of which 353 are currently in force. The participation in RTAs is also ubiquitous with all WTO members taking part in at least one regional trade accord. From a chronological perspective, the emergence of international trade regionalism can be divided into three phases. The first wave of trade regionalism occurred in the 1950s and 1960s (WTO 2011) when post-war Europe started embarking on the journey of German-Franco reconciliation and regional integration lasting till today. The transformation of the European Coal and Steel Community into the European Economic Community (EEC) and the subsequent creation of the supposedly rival pact, the European Free Trade Association in 1957–1958, together with the development of the Andean Pact and the Central American Common Market among mostly developing countries, marked this phase of regional trade liberalisation and integration. In the early to mid-1990s, the "second wave" of trade regionalism (Bhagwati 1999) took place in a post-Cold War bi-polar world. The Southern Cone Common Market (Mercosur) was set up in 1991; the Association of Southeast Asian Nations (ASEAN) Free Trade Area and the European Single Market came into existence in 1993; the North American Free Trade Agreement (Tomlin and Cameron 2000; Hufbauer and Schott 2005), the Common Market for Eastern and Southern Africa and the African Economic Community were established in 1994. The latest wave of trade regionalism began in the mid-2000s. This wave was underpinned by mega-free trade agreements (mega-FTAs) which are in a category of their own by virtue of their size, scope, depth, impact and implication. Mega-FTAs can be defined as "deep integration partnerships between countries or regions with a major share of world trade and foreign direct investment (FDI), and in which two or more of the parties are in a paramount driver position, or serve as hubs, in global value chains" (Meléndez-Ortiz 2014). The most systemically influential mega-FTAs were to be the Trans-Pacific Partnership (TPP), the Regional Comprehensive Economic Partnership (RCEP) and the Transatlantic Trade and Investment Partnership (TTIP). While the negotiation for TTIP lapsed, the TPP agreement known now as the Comprehensive and Progressive Agreement for Trans-Pacific Partnership (CPTPP) with the withdrawal of the United States and the RCEP-minus-India have both entered into force with profound economic implications for participants and the world economy at large

(Petri et al. 2021; Jiang and Yu 2021). It is worth stressing that RCEP region is slated to be the world's largest regional trade bloc. Calls have been made for an orderly merger of the CPTPP and RCEP to form the Free Trade Area of the Asia-Pacific (Ji et al. 2018; Ji and Rana 2019).

As with trade regionalism, it was Europe that took in the lead in championing financial regionalism (Rhee et al. 2013). The first regional financial safety net (RFSN) was the EEC Medium-Term Financial Assistance arrangement established in 1971 to offer medium-term financial assistance for balance of payments difficulties confronting EEC members. It evolved into the European Financial Stabilisation Mechanism in 2010 which was later subsumed (together with the European Financial Stability Facility) by the wider European Stability Mechanism, a permanent crisis resolution mechanism for the eurozone countries, in 2012 (Bauer and Herz 2020). In the Gulf region, the Arab Monetary Fund was established in 1976 as a sub-working group of the Arab League; it was charged with correcting balance of payments disequilibria and promoting exchange rate stability. In Latin America, *Fondo Latinoamericano de Reservas* (Latin America Reserve Fund) was founded in 1989, to replace the smaller Andean Reserve Fund, and to provide balance of payment support as well as to harmonise monetary, fiscal and exchange rate policies across member states (Ocampo and Titelman 2012). In Central Asia, the Eurasian Economic Community members established an anti-crisis instrument—the EurAsEC Anti-Crisis Fund—in 2009 to counteract the effects of the Global Financial Crisis (GFC) and promote economic integration. The fund was renamed as the Eurasian Fund for Stabilisation and Development in 2015. The establishment of regional financial safety net in Asia is comparatively more recent. An ASEAN Swap Arrangement (ASA) was set up in 1977 to provide mutual liquidity support among members' central banks and monetary authorities in case of balance of payment difficulties. ASA paved the way for the adoption of the Chiang Mai Initiative (CMI) in 2000 in the aftermath of the Asian Financial Crisis (AFC) of 1997–1998. The CMI was multilateralised in 2010 to become the Chiang Mai Initiative Multilateralisation (CMIM)[3] (Sussangkarn 2011; Park 2017;

[3] At this point, the CMIM is designed to supplement the IMF financing. Its nature of a "self-help" mechanism has been gradually increased from 10%, 20% in 2010, 30% in 2014. As of 2021, the delinked portion stands at 40%. This is also reflecting the progress of regionalism. However, it will take a long time for Asia to reach 100% and to form its own financial regionalism due to geopolitical reasons.

Pitakdumrongkit 2018). To provide technical support to the operation of the CMIM, the ASEAN+3 Macroeconomic Research Office (AMRO) was founded in 2011 as its analysis and surveillance arm (Khor et al. 2021). The utility and effectiveness of the CMIM remain in question as it has never been activated since its establishment.

In the aftermath of the AFC, work on building the fourth pillar of the GEA, the international financial regulation architecture, started with the establishment of the Financial Stability Forum (FSF) as the focal point of financial regulation initiatives. The FSF brought together national financial regulators to discuss internationally accepted financial standards and reduce cross-border regulatory discrepancies but was also criticised for membership politics and exclusiveness because it locked out less developed countries (Liberi 2003). The FSF was upgraded by the Group of Twenty (G20) countries to the Financial Stability Board (FSB) in 2009 in response to the Global Financial Crisis. The FSF comprised only national financial authorities of the Group of Seven (G7) leading industrialised countries, but the FSB comprises countries that form the G20 grouping which incorporates the G7 countries and a handful of leading emerging economies such as China (Kirton 2016), India, South Africa and Brazil. In the process, GEA is also gradually moving away from a rules-based to a more informal network-based system without any legal backing (Benson and Zürn 2019; Roger 2020). The G20, for instance, is a loosely structured leaders' network without a permanent secretariat (Hajnal 2019; Cooper 2010). The FSB is also a network of institutions that focus on international financial regulations from various jurisdictions.

At the height of the GFC, several academics and politicians had made calls for a "New Bretton Woods (NBW)" (Rana 2010; Stiglitz 2008; Rajan 2009; Helleiner 2010) meaning a comprehensive reform of the old GEA. These calls for the NBW did not materialise mainly because the economic rebound from GFC turned out to be faster than expected and complacency set in. There have no such calls during the pandemic period except for the recent proposal by Indonesia to establish a Global Health Agency (Arshad 2022). Looking forward, in the post-pandemic world, the GEA is expected to continue its incremental move towards a more network-based decentralising/multi-layered system where regional institutions work closely with "senior" global institutions. This is because the rise of populism which began after the GFC of 2008–2009 has not subsided. Instead, the severe economic hardships and inequalities caused by COVID-19 have further sharpened social divides and deepened the distrusts. The rise of populist movements has inspired greater scepticism towards globalisation, collective actions, and global IEIs. Preference may be given to sovereign national institutions and regional IEIs. To manage such a decentralised system in which regionalism and multilateralism interact, reforms of institutions at both regional and global levels are required together with actions to promote complementarity between them.

Scope of the Study

The first three aspects of the decentralisation phenomenon outlined above are important, but in this edited volume we focus on the last aspect, or the institutional decentralisation dimension, namely the rise of regional IEIs in the context where "senior" global IEIs already exist. We also focus on the proliferation of new regional institutions in Asia, since the 1990s, where dissatisfaction of dynamic emerging markets with the existing global governance system has been the key driver. This dissatisfaction arose for several reasons. First, with the economic success of China and the BRICS (Brazil, Russia, India, China and South Africa), there was a shift from a uni-polar to a multi-polar world, and these countries demanded a greater voice and role at the IMF and the World Bank.[4] Second, was the difficulty encountered in reforming the governance of the IEIs to give a greater voice to dynamic emerging markets. Kawai and Petri (2010) have applied the theory of clubs to explain this phenomenon. They conclude that the IMF and the World Bank are relatively inflexible institutions, and their governance cannot change quickly even if they wished to. Governance reform of the IMF and the World Bank has, therefore, proceeded at a slow pace. Dissatisfaction with the slow pace of governance reform at the IMF and the policy mistakes made by the IMF in managing the AFC, led the ASEAN+3 countries to initiate regional "self-help" mechanisms or the ASEAN+3 RFSN in 2000. Similarly, the

[4] Partly for this reason, the transformation of the prevailing global economic architecture towards decentralisation and de-Westernisation is structural in nature and unlikely to see fundamental reversals. Neither discrete discontent with specific regional economic arrangement nor intra-architectural discords among constituent institutional actors would propel a return to the erstwhile centralised architecture centred on the Bretton Woods institutions.

slow pace of governance reform at the World Bank partially spurred China to establish the AIIB and the BRICS to launch the NDB.

The slow progress in multilateral trade negotiations and their focus on mainly "at the border" trade issues alone also encouraged Asian countries to sign regional FTAs with various partner countries including the mega-FTAs which also cover twenty-first century "behind the border" issues relevant to supply-chain trade. Finally, in response to former President Trump's "America First" doctrine and his focus on unilateral and bilateral trade, the rest of the world led by the EU, China, and Japan provided collective leadership to champion regionalism.

From the perspective of Asia, the decentralising international monetary architecture comprises the multilateral financial safety net (i.e. the IMF) along with the ASEAN+3 RFSN (comprising the CMIM and AMRO), bilateral, and national financial safety nets (Fig. 3.2 in Chapter 3). The economic development architecture, which consists of the World Bank, regional development banks and vertical development funds, now has the new non-traditional development banks, the AIIB and the NDB (Fig. 3.3 in Chapter 3). The decentralising international trade architecture comprises the WTO, plurilateral and bilateral FTAs and mega-FTAs (CPTPP and RCEP) (Fig. 7.3 in Chapter 7). The sole exception is the international financial regulation architecture in which the FSB and the associated standard-setting bodies (SSBs), continue to remain centralised (Fig. 8.2 in Chapter 8). This is mainly because the governance system of these IEIs is relatively more egalitarian than that of the IMF and the World Bank. The G20 provides oversight of these institutions.

Theoretical Framework and Methodology

The bulk of existing literature on global economic governance and the institutions that underpin it tend to focus on competition between regional and global institutions and frame the adverse consequence of such competition in terms of fragmentation. Morse and Keohane (2014) conceptualise the contemporary multilateralism landscape as one of "contested multilateralism" characterised by "competing coalitions and shifting institutional arrangements, informal as well as formal". Contested multilateralism arises, as their argument goes, when "states and/or non-state actors either shift their focus from existing institutions to another or create an alternative multilateral institution to compete with existing ones" (Morse and Keohane 2014). In this interpretation which is alternatively known as "counter-institutionalisation" (Zürn 2018), newly established institutions are often "revisionist" and rebellious, seeking to overturn the "disadvantageous" status quo. For example, the establishment of the AIIB was seen to challenge the dominance of ADB and the World Bank in that the two Japan-led and Western-led development financing institutions did not serve the infrastructure finance needs of developing countries and China in particular (Wilson 2019). The RTAs are famously compared to "termites" in the multilateral trading system, eating away at the transparency and openness of the global free trade order (Bhagwati 2008). Similar, albeit less rhetorically alarming, are arguments about regional trade deals serving as "stumbling blocks" to multilateralism. Krishna (1998), for example, notes that RTA gives rise to vested interest that opposes multilateral trade liberalisation, thus undermining the WTO's *modus operandi*. To the extent that some RFSNs were created due to frustrations with the programmes offered by the IMF, it is often argued that the relationship between regional and global financial safety nets is competitive and contentious. The Asian Monetary Fund (AMF) proposed by Japan surfaced during the AFC but was opposed by the United States in the interest of buttressing the centrality of the Washington-dominated IMF (Hyun and Paradise 2019). The competitive relationship is also believed to be one of the reasons that Asian countries have sought to reduce the IMF -linked portion to tap CMIM resources.

Viewed through the theoretical lens of contested multilateralism, global economic governance would seem destined for fragmentation in a "regime complex" (Raustiala and Victor 2004). Competition and fragmentation may entail suboptimal governance outcomes such as resource duplication and redundancy (Landau 1969), forum shopping (Murphy-Gregory and Kellow 2016) by rationally opportunistic national governments, race-to-the-bottom in standards (Wang 2017) and inconsistency in rules and norms governing cross-border economic activities (i.e. the "spaghetti bowl" issue). We reject such pessimistic views on global economic governance. We join global governance scholars like Orsini et al. (2013) in arguing that "fragmentation" per se can be "a buzz, a boom or a boost for global governance". In support of this view, Amitav Acharya (2016) asserts that while fragmentation may be "inevitable" in a "multiplex world", "some areas of fragmentation offer major benefits and can be positive or creative", depending on how the fragmentation process is managed. Challenging Acharya on the "inevitability" of fragmentation, C. Randall Henning (2017) argues that fragmented global finance governance architecture can be avoided if guidelines on transparency, specialisation in accordance with comparative advantage and prohibited areas of competition were specified and honoured by regional and global financial organisations. Miles Kahler (2017) on his part contends that "new [regional] organizations offer additional resources for global ends, the benefits of specialization, and innovation that could improve global governance". Aynsley Kellow (2012) adds that such ratchet-up opportunities to improve the quality of global governance would not be available when "a single regime enjoyed a monopoly on governing capacity".

In a series of analytical contributions, Kahler et al. (2016) and Kahler (2017) maintain that regional organisations and initiatives can facilitate the achievement of global public policy goals but present the potential of new risks as well. They propose a benefit-risk analytical framework to determine whether the rise of regional IEIs poses a threat or a boost to the global governance. This method recognises that the decentralisation of the GEA entails both benefits and risks. The tasks of global governance scholars and practitioners alike are to find out ways of managing the process and "increasing benefits and decreasing risks" associated with the decentralisation process in the furtherance of the effectiveness, inclusiveness and legitimacy of global economic governance. Our edited volume adopts this methodology and examines whether decentralisation due to the presence of regional alternative in the presence of "senior" global IEIs leads to improved or fragmented governance outcomes in the policy domains of monetary and financial, development finance and international trade governance. In each of the policy domains under study, we detail how institutional decentralisation occurred and highlight the benefits and risks of decentralisation, before making a judgement as to whether benefits outweigh risks or vice versa. Then we make policy recommendations to shape and manage the decentralisation process to increase the benefit-risk ratio. Crucial to our analysis is the notion that there could be complementarity between regional IEIs, on the one hand, and between regional IEIs and their global counterparts, on the other. Indeed, as Gehring and Faude (2014) note, complementarity and division of labour, spontaneous or institutionalised, between IEIs allow for the emergence of order and stability within the decentralising GEA.

We and our contributors used three research methods in this volume. First, we conducted desk research to explain and analyse the creation and development of multi-layered governance architectures in the areas of finance, trade and development finance. Second, we used content analysis of official documents from global and regional institutions to analyse the extent to which cooperation and "healthy" competition will, in our view, define the relationship between global and regional institutions, as well as the limits to said cooperation. Third, we interviewed staff of international institutions and government officials including the IMF, World Bank, ADB and AIIB and the Singapore -based AMRO and APEC Policy Support Unit, for background purposes, and to clarify and support specific arguments.

Chapter Overviews

The volume comprises eight chapters organised along thematic lines, each focusing on one and at times two policy areas that are relevant to global and/or regional economic governance.

In Chapter 2, "The Evolution of Global Oversight Institutions: From the Library Group to the Group of Twenty", Xianbai Ji examines the evolution of the twin global steering committees overseeing the functioning of the GEA, namely the G7/8 and G20. First, Ji traces the evolution from the Library Group to the G7/8 and to the G20 from the 1970s to present day. The legitimacy of the global steering group was enhanced with the expansion in participation in global economic decision-making as not only the old Western powers but also the newly empowered countries from the global South now have a say over the conduct of international economic and financial relations. However, that benefit came at the expense of the effectiveness of global economic governance in that the G20 has greater membership heterogeneity than the G7 which has been underpinned by like-mindedness and interest compatibility. Ji argues that both the G7/8 and G20 as self-select elite governance groups suffer from varying degrees of substantive, input and output legitimacy—components of what can be referred to as "whole-process legitimacy". He then evaluates various proposals that are made to enhance the effectiveness-legitimacy nexus for mainly the G20. He concludes the chapter by suggesting that the two G-groupings should refocus and reposition themselves as global oversight bodies, promoting not only mutual complementarity among themselves but also between themselves and a wide swath of functional international governance institutions. Given that the G20 has greater input legitimacy than the G7, he argues that the G20 should focus on the provision of truly global public goods such as monetary and financial stability, trade openness, global poverty reduction, and pandemic control. The G7 should focus on geopolitical issues, peace, stability and other areas of interest to industrial countries. In the provision of global public goods, the G20 should also consider the role of specialised international institutions that have a proven track record and define complementary roles. The G20 was not meant to save the world from all its problems, after all.

In Chapter 3, "International Monetary and Economic Development Architectures: Complementarity Between Global and Regional Institutions", Pradumna B. Rana and Ramon Pacheco Pardo explain why despite over 20 years in the making, the ASEAN+3 RFSN has not yet been utilised. In contrast to RFSNs in other parts of the world which were used during the pandemic, the ASEAN+3 RFSN saw no action. Rana and Pacheco Pardo argue that, at best, the ASEAN+3 RFSN could be sufficient to manage a moderate financial crisis in a single country but not a serious crisis with contagion to neighbouring countries. The latter will require a more structured form of cooperation between the ASEAN+3 RFSN and the IMF, similar to the arrangement that was set up in Europe to manage the eurozone crisis. Building on the broad principles issued by the G20, the AMRO and the IMF have signed a MOU with each other and are gradually deepening cooperation with each other.

Rana and Pacheco Pardo then argue that there are functional complementarities between the ASEAN+3 RFSN and the IMF, and between the non-traditional development banks (AIIB and NDB) and the World Bank. A degree of "healthy" competition in the form of resource additionality also exists between the regional institutions and their global counterparts which is beneficial to financial governance. Rana and Pacheco Pardo do not find evidence of "unhealthy" competition which increases the risk of fragmentation of the global financial architecture.

Rana and Pacheco Pardo conclude that the benefits of decentralisation and creation of new regional institutions appear to have outweighed the risks. The decentralisation of the global financial architecture has not led to its fragmentation and deterioration of global economic governance, so far. Rana and Pacheco Pardo caution, however, that there are limits to this argument due to the history of the establishment of regional institutions, the gap between rhetoric and reality, and the evolving geopolitical forces including the US veto power over the IMF and the on-going US-China trade war.

Looking forward, Rana and Pacheco Pardo argue that in the post-pandemic period both the global financial safety net and the economic development architecture will continue to move incrementally towards a network-based decentralised/multi-layered system where global and regional institutions work closely with a "senior" global institution. They note that in order to manage such a process, reforms at both global and regional levels are required together with actions to promote complementarity between the two.

In Chapter 4, "Promoting Development Bank Complementarity in Asia", Xianbai Ji assesses the prospect of complementarity between the AIIB and ADB in jointly providing regional public goods in relation to development financing and assistance in Asia. Based on the collaborative experiences of the European Investment Bank and the European Bank for Reconstruction and Development, the chapter recommends that ADB and the AIIB should form a tri-partite coordination mechanism along with global or regional institutions to promote cooperation, develop complementary portfolios in terms of sectoral exposure and geographical coverage and co-fund projects to catalyse greater inter-agency cooperation. The resulting synergies will have potential to stitch the two institutions into an inter-dependent and coherent development finance structure in Asia and beyond.

In Chapter 5, "Reforming the Global Reserve System", Pradumna B. Rana and Elgin Chan argue that one of the ways of reforming the present global reserve system (GRS) based on the "fiduciary" or "fiat" US dollar is to strengthen the emerging RFSNs in various parts of the world. They begin by arguing that the present system faces several fundamental problems that have been highlighted by the Global Financial Crisis. These include the asymmetric adjustment problem, inequity bias, and the Triffin Dilemma. It is further argued that if Keynes' proposal to establish an International Clearing Union and the bancor offered during the debated that led to the Bretton Woods conference had been accepted, some of these problems would not have occurred.

Policymakers and academics have put forward a number of proposals to reform the GRS. These are moving to a multiple currency reserve system, gradually establishing an SDR-based IMF, strengthening RFSNs, and establishing a new institution to issue SDRs in a fair and equitable manner. While the multiple currency system provides an opportunity for diversification and risk reduction, it does not address the three problems associated with the present GRS. Also establishing a new institution is not feasible politically as the IMF still exists. Rana and Chan conclude that the two feasible options in reforming the GRS are, therefore, to pursue incremental reforms in the way that SDRs are issued and allocated by the IMF and to strengthen the emerging RFSNs in various parts of the world. These approaches will take time to bear fruit which means that the hegemony of the US dollar will continue for some time yet in the future.

In Chapter 6, "The Evolving International Monetary System: Will Dollar Hegemony Outlive the Digital Revolution?", Xueying Wang, Dongsheng Di and Ruiling Liu examine the evolution of the global monetary order marked by the dominance and hegemony of the US dollar as the internationally recognised reserve asset and transaction currency. They probe the pros and cons associated with the US dollar hegemony and outline a few adverse consequences from the perspective of the world as a whole and developing countries (including China) in particular. Dangers from expansionary US domestic fiscal policies, the fragile China-US symbiotic relations in the monetary and financial sphere and the conflict potential of world politics have been identified by the authors as risks to the prevailing dollar-based international monetary order. Wang, Di and Liu also look into the possibility of digital currency replacing conventional banknotes such as the greenback as the new global currency. The conclusion they reach is that digital currencies will not pose an existential threat to the predominance of the US dollar. The chapter concludes by making the case for cooperative relationship between Beijing and Washington to gradually improve the international monetary system.

In Chapter 7, "Managing the Decentralising International Trade Architecture", Pradumna B. Rana, Wai-Mun Chia and Xianbai Ji argue that global international governance is in flux. The centralised international trade architecture of the post-Bretton Woods era is decentralising as there has been a proliferation of new regional institutions that are being established for various reasons. They argue that decentralisation per se is neither good nor bad: It depends on whether there is "healthy" competition and functional complementarity between the WTO and RTAs on one hand and "unhealthy" competition on the other. The authors find that, so far, the benefits of new regional institutions and trade decentralisation have outweighed the risks, and global trade governance appears to have improved.

Rana, Chia and Ji recommend several policy actions that the WTO should take to manage the decentralising trade architecture. They argue that the Asian countries, especially those that are members of the G20, should play a greater role in lobbying and driving the needed reforms at the WTO. They note that the broad principles that the G20 had issued to enhance cooperation between RFSNs and the IMF have played a catalytic role in deepening cooperation between the two; G20 should issue similar principles for deepening cooperation between RTAs and the WTO. Finally, now that the RCEP has been ratified, efforts should be made to expand membership in the two mega-FTAs that cover Asia, and eventually institutionalise the complementarity between RCEP, CPTPP, and China's Belt and Road Initiative.

In Chapter 8, "Evolving International Financial Regulation Architecture", Pradumna B. Rana argues that the process of building the international financial regulation architecture (IFRA) started later than the other three pillars of the GEA. The reason for this was that it was not until the 1970s that countries started to deregulate their capital markets and cross-border capital flows and financial globalisation took off. During the 1970s to the mid-1990s, a number of international SSBs were established. Following the Asian Financial Crisis of 1997–1998, the G7 established the Financial Stability Forum (FSF) as mentioned above to coordinate the activities of the international SSBs. Then Rana notes that after the Global Financial Crisis, a root cause of which was regulatory failure in the United States, the G20 upgraded the FSF to the Financial Stability Board (FSB) mainly by increasing its membership to all G20 members including the systemically dynamic emerging markets. The power and authority of the FSB were, however, not increased. The IFRA is, therefore, a loose network of members and jurisdictions.

Rana then points out that the IFRA differs from the other GEA pillars in several important ways. First, the IFRA operates on a sectoral basis with the FSB and global SSBs as the key institutions. Second, systemically important emerging markets of the G20 group (like China, India and Russia) are members of the FSB and the SSBs and they seem quite satisfied with the voice and the role that they have in these institutions and there have been no efforts to establish alternative institutions. Third, the FSB and SSBs are loose networks of member countries and jurisdictions, they are not rules-based. Finally, Rana assesses how the IFRA might evolve in the future: Will it become a rules-based pillar comprising institutions like the proposed World Finance Organization (WFO) with power to sanction like the other GEA pillars or will it continue to be a loose network-based pillar? He argues that at the present time because of rising nationalism and populism mainly in the West and also in other parts of the world, it will not be possible to garner support for a rules-based IFRA. Hence, IFRA will continue as a loose network of institutions. Rana argues that the feasibility of the proposed WFO is also questionable for two reasons. First, in contrast with international trade, there is a notable lack of consensus on the benefits of financial globalisation and hence on setting up a rules-based WFO. Second, despite the interconnected nature of global finance, the costs borne to respond to financial crisis remain concentrated at the national level. Nation-states are, therefore, unlikely to give up control to a supranational body. Despite this finding, Rana argues that FSB should be strengthened significantly, and its authority enhanced as much as possible, so that it can effectively do its job of coordinating the activities of sectoral global SSBs. Also, although they are relatively well-represented in the FSB and global SSBs, more members from systemically important emerging markets should be allocated positions of key leadership in these institutions.

The Role of Asia

The first four summits of the G20 had focused on "crisis prevention and crisis management". These summits were relatively successful in coming up with coordinated monetary and fiscal stimulus packages and in strengthening the international financial architecture. At the fifth summit held in Seoul, Korea, for the first time, issues related to economic development were also included in the purview of the G20. Since then, topics like anti-corruption, infrastructure development, marine litter, water sustainability and cross-border flow of data have found their way to the G20 agenda. These issues have distracted the G20 from performing its "crisis prevention and crisis management" role and the notion of "G20 fatigue" have gained ground. COVID-19 had provided an opportunity to the G20 to promote global cooperation and address one of the most pressing issues facing humanity. However, because of rising populist nationalist movements and the state of relations among several G20 members especially the United States and China, the G20 has been unsuccessful in promoting collective action. The response to the pandemic has, therefore, been individual country-based and weak. The G20 has fallen short not only on fiscal coordination but also on coordination on vaccine roll-outs, debt relief, and in strengthening supply chains. Instead of waiting for the global situation to change and US-China relations to improve, Asian countries especially those that are members of the G20 (China,

India, Indonesia, Korea, Japan and Australia) should strengthen partnership among themselves and attempt to improve the global order. They should coordinate, lobby and play a more active role in the deliberations of the G20 and encourage it to (i) implement the required reforms to enhance the G20's "input" and "output" legitimacy and to streamline its agenda, (ii) lobby and promote reforms of global IEIs including those related to governance and (iii) promote complementarity between global and regional international economic institutions. The six principles that the G20 issued for promoting cooperation between the IMF and RFSNs have led to encouraging progress in IMF-CMIM collaboration. The G20 should also develop similar principles for WTO-RTA cooperation and let WTO implement it (Chapter 7).

Asian countries should also establish more regional institutions to support the decentralising GEA. In the area of macroeconomic stability, the region has the ASEAN+3 RFSN comprising the CMIM and AMRO. But as already mentioned, despite being over 20 years in the making, the ASEAN+3 RFSN has yet to be utilised. Efforts are required to establish a centralised reserve pool to replace the "self-managed" arrangement where reserves are held by individual central banks and monetary authorities. The decision-making system to trigger disbursements of CMIM funds also needs to be streamlined. Managing a crisis with contagion to neighbouring countries requires a more structured form of cooperation between the IMF and ASEAN+3 RFSN (Chapter 3).

In the area of international trade, the region is home to two mega-FTAs, the CPTPP and RCEP (the largest FTA by GDP and population covered). Asian countries should expedite the implementation of RCEP and eventually merge the CPTPP and RCEP to form the Free Trade Area of the Asia-Pacific. The complementarity between RCEP, CPTPP and the Belt and Road Initiative should also be institutionalised (Chapter 7).

In the area of international financial regulation architecture, Asian countries should consider establishing the proposed Asian Financial Stability Board (AFSB). The AFSB would provide a forum for broader information sharing in the areas of macroeconomic and financial stability by including financial regulators, as well as finance ministries and central banks. The AFSB would promote discussions on regional financial vulnerabilities, regional capital flows, common issues for financial sector supervision and regulation, and common efforts at financial integration. The AFSB would focus on capital market rules and regulations (micro-prudential monitoring) and promote the stability of the financial system throughout the region through early warning systems (macro-prudential monitoring). Finally, the AFSB would coordinate Asia's participation in the FSB and other relevant international fora to ensure that the Asian context is adequately understood and addressed (Chapter 8).

References

Acharya, Amitav. 2016. "The Future of Global Governance: Fragmentation May Be Inevitable and Creative." *Global Governance: A Review of Multilateralism and International Organizations* 22 (4): 453–460.

Arshad, Arlina. 2022. "Indonesia Calls for Mutual Agreement Among G-20 on New Global Health Agency." *The Straits Times*. Accessed 26 January 2022. https://www.straitstimes.com/asia/se-asia/indonesia-calls-for-mutual-agreement-at-g-20-on-new-global-health-agency.

Bauer, Christian, and Bernhard Herz. 2020. "Reforming the European Stability Mechanism." *JCMS: Journal of Common Market Studies* 58: 3.

Benson, Robert, and Michael Zürn. 2019. "Untapped Potential: How the G20 Can Strengthen Global Governance." *South African Journal of International Affairs* 26 (4): 549–562.

Bhagwati, Jagdish. 1999. "Regionalism and Multilateralism: An Overview." In *Trading Blocs: Alternative Approaches to Analyzing Preferential Trade Agreements*, edited by Jagdish Bhagwati, Pravin Krishna, and Arvind Panagariya. Cambridge, MA: MIT Press.

Bhagwati, Jagdish. 2008. *Termites in the Trading System: How Preferential Agreements Undermine Free Trade*. Oxford and New York: Oxford University Press.

Bordo, Michael D. 1993. "The Bretton Woods International Monetary System: A Historical Overview." In *A Retrospective on the Bretton Woods System: Lessons for International Monetary Reform*, edited by Michael D. Bordo and Barry Eichengreen. Chicago: University of Chicago Press.

Bordo, Michael D., and Barry Eichengreen, eds. 1993. *A Retrospective on the Bretton Woods System: Lessons for International Monetary Reform*. Chicago and London: The University of Chicago Press.

Castells, Manuel. 2005. "Global Governance and Global Politics." *PS: Political Science & Politics* 38 (1): 9–16.

Cooper, Andrew F. 2010. "The G20 as an Improvised Crisis Committee and/or a Contested 'Steering Committee' for the World." *International Affairs* 86 (3): 741–757.

Delivorias, Angelos. 2016. "The World Bank: Serving Ambitious Goals, but in Need of Reform." Brief. Brussels: European Parliamentary Research Service.

Engen, Lars, and Annalisa Prizzon. 2018. *A Guide to Multilateral Development Banks*. London: Overseas Development Institute.

Gehring, Thomas, and Benjamin Faude. 2014. "A Theory of Emerging Order Within Institutional Complexes: How Competition Among Regulatory International Institutions Leads to Institutional Adaptation and Division of Labor." *The Review of International Organizations* 9: 471–498.

Gordenker, Leon, and Thomas G. Weiss. 1995. "Pluralising Global Governance: Analytical Approaches and Dimensions." *Third World Quarterly* 16 (3): 357–387.

Gotz, Norbert. 2019. "The Emergence of NGOs as Actors on the World Stage." In *Routledge Handbook of NGOs and International Relations*, edited by Thomas Davies. Oxon and New York: Routledge.

Hajnal, Peter I. 2019. *The G20: Evolution, Interrelationships, Documentation.* London: Routledge.

Helleiner, Eric. 2010. "A Bretton Woods Moment? The 2007–2008 Crisis and the Future of Global Finance." *International Affairs* 86 (3): 619–636.

Henning, C. Randall. 2017. "Avoiding Fragmentation of Global Financial Governance." *Global Policy* 8 (1): 101–106.

Hufbauer, Gary Clyde, and Jeffrey J. Schott. 2005. *NAFTA Revisited: Achievements and Challenges.* Washington, DC: Institute for International Economics.

Hyun, Suk, and James F. Paradise. 2019. "Why Is There No Asian Monetary Fund?" ADBI Working Paper Series. Tokyo: Asian Development Bank Institute.

Ji, Xianbai, and Pradumna B. Rana. 2019. "A Deal That Does Not Die: The United States and the Rise, Fall and Future of the (CP)TPP." *Pacific Focus* 34 (2): 230–255.

Ji, Xianbai, Pradumna B. Rana, Wai-Mun Chia, and Changtai Li. 2018. "Post-TPP Trade Policy Options for ASEAN and Its Dialogue Partners: "Preference Ordering" Using CGE Analysis." *East Asian Economic Review* 22 (2).

Jiang, Haiwei, and Miaojie Yu. 2021. "Understanding RCEP and CPTPP: From the Perspective China's Dual Circulation Economic Strategy." *China Economic Journal* 14 (2): 144–161.

Kahler, Miles. 2013. "Rising Powers and Global Governance: Negotiating Change in a Resilient Status Quo." *International Affairs* 89 (3): 711–729.

Kahler, Miles. 2017. "Regional Challenges to Global Governance." *Global Policy* 8 (1): 97–100.

Kahler, Miles. 2018. "Global Governance: Three Futures." *International Studies Review* 20: 239–246.

Kahler, Miles, C. Randall Henning, Chad P. Bown, Hongying Wang, Erik Voeten, and Paul D. Williams. 2016. *Global Order and the New Regionalism.* New York: The Council on Foreign Relations.

Kapur, Devesh, John P. Lewis, and Richard Webb, eds. 1997. *The World Bank: Its First Half Century. Volume 1: History. Volume 2: Perspectives*. Washington, DC: Brookings Institution.

Kawai, Masahiro, and Peter A. Petri. 2010. "Asia's Role in the Global Economic Architecture." ADBI Working Paper 235. Tokyo: Asian Development Bank Institute.

Kellow, Aynsley. 2012. "Multi-level and Multi-arena Governance: The Limits of Integration and the Possibilities of Forum Shopping." *International Environmental Agreements: Politics, Law and Economics* 12: 327–342.

Khor, Hoe Ee, Diwa C. Guinigundo, and Masahiro Kawai, eds. 2021. *Trauma to Triumph—Rising from the Ashes of the Asian Financial Crisis*. Singapore: World Scientific.

Kindleberger, Charles P. 2013. *The World in Depression, 1929–1939*. 40th Anniversary ed. Berkeley: University of California Press.

Kirton, John J. 2016. *China's G20 Leadership*. London: Routledge.

Krishna, Pravin. 1998. "Regionalism and Multilateralism: A Political Economy Approach." *The Quarterly Journal of Economics* 113 (1): 227–250.

Landau, Martin. 1969. "Redundancy, Rationality, and the Problem of Duplication and Overlap." *Public Administration Review* 29 (4): 346–358.

Liberi, Jason. 2003. "The Financial Stability Forum: A Step in the Right Direction…Not Far Enough." *University of Pennsylvania Journal of International Law* 24 (2): 549–575.

Luckhurst, Jonathan. 2018. *The Shifting Global Economic Architecture: Decentralizing Authority in Contemporary Global Governance*. Cham: Palgrave Macmillan.

Mallaby, Sebastian. 2004. *The World's Banker: A Story of Failed States, Financial Crises, and the Wealth and Poverty of Nations*. New York: Penguin Press.

Meléndez-Ortiz, Ricardo. 2014. "Mega-regionals: What Is Going On?" In *Mega-regional Trade Agreements Game-Changers or Costly Distractions for the World Trading System?*, edited by Anabel González. Geneva: World Economic Forum.

Morse, Julia C., and Robert O. Keohane. 2014. "Contested Multilateralism." *The Review of International Organizations* 9: 385–412.

Murazzani, Maaria Ludovica. 2009. "NGOs, GLobal Governance and the UN: NGOs as "Guardians of the Reform of the International System"." *Transition Studies Review* 16: 501–509.

Murphy, Hannah, and Aynsley Kellow. 2013. "Forum Shopping in Global Governance: Understanding States, Business and NGOs in Multiple Arenas." *Global Policy* 4 (2): 139–149.

Murphy-Gregory, Hannah, and Aynsley Kellow. 2016. "Forum Shopping and Global Governance." In *Rethinking International Institutions: Diplomacy and*

Impact on Emerging World Order, edited by Wilhelm Hofmeister and Jan Melissen. Singapore: World Scientific.

Ocampo, José Antonio, and Daniel A. Titelman. 2012. "Regional Monetary Cooperation in Latin America." ADBI Working Paper No. 373. Tokyo: Asian Development Bank Institute.

Orsini, Amandine, Jean-Frédéric Morin, and Oran Young. 2013. "Regime Complexes: A Buzz, a Boom, or a Boost for Global Governance?" *Global Governance: A Review of Multilateralism and International Organizations* 19 (1): 27–39.

Park, Young-Joon. 2017. "Strengthening ASEAN 3 Regional Financial Arrangements: A New Framework Beyond CMIM." *East Asian Economic Review* 21 (1): 59–80.

Petri, Peter A., Michael G. Plummer, Shujiro Urata, and Fan Zhai. 2021. "The Economics of the CPTPP and RCEP: Asia Pacific Trade Agreements Without the United States." In *The Comprehensive and Progressive Agreement for Trans-Pacific Partnership: Implications for Southeast Asia*, edited by Cassey Lee and Pritish Bhattacharya. Singapore: ISEAS Publishing.

Pitakdumrongkit, Kaewkamol. 2018. *Negotiating Financial Agreement in East Asia Surviving the Turbulence*. London: Routledge.

Rajan, Raghuram G. 2009. *A New Bretton Woods?* Washington, DC: World Bank.

Rana, Pradumna B. 2010. "Evolving Global Economic Architecture: Will We Have a New Bretton Woods?" RSIS Working Paper. Singapore: S. Rajaratnam School of International Studies.

Rana, Pradumna B. 2014. "From a Centralized to a Decentralized Global Economic Architecture: An Overview." In *New Global Economic Architecture: The Asian Perspective*, edited by Masahiro Kawai, Peter J. Morgan, and Pradumna B. Rana. Cheltenham and Northampton: Edward Elgar.

Raustiala, Kal, and David G. Victor. 2004. "The Regime Complex for Plant Genetic Resources." *International Organization* 58 (2): 277–309.

Rhee, Changyong, Lea Sumulong, and Shahin Vallée. 2013. "Global and Regional Financial Safety Nets: Lessons from Europe and Asia." In *Responding to Financial Crisis. Lessons from Asia Then, the United States and Europe Now*, edited by Changyong Rhee and Adam S. Posen. Washington, DC: Peterson Institute for International Economics.

Roger, Charles B. 2020. *The Origins of Informality: Why the Legal Foundations of Global Governance Are Shifting, and Why It Matters*. Oxford: Oxford University Press.

Ruhlman, Molly. 2019. "NGOs in Global Governance." In *Routledge Handbook of NGOs and International Relations*, edited by Thomas Davies. Oxon and New York: Routledge.

Steil, Benn. 2013. *The Battle of Bretton Woods: John Maynard Keynes, Harry Dexter White, and the Making of a New World Order*. Princeton: Princeton University Press.

Stephen, Matthew D. 2017. "Emerging Powers and Emerging Trends in Global Governance." *Global Governance: A Review of Multilateralism and International Organizations* 23 (3): 483–502.

Stiglitz, Joseph E. 2008. "The Next Bretton Woods." Project Syndicate. Accessed 16 January 2022. https://www.project-syndicate.org/commentary/the-next-bretton-woods.

Sussangkarn, Chalongphob. 2011. "Chiang Mai Initiative Multilateralization: Origin, Development, and Outlook." *Asian Economic Policy Review* 6 (2): 203–220.

Tomlin, Brian W., and Maxwell A. Cameron. 2000. *The Making of NAFTA: How the Deal Was Done*. Ithaca: Cornell University Press.

Vonyó, Tamás. 2008. "Post-war Reconstruction and the Golden Age of Economic Growth." *European Review of Economic History* 12: 221–241.

Wang, Hongying. 2017. "New Multilateral Development Banks: Opportunities and Challenges for Global Governance." *Global Policy* 8 (1): 113–118.

Wangwe, Samuel, and Hiroshi Kawamura. 2018. "The 1960s: High Growth, High Hopes, and Looming Structural Imbalances." In *The World Economy Through the Lens of the United Nations*, edited by José Antonio Ocampo, Anis Chowdhury, and Diana Alarcón. Oxford: Oxford University Press.

Wilson, Jeffrey D. 2019. "The Evolution of China's Asian Infrastructure Investment Bank: From a Revisionist to Status-Seeking Agenda." *International Relations of the Asia-Pacific* 19 (1): 147–176.

WTO. 2011. "The WTO and Preferential Trade Agreements: From Co-existence to Coherence." World Trade Report 2011. Geneva: World Trade Organisation.

Zürn, Michael. 2018. "Contested Global Governance." *Global Policy* 9 (1): 138–145.

CHAPTER 2

The Evolution of Global Oversight Institutions: From the Library Group to the Group of Twenty

Xianbai Ji

Introduction

The contemporary global economic architecture established gradually after the United Nations Monetary and Financial Conference, colloquially known as the Bretton Woods Conference, in 1944 (Steil 2013) enabled accelerated worldwide economic recovery (Wangwe and Kawamura 2018) based on a rules-based, market-oriented liberal international economic order. That architecture was overseen initially by the Group of Seven (G7) leading industrialised rich nations from the West (i.e. the United States, the United Kingdom, France, Germany, Japan, Italy, Canada and the European Union). As the world political economy became multi-polarised and economic globalisation deepened (Wade 2011), the world called for a more representative, responsive and legitimate oversight institution at the

X. Ji (✉)
School of International Studies, Renmin University of China, Beijing, China
e-mail: xbji@ruc.edu.cn

P. B. Rana and X. Ji (eds.), *From Centralised to Decentralising Global Economic Architecture*, https://doi.org/10.1007/978-981-19-2041-7_2

helm of the global economic system. Hence enter the Group of Twenty (G20) systematically important economies from across the major regions of the globe—a quasi-expansion of the G7 (Postel-Vinay 2014). The G20 countries declared themselves to be the "premier forum" for international economic coordination and cooperation at the 2009 Pittsburgh Summit.

The parallel yet symbiotic relationship between the G7 and the G20 as co-governors of world economic affairs raises a series of important questions. How did the G7 come about in the first place? What drove the transformation from the G7 to the G20? Since the G7 representatives are more cohesive and likeminded than the G20 which is marked by economic, political and geographic heterogeneity, does the evolution from the G7 to the G20 involve a trade-off between legitimacy and effectiveness as far as global governance is concerned? How can the G20 be further reformed to enhance all-round legitimacy? Neither the G7 nor the G20 is meant to save the world from all its problems; they are instead situated within an international regime complexity. Given their limited resources and informal nature, is there a scope for the two leadership forums to leverage complementarity with other specialised international institutions and agencies to jointly provide global public goods?

In this chapter, we provide some preliminary thoughts on those research questions. The remainder of the chapter is organised as follows. The next section traces the geneses of the G7 and its predecessor, the Library Group, in the 1970s and describes the evolution from the G7 to the G20. Also included is an introduction of the assortment of governance tasks they each undertook as they progressively expanded their mandates. The chapter then focuses on the notion of legitimacy. The G7 is widely known to be a self-appointed elite forum that aspires to make economic decisions on behalf of other nations. Much the same can be said about the G20. Addressing their substantive, input and output legitimacy deficits are, therefore, crucial for the Gx's political sustainability and practical utility in the future of global governance. The section before conclusion is devoted to a discussion of the cooperative relationship between the two Gs and other international economic institutions for the ultimate objective of effective and responsive global economic governance.

From the Library Group to the G20

At the Bretton Woods Conference, delegates from 44 allied nations agreed to an international monetary system based on gold-dollar convertibility and pegged exchange rates between the dollar and other currencies (Cesarano 2006). The system worked well between the 1940s and 1960s when a hegemonic United States provided global liquidity and stability to turbocharge post-war economic reconstruction and development and underwrite the flourishing international commerce. However, as the United States became mired in the protracted Vietnam War, the Triffin dilemma undermined confidence in the value of dollar and countries such as France rushed to cash in dollar for gold, the system collapsed. In 1971, the United States made an unexpected decision to delink gold and dollar (i.e. the Nixon Shock), leaving the dollar-dominated international monetary order in disarray. In order to coordinate monetary policies of major Western countries, then US Treasury Secretary George Shultz invited his fellow counterparts from Britain, France and West Germany for a private meeting at the White House library (Shultz 1993), hence the nickname "Library Group". The Library Group of four nations soon expanded to include Japan and Italy (G6).[1] At the initiative of France, the G6 convened its inaugural summit at the level of head of state and government in 1975. Canada started to participate in summitry in 1976, forming the G7. The European Communities (predecessor to the European Union) joined in the third year of the group's existence, 1977, as a "non-enumerated" participant (Debaere and Orbie 2013).

The G7 does not have a permanent secretariat, and the rotating presidency country[2] has the power to set the agenda. The initial focus of the G7 summitry was predominately economic, covering issues of mutual or global concern such as world trade, monetary matters, raw materials and commodity price (Hajnal 2007). This was appropriate given the prevailing

[1] The present study's description of the emergence of the G7 through the Library Group only tells part of the story. The vision and initiative were also that of Henry Kissinger who had in mind from the start the model of the Concert of Europe. But unlike Shultz, Kissinger was thinking of leveraging Western summitry to advance the geopolitical agenda of the West.

[2] Annual presidency rotates in this order with each new term starting on 1 January of the year: France, United States, United Kingdom, Russia (suspended), Germany, Japan, Italy and Canada.

mix of international and national circumstances. At the time, the international monetary order was in flux, the rise of protectionism threatened the vitality of international trade and the escalating inflation in the West resulting from oil shocks of the 1970s had stirred up domestic instability and youth unemployment. Indeed, approximately ten G7 Summits in a row till mid-1980s placed emphasis on reducing dependence on imported oil to achieve noninflationary economic revival and job creation. During this period, non-economic, strategic and geopolitical topics (e.g. terrorism, Arab–Israeli conflict and arms control) also crept into the G7's expanding agenda, so did issues of concern like narcotics, environmental protection and scientific advancement.

As the Cold War came to an end in the late 1980s, the G7 ascribed itself a role of assimilating the former Soviet republics into the capitalist world, converting them from centrally planned to free-market economies. In 1994, Russia began playing a part in G7 processes that addressed political developments. The group was thus known as the "Political Eight" till 1998 when Russia was formally admitted as a full member of the enlarged Group of Eight (G8). While being a member, the relationship between Russia and the G7 countries remained largely aloof after a short honeymoon period. Russia's preoccupation was in the energy domain (Panova 2007). Finance ministers, central bank governors and other ministerial officials responsible for economic management still met at the G7 level without Russia's participation. It was telling that Russian President Vladimir Putin gave the 2012 G8 Summit in Camp David a miss due to a bitter row between Moscow and Washington over the former's alleged "mistreatment" of demonstrators protesting against the re-election of Putin as president. The strained relationship eventually worsened further in 2014 after the eruption of the Ukraine Crisis which triggered the Russian takeover of Crimea. Russia's membership of the G8 was suspended indefinitely and Russia announced its permanent withdrawal in 2017, formally reverting the grouping's name to "G7". President Donald Trump attempted to re-invite Russia, but the idea was not supported by other G7 leaders.

If the G7's engagement with Russia was by and large unsuccessful, so was its outreach to other dynamic emerging market countries. Noting that non-Western countries could no longer be alienated in global decision-making, in conjunction with the celebration of the 60th anniversary of the founding of the United Nations, the British Prime Minister Tony Blair invited leaders from Brazil, China, India, Mexico and South Africa to the 2005 Gleneagles G8 Summit for a discussion of global economic issues and climate change. However, the five outreach countries were not treated as equal partners and their leaders were escorted out, however politely, when core decisions were deliberated and made (Nelson 2020). As opposed to some analysts' claim (Cooper and Jackson 2008), the nature of the G8's outreach session did not change even with the introduction of the Heiligendamm process in 2007 aimed at institutionalising partnership between the G8 and "the other five" (Navarrete 2008). Between the 2007 Heiligendamm and 2009 L'Aquila Summits, the format was labelled as "G8+5"—instead of G13 as proposed by a veteran observer (Kirton 2008), for there was a fundamental core-periphery unequal relationship between the "8" and the "5" (Ji and Lim 2021).

This situation changed in 2008 with the launch of the more inclusive G20 summitry in the midst of the Global Financial Crisis (GFC). Non-Western countries and major emerging economies "from every region of the globe" were brought into the global decision-making circle. Although the inaugural G20 Summit was held in November 2008 in Washington, DC, the grouping traces its origin to the December 1999 meeting of G20 finance ministers and central bank governors. That meeting was convened against the background of the Asian Financial Crisis (AFC) triggered by the forced floating of Thai baht spreading to neighbouring countries like Indonesia and Malaysia and to South Korea, Russia and Latin America. G8 countries realised that the world economy was so tightly interwoven in the age of economic and financial globalisation that the practice of continuing to deprive systemically important emerging markets of their deserved seats at the global economic high table would not be sustainable. The ministerial G20, however, lived in the shadow of the G8, rubberstamping many of the latter's decisions. The GFC came as a watershed moment in the history of global economic governance. The GFC not only weakened the West's collective economic standing in the world but also led to questions over the G8's ability and sincerity of safeguarding global economic wellbeing and financial stability. The global attention shifted to the newly empowered G20 as a result.

As with the G7/8, the G20 summitry includes the European Union. Spain was not initially invited to attend the 2008 Washington G20 Summit but thanks to France's diplomatic efforts it was categorised in 2010 as a "permanent guest" of the G20 with an implicitly guaranteed place (Matlay 2017).[3] To make the G20 summitry more accessible, representative and participatory, administrative heads of major international institutions such as the United Nations, International Monetary Fund (IMF), World Bank and World Trade Organization (WTO) attend the Summit and the Association of Southeast Asian Nations (ASEAN) also regularly attend G20 Summits. Under the G20 outreach program, the host country can invite up to five representatives from regional groupings of which two must be from Africa (the New Partnership for Africa's Development [NEPAD] and the African Union [AU]) (Cooper and Thakur 2013).

Commensurate with the expansion of participation by countries and international organisations, agenda items for the G20 Summits have increased steadily. The first four G20 Summits were held in G7/8 countries with a relatively narrow mandate of managing the GFC and its aftershocks. These summits were successful in coming up with coordinated monetary and fiscal stimulus packages and in strengthening the international financial architecture. At the fifth summit, South Korea, a non-G7/8 host country that sought to be a bridge between the Global North and the Global South, identified economic development—a topic of key interest of developing countries many of which were unrepresented at the G20 level—as falling within the purview of the G20. That marked a major expansion of the G20's role which initially was confined to one of "crisis responder and manager". In the following years, that newfound enthusiasm for global economic convergence gave way to, albeit for a short period of time, the imperative of saving the eurozone from disintegration, given the deepening sovereign debt crisis among countries that adopt euro as their common currency (Fabig et al. 2014).

The successive outbreaks of Asian, global and eurozone crises prompted the G20 to coordinate monetary and fiscal stimuli and discuss ways to strengthen the international financial architecture, in particular to reform the IMF. Besides beefing up modestly the IMF quotas on several occasions and encouraging it to introduce new credit lines for

[3] The G20 comprises 19 countries plus the European Union. The participating countries are Argentina, Australia, Brazil, Canada, China, France, Germany, India, Indonesia, Italy, Japan, Mexico, Russia, Saudi Arabia, South Africa, South Korea, Turkey, the United Kingdom and the United States. Spain attends the G20 Summits as a permanent guest. The Presidency also invites representatives of international economic institutions, regional organisations and guest countries to the G20 Summit.

crisis prevention (namely the Flexible Credit Line and the Precautionary Credit Line), the G20 took the matter of undertaking IMF governance reform—an unfinished job at the G7/8—in its own hands. In 2010, the G20 sanctioned a proposal to reallocate some 6% of quotas (hence voting power) from the IMF's overweight northern shareholders to dynamic emerging members. The proposed reform faced enormous political resistance (Lesage et al. 2013) and became a reality only in 2016 after the US Congress gave its consent belatedly. With the reform, China jumped to the third spot at the Fund and other dynamic emerging markets like Brazil and Russia are among the top ten shareholders (IMF 2017). As part of the ongoing "chairs and shares" reform (Truman 2006) for enhancing the IMF's credibility, legitimacy and effectiveness, the Western domination in the IMF's management structure was also lessened. The Fund's Executive Board now consists of elected as opposed to appointed directors and developed European countries have reduced their combined Board representation by two chairs. The election of Managing Director is to be merit-based and open to candidates from all nationalities that are members of the IMF, legally proscribing Europe's monopoly over the position.

After some early successes, when complacency and normalcy set in with the subsiding of the economic crises, the notion of "G20 fatigue" (Cooper and Schrumm 2011) gained ground. Calls for the establishment of a small, dedicated secretariat (Cooper and Bradford 2010; Bishop and Payne 2021; Rana and Ji 2018) were rejected repeatedly, seemingly in defence of what is referred to as "global informalism" (Slaughter 2021) embodied in the G20 *modus operandi*. Countries like the United States were particularly against the creation of a bureaucratic secretariat, arguing that the grouping should stay informal and agile with a flexibly defined agenda (Sinha and Nataraj 2013). As such, the G20 relies on leaders' personal representatives, known as sherpas, together with finance ministers and central bank governors to informally coordinate the work. Meanwhile the G20 drifted to a few relatively medium- and long-term development issues that detracted from its ability to perform the desired role of facilitating "strong, sustainable and balanced growth". These included topics such as anti-corruption, infrastructure development, marine litter, water sustainability and cross-border flow of data. The COVID-19 pandemic provided an opportunity for the G20 to promote global cooperation to address one of the most pressing issues facing humanity. At a virtual meeting organised in March 2020, the G20 leaders pledged to do whatever it took to overcome the crisis, but only a few weak commitments emerged. One of these was the Debt Service Suspension Initiative (DSSI) rolled out in collaboration with the IMF and the World Bank (World Bank 2021) to ensure that eligible developing debtor countries were not squeezed by the economic pressure of repaying debt on the one hand and the domestic financial demand of fighting the infectious diseases on the other. But unfortunately, the DSSI (having been renewed once) was not extended at the G20 Rome Summit in November 2021. At Rome, the advanced countries' agenda of slowing climate change and de-carbonising national economies took precedent over the developing countries' call for vaccine inequality and justice and financial assistance from the IMF (Rana 2021b). The divergence of interests between the G20's advanced and developing members thus casts a long shadow over the grouping's long-term viability and legitimacy.

Strengthening the Gx's "Whole-Process Legitimacy"

G-based global coordination proved successful in mobilising large stimulus packages at the time of the GFC. Unfortunately, the G20 has not been successful in promoting global cooperation to mobilise financial and medical resources to assist in the global fight against the coronavirus in part because of rising nationalism and protectionism.[4] Therefore, there is an urgent need to strengthen the G20 for it to be effective, responsive and above all, legitimate. It has been suggested quite insightfully that the G20 like any other international organisation essentially grapples with the intricate task of maintaining a right balance between like-mindedness, representativeness and effectiveness (Patrick 2010).[5] Indeed, these three interlocking organising constructs point to three dimensions of international organisational legitimacy, namely substantive legitimacy, input legitimacy and output legitimacy.

[4] Efforts by the G7 alone to supply global public goods like vaccine were not successful either as was the case during the Cornwall Summit. G7 leaders agreed to provide one billion vaccine doses to low and low-middle income countries over the 2022, but then this was believed to fall far short of the amount ($11 billion) needed (Wise 2021).

[5] Some scholars refer to this as the "effectiveness-legitimacy nexus". See Ulfgard and Vega (2019) and Subacchi and Pickford (2011).

Substantive Legitimacy

An organisation is often seen as legitimate if its formation and subsequent operation and adaptation constantly appeal to the evolving need and promote shared interests and beliefs of its member countries (Zaum 2016). Simply stated, an organisation has to be dynamically fit for purpose and always in a shape that its members need it to be. The development of the G7/8 illustrates this substantive dimension of legitimacy well. The Library Group started out as an informal gathering of finance ministers in charge of exchange rate policies when there was the need for international monetary coordination. In the 1970s and 1980s, preoccupations of the G7 included jointly economising on imported fossil fuel energy consumption and safeguarding youth employment while economic recovery from the oil crises was the common purpose. During the post-Cold War era, the G7 was seen as useful in presenting a united Western front in geopolitical terms and a seemingly prosperous economic bloc to the former Soviet republics looking for a new, aspiring ideological and economic anchor for their future development path. Into the twenty-first century, at a time when the bloc's collective economic and geopolitical weights are unmistakeably on a downward trend, the G7 remains relevant from the perspective of its members for being a bulwark of open societies and liberal market-democracies against the advancement of the so-called illiberal or authoritarian forces across the globe. The latest phase of development is best captured by the articulated initiative to build a D10 (Democracies Ten including G7 countries plus India, South Africa, and Brazil) and a summit of/for democracy on the pre-existing basis of the G7 (Jain et al. 2021). Needless to say, the high degree of like-mindedness among the G7 countries is key to the unity of purpose within the G7, contributing to its substantive legitimacy over time.

The road travelled so far by the G20 bears some witness to the link between legitimacy and like-mindedness, if only through a negative example. In both 1999 and 2008, there were widely and deeply appreciated convictions among both major established and rapidly emerging countries that the task of preventing and resolving regional and global financial crises could best be accomplished cooperatively and multilaterally. The convenient convergence of interests enkindled the launches of the G20 initially as a ministerial process and later as a summitry. The world celebrated the accomplishment of the G20 in terms of forbidding countries adopting self-centred, beggar-thy-neighbours monetary, trade and fiscal policies that would push a dangerous descent from the Great Recession of 2008–2009 to a devastating full-fledged Great Depression reminiscent of the turmoil in the 1930s (Drezner 2014). However, once the shared anxiety arising from the risk of financial contagion receded in the minds of national policymakers, the sense of global solidarity and the consensus around topical focus dissipated substantially and with them the substantive legitimacy of the G20. Country hosts are at liberty to select and expand annual agendas as they wish, leading to a lack of coherent overarching themes. And the problem is compounded and exacerbated by the notable heterogeneity in the economically, (geo)politically, demographically and ideologically diverse G20 membership (Lesage 2017). Due to low like-mindedness coupled with high host discretion, the G20 has increasingly failed to garner collaborative efforts to address the most pressing issue of the day.

Input Legitimacy

Legitimacy of an international governance organisation is customarily understood to be causally correlated with representation and the chance of participation by those who are affected by its actions (Buchanan and Keohane 2006). An international organisation is legitimate if it ensures sufficiently broad representation—and conversely illegitimate if it cannot guarantee the case. The conundrum of input illegitimacy has been haunting the G7/8 and the G20 since their inceptions as self-appointed elite governance clubs (Cooper 2014; Rana 2011; Wouters and Kerckhoven 2017). Nevertheless, each grouping has taken some steps to mitigate input legitimacy deficits.

Although the G7/8 did not accept membership applications by countries like the Netherlands, Belgium, Spain, Australia and Indonesia (Kirton 1995), an effective extension of insider status to a greater cluster of European countries was realised by allowing countries holding the presidency of the European Council to take part in the summits. An improvement in representation took place in the mid-1990s when heads of the United Nations and Bretton Woods institutions began attending more regularly G7/8 Summits as guests of the chair. Prior to the 2005 Gleneagles G8 Summit (which kicked off the G8+5 process as noted), an earlier breakthrough was achieved with the 2003 Evian-les-Bains Summit when the reformist French President Jacques Chirac convened a historic

Enlarged Dialogue Meeting that involved not only international organisations but also leaders from Asia, Latin America, Morocco (Chair of the Group of 77) and Switzerland—on the justification that the G8 did not "have any particular legitimacy" (n'avait pas de légitimité particulière) and needed to listen to the world. The input legitimacy was further enhanced when leaders from Africa and its attendant institutions (e.g. the African Union) and major developing nations were invited to the "extended family" of the G7. But as the world increasingly split along ideological lines, there was a heavy emphasis by the G7, when deciding on invitees, on balancing like-mindedness and representation to make sure that the pursuit of the latter did not come at the expense of the former. The result was that recent invitees were confined to democratic countries with regional influence like India, South Korea and Australia. The G20 underwent a similar experience of advancing towards a "cosmopolitan order" within the grouping (Cooper 2014). The presence of leaders from ASEAN, NEPAD, Gulf Cooperation Council (GCC) and Global Governance Group (3G) has become a regular feature of the G20 summitry.

Besides enhancing participation across countries, there has been a drive to enhance participation within nations; the G7/8 and the G20 have mounted extensive outreach programmes to the business community and civil society[6] at large to enhance their claim to (input) legitimacy. For example, the International Chamber of Commerce which calls itself the most representative business organisation in the world has followed and provided input to the Gx processes (Hajnal 2007). Also seen as the interlocutors between the G-summitry and the private sector are civil society organisations. The establishment of a plethora of engagement groups such as the Business20 (B20), Labour20 (L20), Think20 (T20), Civil20 (C20), Women20 (W20), Science20 (S20), Urban20 (U20) and Youth20 (Y20) and their G7/8 equivalents is enriching the Gx universe. Notably, each engagement may hold its own alternative or parallel summits and transmit their resolutions and recommendations to Gx officials (Hajnal 2015). Recent examples include the People's Summits (on global justice), Religious Leaders' Summits (on inter-faith harmony and reconciliation) and Women's Summit (on gender equality).

[6] For an account of the involvement of civil society in global governance, see Scholte (2016).

Output Legitimacy

The Gx's output legitimacy hinges on whether it is able to effectively translate pledged organisational objectives and commitment into concrete governance outcomes. Many have lamented the "waning" effectiveness of the G7/8 and the G20, denouncing them to be merely irrelevant, toothless talkfests (Vestergaard and Wade 2012; Cooper 2010) especially after they broadened mandates far beyond "crisis management/prevention" (Bremmer and Roubini 2011). Such criticisms are predicated on an adherence to the known correlation between the availability of constitution and the effectiveness of an organisation. Formal intergovernmental organisations and supranational ones founded on treaties (which have to be ratified by the legislative branches of member governments)–with strong legal personality, binding enforcement capacity, and operational and policy autonomy—tend to wield greater compliance power than informally and loosely organised entities like the Gx. The absence of formal, sovereignty-constraining rules at the G7/8 and the G20 aggravates the risk of countries manipulating the Gx to advance narrow national interest—a key concern that is believed to undermine international organisational performance (Lall 2017; Mitchell and Hensel 2007).

In a break from those received wisdom, however, some scholars empirically monitoring the performance of the Gx argue that the G7/8 and the G20 actually fared much better than widely appreciated—"The G7/8 retains its capacity as a concert for its leaders' deliberation and its good track record for delivering on the pledges they make. The G20 has substantially enhanced its delivery performance" (Larionova et al. 2015). Contributing to the better-than-presumed effectiveness at the Gx fronts is their uniquely instituted assessment-cum-monitoring mechanisms. The G7/8 relies on a multi-year, intergovernmental joint assessment approach to provide an account of what the grouping has done. In 2009, the G8 Accountability Working Group was unveiled with an eye to building a system of accountability. In the following year, the G8 released the Muskoka Accountability Report, beginning to assess the implementation of G8's commitments, individually or collectively pledged, with regard to development and related goals. Since then, the G7/8 issues comprehensive accountability reports to take stock of actions and achievements every three years, along with sector-focused accountability reports in the interim years (G7 Accountability Working Group 2021).[7]

The G20, on the other hand, adopts a mutual assessment approach, empowering each member to evaluate if other G20 countries have lived up to their promises. The peer-pressure-based mechanism is known as the Mutual Assessment Process (MAP), with clear parallels with IMF's Multilateral Consultation on Global Imbalance procedure (Faruqee and Srinivasan 2012) and the European Union's Macroeconomic Imbalances Procedure (Rommerskirchen and Snaith 2018). Despite the purported mutuality, MAP in effect is conducted by delegating monitoring and surveillance authority to the IMF. On top of providing data, the IMF coordinates G20-level macroeconomic policy coordination and compliance by providing technical assistance and policy advice (Bird 2017).

Whole-Process Legitimacy

Notwithstanding their efforts to bring about enhanced legitimacy, being global steering committees requires the Gx to command what can be termed "whole-process legitimacy" that brings together substantive legitimacy with input and output legitimacy and places additional emphasis on accountability and transparency.

On substantive legitimacy, the Gx needs to make sure that it is poised to address the most pressing issue commonly facing the world instead of relatively trivial issues important only to a small subset of countries. The G20 has at its disposal a diverse array of dedicated working groups and tasks forces organised along functional and thematic lines but not one charged with pinpointing the most overriding issues and priorities that ought to be dealt with in the summits. The G20 needs to do its best to refocus its agenda which is currently suffering from mission creep and reassert its leadership on issues like climate change, global health and international financial system reform.

In terms of input legitimacy, there could be scope for the G20 to further reduce overrepresentation by European countries (Rana 2011) which have a seat at the G20 high table as G7/8 countries, presidency

[7] The G20 has also established a G20 Development Working Group Accountability Framework. The Framework is based on a methodology for evaluating agreed and new G20 development impact in line with sherpas' guidance (G20 2014). Such mechanism also helps to boost the G20's output legitimacy.

of the European Council, permanent invitees and ad hoc guests. Gaining entry into the G20 is demonstrably more difficult and strenuous for other countries. The G20 should categorically announce that representatives from Africa (African Union and NEPDA), West Asia and Middle East (GCC), Central Asia (Commonwealth of Independent States), East and Southeast Asia (ASEAN), Oceania (Pacific Islands Forum), Americas (Mercosur and Pacific Alliance), and the cross-regional 3G will be invited, ending the unhelpful guessing game of who will or not be invited (Rana 2011). Rana also argues that a system of indirect participation should be considered. For example, South Africa has set up a Committee of Ten finance ministers and central bank governors from around Africa to support its participation in G20. Brazil could adopt a similar approach in Latin America, India in South Asia and Australia in the South Pacific.

Needless to say, apart from making the summitry more representative, it is also crucial to facilitate productive and constructive dialogue between the G20 members, core and extended, with non-G20 members (Callaghan et al. 2014). In this regard, MAP should incorporate quantifiable indicators gauging the quality of outreach activities by the presidential Troika.[8]

As to output legitimacy, the G7 should go beyond the traditional approach of self-assessment. One way forward might be for it to learn from the G20. It can consider assigning an independent auditing role to such credible and autonomous organisations like the United Nations Security Council given its focus on geopolitics and development. For the G20, it should increase the public accessibility and accountability of the MAP results through readily digestible reporting (English et al. 2012). In the short-run and in the long-run, it should come up with "better measures", "better concepts" and "better mechanism" in the words of John Kirton (2015) to comprehensively and systemically shore up output legitimacy. Importantly, in addition to commitments written in one Gx communique for a specific year, the scope of effectiveness evaluation should include cumulative commitments made throughout a certain time period across summits. This approach allows tracking of implementation

[8] The presidency of the G20 rotates annually among its members, with the country that holds the presidency working in conjunction with its immediate predecessor and successor, in an arrangement known as Troika, to ensure the continuity of the agenda.

progress and offers a more flexible way for the Gx to prove its effectiveness and whole-process legitimacy (spanning substantive, input and output dimensions).

Promoting Complementarity Within Gx and Between Gx and Other Global Bodies

The G7 and the G20 do not exist in isolation. They are situated within a complex galaxy of partially overlapping international governance institutions that form "regime complexes" (Orsini et al. 2013). Prior research points out that within institutional complexes, the emergence of an internal order formed on the basis of mutual adaptation and division of labour among elemental entities is possible and conducive to the accomplishment of collective institutional governance objectives, overcoming fragmentation and competitive dynamics (Gehring and Faude 2014).

Going forward, the G7 and the G20 can help cultivate an order within the global governance complex by dividing roles in accordance with their distinctive comparative advantages. The G20's membership collectively accounts for 85% of the world's GDP and 75% of its population, while the corresponding figures for the G7 are 40 and 10% respectively. The G20, therefore, has greater input legitimacy than the G7. Accordingly, the G20 should focus on the provision of truly global public goods such as monetary and financial stability, trade openness, global poverty reduction and pandemic control.[9] The G7 should focus on geopolitical issues, peace, stability and other areas of interest to industrial countries. The G7 should also bring in policy perspectives and development and industrialisation experiences of the developed countries to the G20 discussions. This thematic functional division of labour between the G7 and the G20 will better ensure that the demand for an entire spectrum of global public goods from political stability to economic prosperity to environmental sustainability is covered. This division of labour requires close cooperation and coordination between the G20 and the G7 and seems to be a prerequisite for bridging differences between the emerging market and developing countries and the major established powers on core

[9] Containment of a pandemic is a global public good and needs coordinated global responses with common narratives on the challenges to be tackled. One reason for the weak outcome of the G7 Cornwall UK Summit in 2021 was that this issue should have been addressed instead by the more inclusive G20 rather than the G7 (Rana 2021a).

global governance issues. Otherwise, either the tyranny of the developed countries in the northern hemisphere or the tyranny of the developing countries of the southern hemisphere would prevail over the benign outcome of "complementary multilateralism" (Ji, 2022) derived from a collaborative G7-G20 partnership.

Moreover, neither the G7 nor the G20, even with due enactment of the prescribed reforms, is meant to save the world from all its problems on its own. There are other specialised international institutions and agencies that have done a decent job like the IMF (macroeconomic stability and crisis resolution), WTO (trade liberalisation, transparency and openness), World Bank (development mentorship and financing), World Health Organisation (global health and pandemic control), United Nations Environment Programme (climate change and sustainable development), Food and Agriculture Organization (food security and famine prevention), International Labour Organisation (workers' rights), Interpol (counter-terrorism and transnational crime), International Criminal Court (violence against humanity), International Committee of the Red Cross (humanitarian actions), United Nations High Commissioner for Refugees (protection of internationally displaced persons and refugees) and International Telecommunication Union (communication) and their regional replicas and non-governmental functional equivalents. Given their limited resources, the G7 and the G20 should refocus and reassert their shared mandate as global oversight and coordination bodies at the apex of global governance. Oversight and global coordination would be improved if the Gx could promote cooperation and complementarity between global institutions and between global and regional and non-governmental institutions so that they can function in mutually supportive ways.[10] For instance, Chapter 3 of the present book offers an account of how the G20 has promoted cooperation between the IMF as global financial safety net and the Chiang Mai Initiative Multilateralisation as regional financial safety net; Chapter 7 makes a similar case for targeted G20 interventions on international trade to promote cooperation between the WTO and regional free trade accords.

[10] In this regard, some scholars suggest that the Gx, especially the G20, commands network power of forging consensus and enabling convergence of international standards across international organizations (Cho and Kelly 2012).

Conclusion

The global economic governance architecture is becoming multi-layered and decentralised. Sitting at the top of such architecture are two global oversight and coordination focal points—the G7 countries of major industrial democracies and the G20 systematically important countries. They are the de facto co-governors of world affairs despite being informal leadership clubs without legal personality or standing bureaucracy.

The histories and evolutions of the G7 and the G20 show significant parallels. The G7 arose in the midst of global monetary disorder and in the aftermath of the oil crises in the 1970s. The G20 emerged in response first to the AFC of the late 1990s and then to the GFC of the late 2000s. Notably, the creation of the G20 signifies that the balance of economic, financial and geopolitical power is shifting towards the dynamically emerging economies, and both global governance and economic policy thinking are moving in tandem with the tectonic shift. Furthermore, both groupings have experienced mission creep. The G7 stepped over its core mandate on macroeconomic coordination, bringing non-economic issues under its purview. The G20's expansion in mandate occurred primarily within the economic and financial sphere. This allows for a carefully crafted division of labour between the G7 and the G20 with the former claiming responsibility on non-economic issues and the latter taking the lead on the economic aspects of the multifaceted global governance endeavour. The G7 and the G20 can also better fulfil their roles by focusing on a division of labour that cultivates cooperation and functional complementarity with other institutions for global economic governance that have already contributed to global governance in their own way.

That said, both the G7 and the G20 suffer from varying degrees of legitimacy deficits in terms of substance, input and output. Buttressing the Gx's whole-process legitimacy warrants tackling the three interwoven dimensions of international institutional legitimacy in a holistic manner. To remedy substantive illegitimacy, the Gx should ensure that they address the most pressing challenge of the day, otherwise they would be obsolete sooner or later. To address input illegitimacy, expanding representation and enhancing outreach programmes would go a long way to strengthen the authority and rightfulness of the two essentially self-appointed groups. To make up for the shortfalls in output legitimacy, the Gx need to put forward innovative ways to improve compliance and effectiveness.

References

Bird, Graham. 2017. "Assessing the G20's Mutual Assessment Process: A MAP but Little Direction." *World Economics Journal* 18 (2): 83–106.

Bishop, Matthew Louis, and Anthony Payne. 2021. "Steering Towards Reglobalization: Can a Reformed G20 Rise to the Occasion?" *Globalizations* 18 (1): 120–140.

Bremmer, Ian, and Nouriel Roubini. 2011. "A G-Zero World: The New Economic Club Will Produce Conflict, not Cooperation." *Foreign Affairs* 90 (2): 2–7.

Buchanan, Allen, and Robert O. Keohane. 2006. "The Legitimacy of Global Governance Institutions." *Ethics & International Affairs* 20 (4): 405–437.

Callaghan, Mike, Daniela Strube, Emmanuel Nnadozie, Azamat Abdymomunov, Gary Hawke, Ron Duncan, and Raymond Saner. 2014. G20 Outreach and Non-G20 Member Views on the G20. In *G20 Monitor*. Sydney: Lowy Institute for International Policy.

Cesarano, Filippo. 2006. *Monetary Theory and Bretton Woods: The Construction of an International Monetary Order*. Cambridge: Cambridge University Press.

Cho, Sungjoon, and Claire R. Kelly. 2012. "Promises and Perils of New Global Governance: A Case of the G20." *Chicago Journal of International Law* 12 (2): 491–562.

Cooper, Andrew F. 2010. "The G20 as an Improvised Crisis Committee and/or a Contested 'Steering Committee' for the World." *International Affairs* 86 (3): 741–757.

Cooper, Andrew F. 2014. "The Group of Twenty: Input and Output Legitimacy, Reforms and Agenda." In *New Global Economic Architecture: The Asian Perspective*, edited by Masahiro Kawai, Peter J. Morgan, and Pradumna B. Rana. Cheltenham and Northampton: Edward Elgar.

Cooper, Andrew F., and Colin I. Bradford. 2010. The G20 and the Post-Crisis Economic Order. In *CIGI G20 Papers*. Waterloo: Centre for International Governance Innovation.

Cooper, Andrew F., and Kelly Jackson. 2008. "The Incremental Transformation of the G8 through the Heiligendamm Process." *Studia Diplomatica* 61 (2): 79–88.

Cooper, Andrew F., and Andrew Schrumm. 2011. "Reconciling the Gs: The G8, the G5, and the G20 in a World of Crisis." In *Global Financial Crisis: Global Impact and Solutions*, edited by Paolo Savona, John J. Kirton and Chiara Oldani. Surrey and Burlington: Ashgate.

Cooper, Andrew F., and Ramesh Thakur. 2013. "The G20 as the Answer to the Crisis of Global Governance." In *The Group of Twenty (G20)*. London and New York: Routledge.

Debaere, Peter, and Jan Orbie. 2013. "The European Union in the Gx System: Representation and Coordination." In *Routledge Handbook on the European Union and International Institutions: Performance, Policy, Power*, edited by Knud Erik Jørgensen and Katie Verlin Laatikainen. London: Routledge.

Drezner, Daniel W. 2014. *The System Worked: How the World Stopped Another Great Depression*. New York: Oxford University Press.

English, Kevin, Xenia Maren Menzies, Jacob Muirhead, and Jennifer Prenger. 2012. A Map for Strengthening the G20 Mutual Assessment Process. In *CIGI Junior Fellows Policy Brief Series*. Waterloo: Centre for International Governance Innovation.

Fabig, Holger, Yannick Kirchhof, and Inka Zippe. 2014. "Overcoming the Euro Area Crisis—Reforms and Results." In *Global Cooperation Among G20 Countries: Responding to the Crisis and Restoring Growth*, edited by Michael Callaghan, Chetan Ghate, Stephen Pickford, and Francis Xavier Rathinam. New Delhi: Springer.

Faruqee, Hamid, and Krishna Srinivasan. 2012. "The G-20 Mutual Assessment Process—A Perspective from IMF Staff." *Oxford Review of Economic Policy* 28 (3): 493–511.

G7 Accountability Working Group. 2021. "G7 Carbis Bay Progress Report: Advancing Universal Health Coverage and Global Health Through Strengthening Health Systems, Preparedness and Resilience." Accessed 1 December 2021. https://assets.publishing.service.gov.uk/government/uploads/system/uploads/attachment_data/file/990319/G7_Carbis_Bay_Report.pdf.

G20. 2014. "G20 Development Working Group Accountability Framework." Accessed 18 January 2022. http://www.g20.utoronto.ca/2014/g20_development_working_group_accountability_framework.pdf.

Gehring, Thomas, and Benjamin Faude. 2014. "A Theory of Emerging Order Within Institutional Complexes: How Competition Among Regulatory International Institutions Leads to institutional Adaptation and Division of Labor." *The Review of International Organizations* 9: 471–498.

Hajnal, Peter I. 2007. *The G8 System and the G20: Evolution, Role and Documentation*. Aldershot: Ashgate.

Hajnal, Peter I. 2015. "G7/8 and G20 Accountability and Civil Society." In *The G8-G20 Relationship in Global Governance*, edited by Marina Larionova and John J. Kirton. Abingdon and New York: Ashgate.

IMF. 2017. IMF Quotas. Washington, DC: International Monetary Fund.

Jain, Ash, Matthew Kroenig, Tobias Bunde, Sophia Gaston, and Yuichi Hosoya. 2021. *From The G7 To A D10—Strengthening Democratic Cooperation For Todays Challenges*. Washington, DC: Atlantic Council.

Ji, Xianbai, and Guanie Lim. 2021. "The Chinese Way of Reforming Global Economic Governance: An Analysis of China's Rising Role in the Group of Twenty (G-20)." *The Chinese Economy* online first. https://doi.org/10.1080/10971475.2021.1972546.

Ji, Xianbai. 2022. "How Global Summitry Evolves: The Complementary Multilateralism Perspective." *The Chinese Journal of International Politics* 15 (3): 289–312. https://doi.org/10.1093/cjip/poac011

Kirton, John J. 1995. "The Diplomacy of Concert: Canada, the G7 and the Halifax Summit." *Canadian Foreign Policy* 3 (1): 63–80.

Kirton, John J. 2008. "From G8 2003 to G13 2010? The Heiligendamm Process's Past, Present, and Future." In *Emerging Powers in Global Governance: Lessons from the Heiligendamm Process*, edited by Andrew F. Cooper and Agata Antkiewicz. Waterloo: Wilfrid Laurier University Press.

Kirton, John J. 2015. "Advancing G8 and G20 Effectiveness Through Improved Accountability Assessment." In *The G8-G20 Relationship in Global Governance*, edited by Marina Larionova and John J. Kirton. Abingdon and New York: Ashgate.

Lall, Ranjit. 2017. "Beyond Institutional Design: Explaining the Performance of International Organizations." *International Organization* 71: 245–280.

Larionova, Marina V., Mark Rakhmangulov, and Andrey Shelepov. 2015. "Assessing G7/8 and G20 Effectiveness in Global Governance." In *The G8-G20 Relationship in Global Governance*, edited by Marina Larionova and John J. Kirton. Abingdon and New York: Ashgate.

Lesage, Dries. 2017. "From Washington to Hangzhou: Does the G20 Live Up to Its Potential?" *Studia Diplomatica* 68 (3): 65–78.

Lesage, Dries, Peter Debaere, Sacha Dierckx, and Mattias Vermeiren. 2013. "IMF Reform After the Crisis." *International Politics* 50: 553–578.

Matlay, Lyubava. 2017. "Spain as a Permanent Invited Participant of G-20 (2009–2017)." *SHV* 3 (2): 7–13.

Mitchell, Sara McLaughlin, and Paul R. Hensel. 2007. "International Institutions and Compliance with Agreements." *American Journal of Political Science* 51 (4): 721–737.

Navarrete, Jorge Eduardo. 2008. G8 and "The Other Five": Creating a Constructive Relationship—The Role of Mexico. In *FES Briefing Paper 5*. Berlin: Friedrich-Ebert-Stiftung.

Nelson, Rebecca M. 2020. International Economic Policy Coordination at the G-7 and the G-20. In *CRS Report*. Washington, DC: Congressional Research Service.

Orsini, Amandine, Jean-Frédéric Morin, and Oran Young. 2013. "Regime Complexes: A Buzz, a Boom, or a Boost for Global Governance?" *Global Governance* 19 (1): 27–39.

Panova, Victoria V. 2007. "Russia and the G8: Matured Partnership." In *Financing Development: The G8 and UN Contribution*, edited by Michele Fratianni, John J. Kirton and Paolo Savona. Aldershot and Burlington: Ashgate.

Patrick, Stewart. 2010. "The G20: Shifting Coalitions of Consensus Rather Than Blocs." In *Global Leadership in Transition: Making the G20 Effective and Responsive*, edited by Colin Bradford and Wonhyuk Lim. Seoul and Washington, DC: Korea Development Institute & The Brookings Institution.

Postel-Vinay, Karoline. 2014. *The G20: A New Geopolitical Order*. Basingstoke: Palgrave Macmillan.

Rana, Pradumna B. 2011. "A Proposal to Enhance the G20's "Input" Legitimacy." VoxEU. Accessed 11 November 2021. https://voxeu.org/article/proposal-enhance-g20-s-input-legitimacy.

Rana, Pradumna B. 2021a. Covid-19: Time for Emergency G20 Summit. In *RSIS Commentary*. Singapore: S. Rajaratnam School of International Studies.

Rana, Pradumna B. 2021b. Is the G20 Breaking Up? In *RSIS Commentary Series*. Singapore: S. Rajaratnam School of International Studies.

Rana, Pradumna B., and Xianbai Ji. 2018. G20 at Ten: Time for Greater Multilateral Role. In *RSIS Commentary Series*. Singapore: S. Rajaratnam School of International Studies.

Rommerskirchen, Charlotte, and Holly Snaith. 2018. "Bringing Balance to the Force? A Comparative Analysis of Institutionalisation Processes in the G20's Mutual Assessment Process and the EU's Macroeconomic Imbalances Procedure." *New Political Economy* 23 (4): 391–406.

Scholte, Jan Aart. 2016. "Relations with Civil Society." In *The Oxford Handbook of International Organizations*, edited by Jacob Katz Cogan, Ian Hurd and Ian Johnstone. Oxford: Oxford University Press.

Shultz, George P. 1993. *Turmoil and Triumph: My Years as Secretary of State* New York: Charles Scribner's Sons.

Sinha, Rohit, and Geethanjali Nataraj. 2013. *Doesn't G20 Need a Secretariat?* New Delhi: Observer Research Foundation.

Slaughter, Steven. 2021. "Global Informalism and the G20." *Journal of International Relations and Development* 24: 533–554.

Steil, Benn. 2013. *The Battle of Bretton Woods: John Maynard Keynes, Harry Dexter White, and the Making of a New World Order*. Princeton: Princeton University Press.

Subacchi, Paola, and Stephen Pickford. 2011. Legitimacy vs Effectiveness for the G20. A Dynamic Approach to Global Economic Governance. In *International Economics Briefing Paper*. London: Chatham House.

Truman, Edwin M. 2006. "Rearranging IMF Chairs and Shares: The Sine qua non of IMF Reform." In *Reforming the IMF for the 21st Century*, edited by Edwin M. Truman. Washington, DC: Peterson Institute for International Economics.

Ulfgard, Rebecka Villanueva, and Bernadette Vega. 2019. "The Effectiveness-Legitimacy Nexus in the G20's Development Working Group: A View from Mexico." *South African Journal of International Affairs* 26 (4): 621–641.

Vestergaard, Jakob, and Robert H. Wade. 2012. "Establishing a New Global Economic Council: Governance Reform at the G20, the IMF and the World Bank." *Global Policy* 3 (3): 257–269.

Wade, Robert H. 2011. "Emerging World Order? From Multipolarity to Multilateralism in the G20, the World Bank, and the IMF." *Politics & Society* 39 (3): 347–378.

Wangwe, Samuel, and Hiroshi Kawamura. 2018. "The 1960s: High Growth, High Hopes, and Looming Structural Imbalances." In *The World Economy Through the Lens of the United Nations*, edited by José Antonio Ocampo, Anis Chowdhury and Diana Alarcón. Oxford: Oxford University Press.

Wise, Jacqui. 2021. "Covid-19: G7 Vaccine Promises Fail to Meet Scale of Challenge, Say Critics." *BMJ* 373: 1520.

World Bank. 2021. "COVID 19: Debt Service Suspension Initiative." Accessed 3 June 2021. https://www.worldbank.org/en/topic/debt/brief/covid-19-debt-service-suspension-initiative.

Wouters, Jan, and Sven Van Kerckhoven. 2017. "The Gx Contribution to Multilateral Governance: Balancing Efficiency and Inclusiveness." *Studia Diplomatica* 68 (3): 45–64.

Zaum, Dominik. 2016. "Legitimacy." In *The Oxford Handbook of International Organizations*, edited by Jacob Katz Cogan, Ian Hurd and Ian Johnstone. Oxford: Oxford University Press.

CHAPTER 3

International Monetary and Economic Development Architecture: Complementarity Between Global and Regional Institutions

Pradumna B. Rana and Ramon Pacheco Pardo

Introduction

Global economic governance is in flux. The institutions and norms set up by the United States (US) and other Western powers such as the International Monetary Fund (IMF), World Trade Organisation (WTO), and the World Bank are being eroded. The economic rise of emerging countries, their newfound diplomatic assertiveness, and contestation of supposedly universal norms are driving a process whereby the organisations launched during the post-World War II period are being challenged by regional

P. B. Rana (✉)
S. Rajaratnam School of International Studies, Nanyang Technological University, Singapore, Singapore
e-mail: prana@ntu.edu.sg

R. Pacheco Pardo
Department of European & International Studies, King's College London, London, UK

P. B. Rana and X. Ji (eds.), *From Centralised to Decentralising Global Economic Architecture*, https://doi.org/10.1007/978-981-19-2041-7_3

organisations and emerging power-led initiatives—especially in East Asia and from China. Or are they?

This chapter will argue that there is a clear potential for and evidence of functional complementarity, and "healthy" competition or cooperation between East Asian regional organisations and China-led governance initiatives on the one hand and existing global institutions on the other. There is less evidence of "unhealthy" competition such as race to the bottom in standards and forum shopping. The chapter underpins its normative case for functional cooperation and "healthy" competition by applying existing theoretical research on the fragmentation of global governance, as well as by presenting empirical evidence of existing cooperative efforts. Nonetheless, the chapter will argue that there are limits for potential functional complementarity and "healthy" competition between regional and global institutions.[1] These are the history of the establishment of regional institutions, the gap between rhetoric and reality, and the evolving geopolitical forces.

The question of whether East Asian regional institutions in general and China in particular will seek to cooperate with or compete against international institutions is crucial for the future of global economic governance. As Chin and Freeman (2016) posit, the rise of an increasing number of emerging powers has resulted in the contestation of international institution priorities, agenda setting, norms, rules, and principles. Furthermore, the development of multi-layered governance—mixing global, regional, bilateral, and national arrangements—has been portrayed as a defection from global institutions (Cooper et al. 2008).

The case of East Asian regional institutions and China-led institutions merits particular attention. Outside of the European Union (EU), East Asia is the part of the world where regionalism is the strongest.

[1] Indeed, Muhlich and Fritz (2021) challenge the dominant view that the fragmented global financial safety net needs to be coordinated by stitching together different layers. Citing the book "When Things Don't Fall Apart" (Grabel 2018), they insist that the global crisis induced inconsistent and ad hoc discontinuities in global financial governance and developmental finance that are now having profound effects on emerging market and developing economies. Their normative claim is that the resulting incoherence in global financial governance is productive rather than debilitating. In the age of productive incoherence, a more complex, dense, fragmented, and multi-polar form of global financial governance is expanding possibilities for policy and institutional experimentation, policy space for economic development, financial stability and resilience, and financial inclusion. Meanwhile having a big coordination team would lead to "white elephant problem" in practice.

Economic and financial initiatives such as the Chiang Mai Initiative Multilateralization (CMIM), the ASEAN+3 Macroeconomic Research Office (AMRO), the BRICS's Contingent Reserve Arrangement (CRA), or the pan-continental Asian Development Bank (ADB) form an institutional network linking together the countries in the region. Moreover, the CMIM, AMRO, and other financial initiatives such as the Asian Bond Markets Initiative (ABMI) were the direct result of the Asian financial crisis (AFC) and displeasure with the behaviour of the IMF (Pacheco Pardo and Rana 2015). Thus, they are useful case studies.

China, meanwhile, has been portrayed as the strongest disruptor to the existing global governance architecture (Beeson and Li 2016). Beijing has made no secret of its unhappiness with existing global institutions—especially the limited power that China holds, as well as their allegedly pro-Western agenda (Beeson and Li 2016). Furthermore, Chinese authorities have been busy launching potentially alternative institutions. Among them, the Asian Infrastructure Investment Bank (AIIB) and the New Development Bank (NDB) stand out. As with the East Asian financial institutions highlighted above, these two economic institutions are largely the result of discontent with existing Western-led organisations (Wang 2015). Given that the key reason why Beijing has launched these institutions is similar to that of East Asian financial initiatives, it is of analytical interest to understand how these regional institutions are working with their global counterparts. This is what we do in this chapter.

To make our case that the East Asian regional layer and China-led institutions have a clear potential to work in a complementary manner with the global layer while injecting a dose of "healthy" competition, but that there are limits to this cooperation, we focus on the global financial architecture (GFA) defined as the global financial safety net and development finance architectures. The reasons are two-fold. First, financial safety net is an area in which East Asian countries have established institutions whose membership includes countries in the region alone—thus preventing the US from exercising power from the inside. Meanwhile, development finance is an area in which China has taken a decisive lead role and the US and Japan are not part of its recently launched institutions. Thus, we can observe the approach towards global institutions that East Asia and China have taken when independent from direct American—and, in the latter case, Japanese—influence. Second, as already explained, in both of these areas institution-building resulted from displeasure with existing global arrangements. In theory, this would make full-blown "unhealthy" competition more plausible.

In the following section, we will present the theoretical framework underpinning our analysis, as well as a short summary of our methodology. We will then briefly examine factors that have led to the decentralisation of the GFA. This will be followed by an exploration of the emerging multi-layered financial safety net in East Asia. We will then suggest how the East Asian regional layer might cooperate with its global counterpart, and the limits to any potential complementarity and "healthy" competition. This will be followed by a section analysing the decentralising global development finance architecture and China's institutional build-up in this area. We will then analyse the extent to which China-led institutions might cooperate with their global counterparts, as well as, the limits to complementarity and "healthy" competition. A concluding section will briefly summarise our arguments and findings.

Theoretical Framework and Methodology

The growth of regionalism in terms of both the number and scope of regional institutions, together with the increasing assertiveness of emerging powers willing to launch and participate in new institutions, has led to discussions about the so-called contested multilateralism. This term defines the idea that powers dissatisfied with status quo institutions seek to create their own that may challenge the rules and practices of the status quo institution (Morse and Keohane 2014). Contested multilateralism can take two forms: (1) regime shifting, which occurs when dissatisfied powers shift to an alternative institution that they find more favourable (e.g. the World Bank entering the field of global health governance) and (2) competitive regime creation, which occurs when dissatisfied powers create a new formal institution or informal arrangement (e.g. proliferation of security initiatives) (Morse and Keohane 2014). The latter is the case in the regional monetary and economic development institutions in East Asia and China-led initiatives, respectively.

The creation of alternative institutions has the potential of leading to the fragmentation of global governance in multiple areas. Fragmentation refers to the institutional framework in a given policy domain including a patchwork of international institutions with different characters, constituencies, spatial scope, and subject matter (Biermann et al. 2009). A priori, decentralisation seems to have negative connotations because it can lead to exclusion and forum shopping (Zürn and Faude 2013). However, decentralisation is not necessarily negative when we understand that it partially results from functional differentiation linked to the increasing complexity of policy domains and is not merely the consequence of a powerful actor being dissatisfied with existing institutions (Zürn and Faude 2013). This suggests that contested multilateralism is not necessarily related to contestation per se only, but rather can also result from functional needs.

Decentralised global governance and cooperation among institutions are therefore not mutually exclusive. Functional overlap can lead to cooperation resultant from a division of labour among institutions, in turn linked to the members of a particular institution having an interest in a particular division or labour. This fosters institutional adaptation to achieve the desired complementarities (Gehring and Faude 2014). Instead of turning to forum shopping, as much current literature assumes, members of two or more institutions with functional overlap will seek to maximise their participation in multiple institutions. They do so by pressing for adaptation and concomitant division of labour, as the case of agricultural genetically modified organism illustrates (Gehring and Faude 2014).

In the finance architecture, however, existing literature suggests that decentralisation seems to be leading to competition. Regional financial institutions in the EU, East Asia, Latin America, or among the BRICS stem from a displeasure with the IMF. The open and significant differences between EU institutions and the IMF in areas such as the division of labour or debt restructuring, among others, point in this direction (Henning 2017). In the economic development architecture, existing literature suggests that decentralisation is resulting in competition. The AIIB and the NDB are portrayed as focused on the narrower needs of their members and willing to disregard existing conditionality and norms (Kahler 2017).

We disagree with these negative views. Building on the "functional fragmentation" literature just discussed, we will explain how a division of labour is emerging and is likely to continue to develop between East Asian or China-led institutions, on the one hand, and global institutions, on the other. We will show how this has already resulted in incipient institutional adaptation and cooperation. We will argue, however, that cooperation has not entirely eliminated existing limits to cooperation due to geopolitics and a history of limited cooperation across East Asia.

To prove our argument, we use three research methods. First, we conduct desk research to explain and analyse the creation and development of multi-layered governance architectures in the areas of money and economic development. Second, we use content analysis of official documents from global and regional institutions to analyse the extent to which functional complementarity and "healthy" competition will, in our view, define the relationship between global and regional institutions, as well as the limits to said cooperation. We should note that we have also used some desk research for the cooperation and limits analysis, as well as some content analysis for the creation and development of multi-layered architectures sections. Third, we interviewed staff from international institutions and government officials for background purposes, and in some cases to clarify and support specific arguments.

Decentralising Global Financial Architecture

As Kindleberger (1986) has noted, the absence of a rules-based system contributed to the economic instability during the inter-war period that eventually led to the Great Depression of the early 1930s. Thus, the focus of the Bretton Woods conference in 1944 was to establish a set of rules-based global institutions to provide public goods. In the area of money, the IMF was established to provide short-term finance for macroeconomic stability, and the World Bank was established to provide long-term development finance for poverty reduction.

This global financial architecture (GFA) worked well for a number of decades and brought about economic prosperity across different parts of the world. More recently, however, it has tended to (1) decentralise and become more multi-layered with global, regional, bilateral and national economic institutions, and (2) move away from a rules-based to a more informal network-based system (Rana 2014).

A number of factors account for the evolution of a more decentralised GFA. Firstly, there has been a shift from a uni-polar to a multi-polar world, especially the rise of China and its demand and desire to play a greater role in writing global rules and provide financial resources. Secondly, there have been impediments to the effective reform of the governance of global institutions to give a greater voice to emerging powers. Global institutions are relatively inflexible institutions and cannot change even if they wish to. These two factors relate to the idea that global governance decentralisation is partly related to powerful actors being dissatisfied with existing institutions and unwilling to support them. Kawai, Petri, and Sisli-Ciamarra (2009) have applied the theory of clubs to explain this phenomenon. Thirdly, financial globalisation has dramatically changed the environment in which global institutions operate and has also reduced their effectiveness, which is linked to the notion that functionality is a driver behind decentralisation. Kawai and Rana (2009) have argued that preventing and managing a financial crisis in a globalised world needs actions at the global, regional, and national levels.

Decentralisation of the GFA accelerated under the Trump Presidency. The US has for a long time played a lead role in international economic institutions through formal means (e.g. financial contributions) and informal practices and conventions (Foot et al. 2003). But Trump's preference for "fair trade" and "bilateralism" meant reduced US support and commitments for multilateral bodies such as the IMF, the World Bank, and the WTO. At the same time, the BRICS, and China in particular, have expressed interest in filling the gap.

Decentralisation of the GFA would suggest that global and regional institutions compete against each other. Authors focusing on a competitive relationship argue that regional institutions will make their global counterparts obsolete and create opportunities for arbitrage (Rhee et al. 2013; Henning 2017). This notwithstanding, a complementary relationship between the two sets of institutions has evolved for a number of reasons. First, both regional and global institutions have relative comparative advantages in different areas—cross-regional expertise and experience plus institutional memory in the case of the latter, region-specific knowledge, and proximity in the former (Kawai and Rana 2009). Second, the demand for international public goods is big enough for both to co-exist (Desai and Vreeland 2013). Third, the still-limited capacity of regional institutions needs improving—which global institutions can help with (Desai and Vreeland 2013). Fourthly, managing globalisation needs global, regional, and even national institutions (Kawai and Rana 2009). These intertwined reasons are at play in the cases of the global financial safety net and economic development architecture.

Multi-Layered Global Financial Safety Net

Initially, the global financial safety net was centralised and included global institutions only. The architecture which prevailed in the 1970s and 1980s is depicted in Fig. 3.1. It comprised the IMF with the Group of Seven

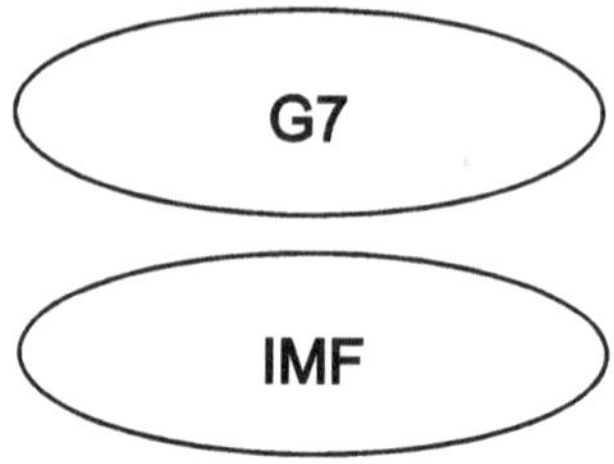

Fig. 3.1 Centralised global financial safety net

(G7) as the oversight body. This architecture was mostly successful in promoting macroeconomic and financial stability, aside from the Latin American debt crisis of the 1980s and the problems with the European Monetary System in the early 1990s.

In the aftermath of the AFC and the Global Financial Crisis (GFC), however, this centralised global financial safety net has become more decentralised—accelerating a trend that in some regions had already started before. The decentralising Global Financial Safety Net (GFSN) comprises the Multilateral Financial Safety Net (IMF), Regional Financial Safety Nets (such as the CMIM, AMRO, and BRICS CRA in Asia), Bilateral Safety Nets (swaps among central banks), and National Financial Safety Nets (reserve accumulation by countries), as depicted in Fig. 3.2. The G20 has also emerged as the oversight body of the GFSN.

Ad Hoc Complementarity Between ASEAN+3 RFSN and the IMF

Before the AFC, the only RFSN in East Asia was the ASEAN swap arrangement (ASA), which was established in 1977 when the original members agreed to a reciprocal currency swap arrangement among themselves. The idea was to provide liquidity support to members experiencing balance of payments difficulties. The maximum amount of liquidity available under the ASA eventually reached $200 million. The size of the ASA was too small to be of use in helping countries manage the AFC though; thus, it was not used.

The AFC led East Asian countries to revisit the issue of a RFSN, mainly because of the way in which the IMF managed the crisis. Four of the crisis-affected countries—Indonesia, Philippines, South Korea, and Thailand—had accepted an IMF programme, while Malaysia went alone. The IMF misdiagnosed the problem and prescribed the wrong medicine (Sussangkarn 2011). It was also believed at the time that the IMF might

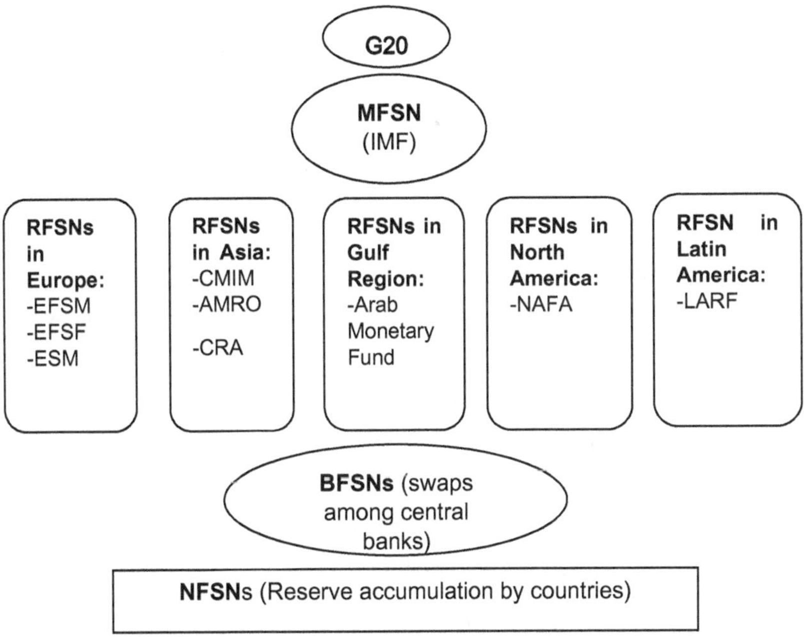

Fig. 3.2 Decentralising GFSN (global financial safety net) (*Notes* AMRO = ASEAN+3 Macroeconomic Research Office; BFSN = Bilateral Financial Safety Nets; CMIM = Chiang Mai Initiative Multilateralization; CRA = Contingent Reserve Arrangement; EFSF = European Financial Stability Facility; EFSM = European Financial Stabilisation Mechanism; ESM = European Stability Mechanism; NAFA = North American Framework Agreement; NFSN = National Financial Safety Net; LARF = Latin American Reserve Fund; RFSN = Regional Financial Safety Net)

not have adequate resources to help countries manage a "capital account" crisis associated with large inflows and sudden reversals of private capital flows (Kawai and Rana 2009).

There was a strong feeling among policymakers in East Asia that a regional financing facility could act as the first line of defence. It could provide short-term liquidity and thereby prevent a crisis in case of speculative attacks (Sussangkarn 2011). As a result, ASEAN+3 Finance Ministers agreed in May 2000 to launch the Chiang Mai Initiative (CMI) as a regional "self- help and support mechanism" to provide "sufficient and timely financial support to ensure financial stability in the East Asia region" (ASEAN+3 Finance Ministers 2000). The CMI expanded the ASA to all ASEAN members. In addition, it set up a bilateral swap network among the ASEAN+3 countries. The ASA was expanded to eventually reach $2 billion. ASEAN+3 countries also signed bilateral swaps among each other and by 2008 there were 16 agreements amounting to $84 billion (Pacheco Pardo and Rana 2015). In March 2010, after the GFC, these were combined and expanded to become the Chiang Mai Initiative Multilateralization (CMIM) or the $120 billion "self-managed reserve pooling arrangement". All ASEAN+3 members (plus Hong Kong, China) contribute to this fund and are eligible to borrow from it in case they face payments problems. Under this arrangement, foreign exchange is earmarked for crisis prevention and crisis management but held in separate national accounts.

Pursuit of complementarity and—as a result—cooperation has been the key focus of the ASEAN+3 RFSN. From the beginning, ASEAN+3 Finance Ministers stipulated that the RFSN in East Asia should "supplement the existing international facilities" (ASEAN+3 Finance Ministers 2000). The way that complementarity was promoted in the CMIM—and its predecessor, the CMI—was by requiring the existence of an IMF-supported programme to provide assistance in excess of a certain percentage of maximum access. Initially, on an ad hoc basis, only ten percent of the maximum access was readily available with 90% linked to an IMF programme. The size of the delinked portion was subsequently increased. The link to the IMF was also intended to address the moral hazard problem in lending and the lack of independent surveillance capacity in the CMI (Pacheco Pardo and Rana 2015).

In the aftermath of the severe credit crunch that the region experienced because of the GFC in 2008, the CMI bilateral swaps were not used. This was because of the small size of the swaps and the absence of a rapid response mechanism to trigger the swaps—each bilateral swap had to be triggered one at a time (Pacheco Pardo and Rana 2015). Leaving technical issues aside, CMI swaps were not used due to the rhetoric-reality gap in East Asia as well. This gap refers to the fact that the rhetoric of economic cooperation in the region is not always matched by its reality in practice (Jones and Smith 2007).

After the GFC, ASEAN+3 took a number of actions to increase financial resources available from its RFSN and to clarify the disbursement procedures. These include (i) doubling its size of CMIM to $240 billion,

(ii) increasing the delinked portion to 30% with a view of increasing it further to 40% subject to review (iii) agreeing to a decision-making process and operational guidelines, and (iv) establishing the ASEAN+3 Macroeconomic Research Office (AMRO) in 2011 as the independent surveillance unit for the CMIM and giving it the status of an international organisation in 2016 with a mandate for surveillance of the member countries either individually or collectively (Chang 2016).

To deal with the fallout from the COVID-19 pandemic, ASEAN+3 governments and central banks provided fiscal and monetary stimulus on an unprecedented scale, in most countries, fiscal policy largely targeted households and businesses, while unconventional monetary policy was used to support financial markets. The size of stimulus packages ranged from 10 to 40% of GDP. The use of direct income support proved useful. The central banks in the region also provided monetary stimulus measures by lowering interest rates. They also provided government guarantees on select banking activities, temporary credit lines, and bought corporate bonds.

In addition to these individual country efforts, actions were also taken to strengthen the CMIM. At a virtual meeting of the ASEAN+3 Finance Ministers and Central Bank Governors in September 2020, the leaders agreed to (i) increase the size of the IMF de-linked portion to 40%, and (ii) decided to use local currencies for CMIM crisis financing on a voluntary and demand-driven basis. They also announced the completion of the CMIM conditionality framework under which, with the analytical support of the AMRO, CMIM, can set conditions for the IMF-delinked portion (ASEAN+3 Finance Ministers and Central Bank Governors 2020). An agreement was also reached on a time limit for swap executions and "the meeting format for the CMIM decision-making body" (AMRO 2021).

Why ASEAN+3 RFSN Was Not Been Used During the COVID-19 Pandemic?

Despite the above actions, the CMIM, the region's financing arrangement, was not utilised during the COVID-19 pandemic. This is in contrast to RFSNs in other parts of the world. For example, the European Stability Mechanism (ESM) supported the provision of health care in a number of member countries through a 240 billion euro facility. Similarly, the LARF, EFSF, and the AMF assisted member countries to partially address the balance of payments difficulties arising from the pandemic (Han and Watanabe 2020).

There are a number of reasons why the CMIM remains unutilised. First, under the new agreement, five ASEAN members—Indonesia, Malaysia, Philippines, Singapore, and Thailand—can borrow a maximum amount of approximately $23 billion each from the CMIM with an IMF programme in place—one-third of which will be the delinked portion—under a single contract at one go (Hill and Menon 2014).[2] These amounts are large compared to the old CMI swaps, but still inadequate to prevent and manage the newer types of capital account crisis associated with large inflows and sudden withdrawal of short-term financial capital. It is unlikely that ASEAN+3 countries will increase their commitments to the CMIM and raise the percentage of the delinked portion without the capacity of AMRO being strengthened significantly for regional surveillance and for designing conditions under which funds can be loaned out—otherwise there could be moral hazard. Although AMRO has come a long way, as a relatively new institution, it still lacks the research capacity, human resources, and experience to serve as an independent surveillance unit.

More important is the speed and efficiency with which requests for assistance can be disbursed (Hill and Menon 2014). The operational guidelines for the CMIM note that decision based on two-thirds majority are to be made within two weeks of the swap request (AMRO 2012).[3] This is unlikely to happen as the CMIM is not a centralised fund, but a "self-managed" arrangement where contributions are held by individual central banks and monetary authorities. Also, the decision rests

[2] With the size of the de-linked portion increasing to 40%, this amount will increase somewhat.

[3] Activation of the "CMIM may be initiated by any CMIM Party by submitting to the CMIM Coordinating Countries a request for the purchase of US dollars or other members' currencies under the CMIM arrangement with its local currency. The Coordinating Countries, in turn, will deliver the swap request notice and other relevant information to the Executive Level Decision Making Body (ELDMB) comprising the deputies and convene a meeting to decide on the swap request. Upon approval, CMIM Parties will proceed with the activation of bilateral swap transactions between each of the swap providing parties and the relevant swap requesting party, in accordance with the terms and pro rata allocation provided in the CMIM Agreement. In any event, determinations required in response to a swap request should be completed within two weeks following the delivery of the swap request notice to the members of the ELDMB" Bangko Sentral ng Pilipinas (2020).

with a non-resident body and there is uncertainty regarding the nature of information and the analysis required to facilitate the decision-making (Sussangkarn 2011). In contrast, bilateral swaps are fast-disbursing and come without explicit conditionalities as they are well-collateralised.

The inadequacies of the CMIM can also be attributed to the just-mentioned rhetoric-reality gap, which means that countries in the region do not match their verbal commitments to cooperation with actual actions. It can also be attributed to geopolitical competition between China and Japan. Getting both of them to agree to their respective financial contributions and a fair distribution of voting ratios already proved difficult (Pitakdumrongkit 2016). Furthermore, both powers seem to now be engaging in competitive bilateral swap arrangement network building through their central banks (Pacheco Pardo 2017). Also funds from the CMIM are linked to the IMF for which there is a stigma, and so Asian countries prefer alternative sources of funding like bilateral swaps from the US FED. These inadequacies, however, are not necessarily an impediment to cooperation with the IMF.

From Ad Hoc to Structured ASEAN+3 RFSN and IMF Cooperation

The present modality of ad hoc cooperation between the ASEAN+3 RFSN (CMIM and AMRO) and IMF is yet to be effective. Even when it is effective, the funds available through this modality may be sufficient only to manage a moderate crisis confined to a single country. In order to manage a more serious crisis with contagion to neighbouring countries, a more structured form of cooperation between the ASEAN+3 RFSN and IMF should be considered similar to the arrangement set up in Europe to manage the eurozone crisis. This framework would involve pooling of financial, human, and technical resources between the ASEAN+3 RFSN and IMF in three cooperative activities (Table 3.1). Our proposal is similar to the one established between the EU and the IMF to fight the Eurozone crisis. Although it was not an ideal system and there were sometimes conflicts between the partners (Darvas et al. 2018), it had a number of positive features which could be adopted in Asia.

To begin with, ASEAN+3 countries seeking financial resources should be required to apply simultaneously to both the IMF and CMIM and the IMF and AMRO should jointly analyse and evaluate the applications. Currently, the analysis and evaluation by the two institutions are separate with AMRO responsible for CMIM funds (AMRO 2012). But AMRO's

Table 3.1 Structured ASEAN+3 RFSN and IMF cooperation

Possible issue/area of cooperation	*Advantages*
CRISIS MANAGEMENT	
1. Simultaneous request for financial assistance from CMIM and IMF and joint analysis and evaluation	• Bring in expertise from outside East Asia to supplement AMRO resources • IMF staff, in theory, would be more dispassionate to regional countries
2. Joint monitoring and surveillance, joint AMRO-IMF missions, and jointly developed conditionality	• Focus on relative comparative advantages (IMF, macro- and macro-financial and cross-regional experience; AMRO, regional financial and capital market developments, and structural reforms)
3. Co-financing (with amounts depending on specific basis) and joint supervision	• Would leverage CMIM funds as IMF funds would also come in
CRISIS PREVENTION	
4. Joint assessment (of eligibility) and co-financing	• Focus on relative comparative advantages • Would leverage CMIM funds as IMF funds would also come in

capacity is limited and it will take a long time to strengthen it. Involving both the IMF and AMRO in the analysis and evaluation process would increase its robustness in two ways. Firstly, experts from outside East Asia would support an understaffed AMRO and would arguably be less politicised than CMIM members. Decisions on applications could therefore be made more rapidly and involving IMF staff who, at least in theory, should feel more dispassionate about the country requesting a CMIM package. A crisis triggering an application for CMIM funds would need a decision to be taken in the shortest period of time and with the smallest moral hazard possible. IMF and AMRO intervention in the decision-making process would help both, since the speediness of AMRO and the robustness and experience of the IMF would produce complementarities.

In addition, a joint application to both the IMF and CMIM would help address the IMF stigma in East Asia. Given the experience of the 1997 AFC, politically it would be very difficult to sell an IMF programme anywhere in East Asia (Robles 2015). Having a joint process together with an ASEAN+3 institution—AMRO—would eliminate the potential duplication in terms of applications, while also lessening the political fallout of any programme the IMF might want to impose. For the IMF, this would limit the potential for forum shopping that ASEAN+3 institutions have brought. It would also require institutional adaptation in the form of working jointly with regional institutions that the IMF has been willing to undertake in the case of Eurozone crisis-related bailout packages.

The second area of cooperation between ASEAN+3 and the IMF would be joint monitoring and surveillance, and conditionality. Given that the IMF and AMRO reports have the common goal of ensuring that signs of financial stress are caught well on time to prevent a possible crisis, it would make sense for the two institutions to combine their capabilities. AMRO, as already noted, has very few staff. But they all come from ASEAN+3 members, giving them familiarity with one or more countries in the region – including relevant language skills and cultural understanding (Sussangkarn 2011). For its part, the IMF is better-resourced and has staff with knowledge about financial systems in different parts of the world (Clegg 2013). Pulling their resources together through joint IMF-AMRO missions and analysis including conditionality would strengthen the surveillance mechanism. The two institutions should focus on their relative comparative advantages—the IMF on macro- and micro-financial and cross-regional experience and the AMRO on regional financial and capital market developments and structural reforms. A division of labour is thus eminently feasible.

The third area of cooperation would be co-financing and joint supervision of liquidity provision programmes. Currently, financing would only come from the CMIM pool (AMRO 2012), which, as already explained above, would probably be insufficient to avert the spread of a financial crisis. Co-financing with the IMF would substantially increase the resources available for ASEAN+3 to deal with a financial crisis. As the experience of joint EU-IMF programmes shows, the percentage of a total rescue package coming from the RFSN and the IMF can be negotiated on a case-by-case basis (European Stability Mechanism 2016). Also, joint supervision of any approved liquidity provision programme would be the natural consequence of joint approval and financing. The institutional adaptation of the IMF to work hand-in-hand with EU institutions could be transposed to the East Asia region.

The timing is also appropriate for a more structured form of cooperation between the IMF and ASEAN+3 RFSN. Following the AFC, Asian countries had the IMF stigma which originated from the feeling of being unfairly treated and being forced to accept inappropriate conditions. This is now changing, and the IMF is invited to ASEAN+3 surveillance meetings together with AMRO. The IMF has also engaged in dialogues with AMRO as part of its outreach activities, although it does not have a formal technical assistance programme (IMF 2013). This engagement should be deepened further to a more structured form of ASEAN+3 RFSN and IMF cooperation as outlined above. The IMF should not reject such offers as it would be seen as being too euro-centric. To reflect Western domination of the IMF, Kapur and Subramanian (2013) had argued that the IMF was not an international but a “Euro-Atlantic Monetary Fund”. Thanks to its ongoing joint initiatives with East Asian institutions, the IMF is addressing this criticism and preventing forum shopping towards its ASEAN+3 counterparts.

AMRO and IMF Cooperation

At its Seoul Summit in November 2010, the G20 had endorsed a set of broad principles to promote a more structured form of cooperation between regional financial safety nets and the IMF (G20 2011). Accordingly, AMRO and IMF have taken a number of steps in this direction, both individually and jointly. AMRO has substantially strengthened its surveillance capacity. In addition to the confidential reports that it presents at ASEAN+3 meetings, it has started posting an annual ASEAN+3 Regional Outlook Report and monthly updates on its web site since 2017. In order to pre-qualify countries for its precautionary facility, the AMRO has also started to compile an Economic Review and Policy Dialogue (ERPD) matrix.

In July 2017, the IMF Board discussed the Policy Paper on Collaboration between Regional Financing Arrangements and the IMF (IMF 2017). Based on its experiences of working with RFSNs in Europe, the Middle East, North America, the former Soviet Union, and CMIM (through its test runs), the IMF derived 7 lessons, 6 principles, and 4 modalities that could be considered in collaborating with RFSNs. Among the lessons two were worth pointing out: (i) enhanced (structured) collaboration between the IMF and RFSNs could be beneficial, and (ii) such collaboration should be “early and evolving”. The IMF Board also discussed a Policy Paper on the Exchange of Documents between the Fund and Regional Financing Arrangements (2018). Accordingly, AMRO and IMF joint activities have also increased in recent years.

In October 2017, AMRO and IMF signed a Memorandum of Understanding (MOU) to promote cooperation in the areas of information exchange, capacity building, and joint seminars (AMRO 2017). This is a good beginning, but the two institutions should build up on this landmark MOU and promote collaboration in the three functional areas of joint analysis and evaluation; joint missions, surveillance, and joint conditionality focusing on the comparative advantages of the two institutions; and co-financing. These are the areas in which a group of RFSNs felt that they could enhance their cooperation with the IMF (Cheng et al. 2018).

In addition, annual High-level Dialogue between RFSNs and the IMF has also been formalised. The focus of the Dialogue in 2020 was, as expected, on possible assistance to member countries to address the adverse impacts of the pandemic. An annual research seminar, where experts from various institutions and academics to discuss issues of common interest was also launched in 2017.

Beyond cooperation, "healthy" competition between the ASEAN+3 RFSN and the IMF is also desirable. As already mentioned, the ASEAN+3 RFSN has not been tested as yet. Co-financing between the IMF and the ASEAN+3 RFSN could substantially increase the resources available to manage a financial crisis. During the recent Eurozone crisis, two separate packages of $142 billion and $130 billion (in current dollars) were put together for Greece and $100 billion for Portugal. Such large amounts of financing might not have been possible without the joint financing from the IMF and the European Stability Mechanism under the "troika" framework (Pacheco Pardo and Rana 2015).

In summary, East Asian countries do not take a competitive approach to relations with global institutions. The ASEAN+3 RFSN might have been created due to unhappiness with the behaviour of the IMF during the AFC and replicate some of its functions, but the CMIM and AMRO have and should take a cooperative approach towards their relations with the multilateral institution, as endorsed by the G20. Functional complementarity and the still-limited capacity of regional institutions are the main reasons behind cooperation.

Limits to Functional Complementarity and "Healthy" Competition Between ASEAN+3 RFSN and IMF

History poses a potential limit to functional complementarity and "healthy" competition between the ASEAN+3 RFSN and the IMF. The former was set up because of the displeasure with the behaviour of the latter by the same East Asian countries that blamed the Washington-based institution for exacerbating the AFC (Pacheco Pardo and Rana 2015). In other words, regime creation in the form of the ASEAN+3 RFSN was the response in the region to the behaviour of the IMF during the crisis. Asian countries have not requested support from the IMF since the AFC—not even during the global financial crisis when several European countries did—suggesting that an underlying IMF stigma, although decreasing, remains in the region. More recently, Myanmar has borrowed funds from the IMF to manage the pandemic.

Rhetoric-reality gap could also limit cooperation between the ASEAN+3 RFSN and the IMF. Many of the announced bilateral and regional safety nets have not been implemented effectively and utilised in times of crisis. For example, when Singapore and South Korea faced a financing constraint at the time of the global financial crisis, they triggered bilateral swap arrangements with the US Federal Reserve instead of activating the CMIM (Pacheco Pardo and Rana 2015). Such steps were repeated during the pandemic as well. These rhetoric-reality gap could limit CMIM-IMF cooperation in the future.

Geopolitical competition could also prevent ASEAN+3 RFSN-IMF cooperation. The US retains veto power over IMF decisions. It can also effectively reject nominations to head the institution and is able to shape financing packages to countries outside of Europe (Weisbrot 2015). Even in the case of recent EU bailout packages, the US helped to shape the IMF's decision to offer debt relief to Athens, since Washington sought to maintain Greece in the Eurozone in spite of opposition from Germany and other EU member states (Weisbrot 2015). American influence over the IMF could certainly derail crisis management cooperation with the CMIM. The ongoing US-China trade war could also lead to a decoupling and more intense "unhealthy" competition and rivalry between US-led and China-led institutions. The Biden administration is seeking to renew its relationship with its allies, while maintaining the tougher US approach taken by the Trump administration.

Decentralising Economic Development Architecture

Over the past 70 years, the economic development architecture has evolved dramatically. From one institution, we now have a multitude of development banks and funds. These include multilateral development banks (MDBs), a variety of sub-regional banks, and a number of specialised vertical funds. A large number of private funds with a development focus have also emerged.

Five stages in the evolution of the global development finance architecture can be noted (Fig. 3.3). The Bretton Woods conference established the World Bank in 1944 to finance post-war reconstruction. The second stage saw the establishment of regional development banks in the 1950s and 1960s, including the Asian Development Bank (ADB) in 1966. This was followed by the emergence of sub-regional development banks, mainly in Latin America. In the fourth stage, from the mid-1970s to the 2000s, specialised vertical funds—such as the International Fund for Agriculture Development—were established to address global issues and private development finance—such as the Gates Foundation—expanded.

The current fifth stage is closely related to the economic emergence of China, along with other BRICS or non-traditional donors. While traditional donors, namely the countries which are members of the

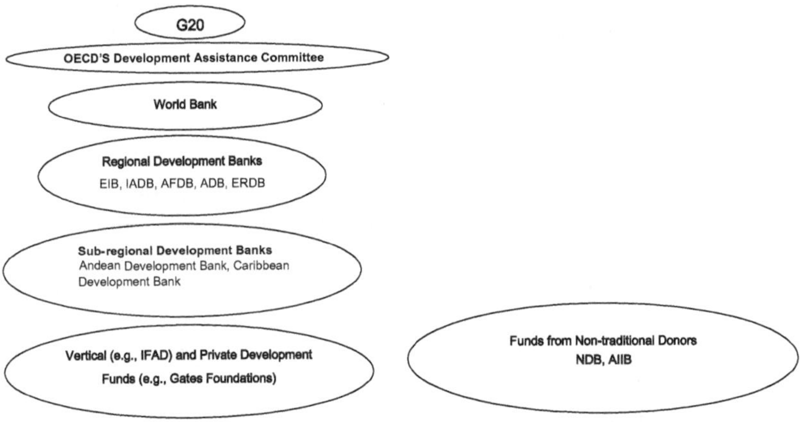

Fig. 3.3 Decentralising economic development architecture (*Notes* ADB = Asian Development Bank; AFDB = African Development Bank; AIIB = Asian Infrastructure Investment Bank; EIB = European Investment Bank; ERDB = European Bank for Reconstruction and Development; IFAD: International Fund for Agricultural Development; NDB: New Development Bank)

Development Assistance Committee (DAC) of the OECD, are financially constrained and are concerned with conserving their resources, non-traditional donors are expanding their bilateral and multilateral assistance (Kragelund 2011). In July 2014, China and the other BRICS formally agreed to launch the NDB, a new non-traditional. Then, in October 2014, China announced the founding of the AIIB—another non-traditional MDB. Both institutions became operational in 2016 and are implementing projects (Table 3.2).

China and Non-traditional MDBs

Beijing has made clear that it sees the AIIB and NDB as complementary to existing MDBs (Xinhua 2014). However, several others see them as a challenge. The AIIB, in particular, has proved to be very controversial. Wary of the potential for this institution to undermine its influence in Asia, the US was opposed to its launch and tried to stop allies from joining in (Beeson and Li 2016). Japan also refused to become a founding member of the AIIB, which Tokyo sees as a threat to the role of the ADB. Geopolitical considerations are the main reason behind the position of the US and Japan. They believe that the AIIB, especially, can undermine their economic power in Asia (Ren 2016).

Notwithstanding this apprehension, the two new MDBs led by China are required for several reasons. First, there is a massive need for infrastructure finance in Asia (Weaver 2015; Reisen 2015). The ADB has estimated that developing Asia will need to invest \$26 trillion or \$1.7 trillion per year for infrastructure development (ADB 2017). Until recently, the World Bank and the ADB were the two key MDBs providing development assistance to Asian countries. As Table 3.3 shows, traditionally the sectorial priorities and areas of operations of these traditional MDBs have been closely correlated with the prevailing development theory.

In the 1960s and 1970s, the prevailing development theory was the Harrod-Domar model which placed emphasis on the need to boost investment in order to achieve higher economic growth. Hence, during this period, both MDBs focused on projects for infrastructure development together with projects in the agricultural sector and those to meet the basic needs of the population. In the 1980s, the Solow model became popular, and the focus shifted to economic policy reforms and economic liberalisation policies. Operations of the MDBs accordingly shifted away from projects to structural adjustment loans to support economic reforms

Table 3.2 Details on traditional and non-traditional MDBs

	WB	*ADB*	*AIIB*	*NDB*
Headquarter	Washington D.C., US	Metro Manila, Philippines	Beijing, China	Shanghai, China
Founding/ present members	Present members, 189 members for IBRD, and 173 for IDA	31 founding members 68 members in 2018 a. 49 regional members b. 19 non-regional members	31 founding members 103 members in 2020 a. 46 regional members b. 39 non-regional members c. 18 prospective members	5 BRICS countries: a. Brazil b. Russia c. India d. China e. South Africa Membership open to non-BRICS
Operational from	IBRD from 1946 IDA from 1960	19 December 1966	April 2016	April 2016
Geographic focus	Global	Asia–Pacific	Asia–Pacific	BRICS countries and other developing countries
Objective	Providing a long-run capital to member countries for economic reconstruction and development	Fostering economic growth and cooperation in the region of Asia and the Far East	Infrastructure financing in developing countries, especially in Asia	Mobilising resources for infrastructure and sustainable development projects in BRICS and other developing countries around the world

(continued)

Table 3.2 (continued)

	WB	*ADB*	*AIIB*	*NDB*
Authorised, subscribed, and paid-up capital	Initial authorised capital $10 billion: Now $280bl **Paid-up capital: $14 billion**	Initial authorised capital: $100 billion • Japan, 15.68% • United States, 15.57% • China, 6.47% • India, 6.34% **Paid-up capital: $5.9 billion**	Initial authorised capital $100 billion Initial subscribed capital: $50 billion • China, $29.7b • India, $8.3b • Russia, $6.5b **Paid-up capital: $10 billion**	Initial authorised capital: $100 billion Initial subscribed capital: $50 billion Divided equally among 5 members (Brazil, Russia, India, China, South Africa) **Paid-up capital: $10 billion**
Voting power	Approval of at least 85% required for major decisions 1. US 15.85% 2. Japan 6.84% 3. China 4.42% 4. Germany 4.00% 5. United Kingdom 3.75% 6. France 3.75%	1. Japan 12.84% 2. United States 12.75% 3. China 5.48% 4. India 5.39%	Approval of at least 75% required for major decisions 1. China 26.06% 2. India 7.51% 3. Russia 5.93% 4. Germany 4.15%	All members have equal voting power with no veto power
Governance structure	The Bank has a Board of Governors, Executive Directors, a President, and other officers and staff	The Bank has a Board of Governors, a Board of Directors, a President, one or more Vice-Presidents, and other officers and staff	The Bank has a Board of Governors, a Board of Directors, a President, one or more Vice-Presidents, and other officers and staff Board of Directors are non-resident	The Bank has a Board of Governors, a Board of Directors, a President, Vice-Presidents as decided by the Board of Governors, and other officers and staff

	WB	*ADB*	*AIIB*	*NDB*
Annual lending (% infrastructure)	$33.5 billion (35%)	$13.3 billion (55%)	About $1.5 billion in 2016: $10–15 billion in the first 5–6 years	–
Priority sectors	Education, health, public administration, infrastructure, financial and private sector development, agriculture, and environmental and natural resource management	Infrastructure, healthcare services, financial and public administration systems, tackling climate change related problems, and managing of natural resources	Infrastructure construction in Asia, regional connectivity, and economic cooperation	Infrastructure and development projects in BRICS countries

Source Authors from various sources

Table 3.3 Traditional MDBs changing priorities and operations

	1960s	*1970s*	*1980s*	*1990s*	*2000s*
Prevailing Development Theories and Ingredients	Harrod-Domar Model (Investment)	Harrod-Domar and New Growth Theory (Human Capital)	Solow Model (Policy Reforms/Environment)	Holistic approach to development, country ownership, and networking	Holistic approach to development, country ownership, and networking
World Bank	1950: Reconstruction of Europe and beyond 1960s and Beyond: Economic growth of developing countries	Infrastructure and Basic Needs a. Health b. Education c. Shelter	Economic Liberalisation Policies: Washington Consensus	Social development (focusing on Millennium Development Goals) After Cold War: Pursuit of Aid effectiveness a. New Development Paradigm b. Policy Dialogue c. Country ownership, country driven strategies d. Good governance e. Partnership among donors	Social development (focusing on Social Sustainability and Inclusion)
Lending Modalities	Projects/Technical Assistance	Sector Loans	Structural Adjustment Loans	Country Assistance Strategies	Comprehensive Development Framework Preparation of Poverty Reduction Strategy Papers

	1960s	*1970s*	*1980s*	*1990s*	*2000s*
Asian Development Bank	Infrastructure Food Production and Rural Development	Education, Health, Infrastructure, and Industry	Structural Adjustment Loans a. Private sector operation b. Energy (after oil shocks) c. Gender d. Microfinance e. Urban Planning f. Health	Broad-based development Regional Cooperation and Integration	Broad-based development and Regional Cooperation and Integration

Source Authors from various World Bank and ADB sources

and to promote the private sector. In the 1990s, the focus of development efforts shifted yet once again to country ownership to enhance development effectiveness by building networks and interconnectedness (Killick 1997). Hence, during the decades of the 1980s and 1990s, developing countries in Asia were deprived of infrastructure projects from the World Bank and ADB.

Reflecting the above trends, MDBs currently account for only ten percent of global infrastructure provision (about $40 billion in 2013) and their investment in infrastructure has declined considerably as a share of total investment in recent decades (Humphrey 2015). The share of infrastructure in total investment of the World Bank fell from about 70% in the 1960s to about 30% in the 2000s. The fall was less dramatic in the case of the ADB, from 55% in the 1960s to about 50% in the 1980s. At the same time, however, demand for infrastructure finance has increased greatly in Asia (Inderst 2016). To address this situation, the AIIB and NDB have a clear focus on infrastructure building. This points towards functional fragmentation and functional needs being one of bases for the creation of new institutions.

Second, the governance structure at many MDBs—particularly at the World Bank—was designed as part of an economic and political order that no longer exists. The governance of the World Bank has not kept pace with the rising economic and political clout of China and other emerging powers (Reisen 2015; Weaver 2015). Even post-global financial crisis voting share reforms were insufficient to give Beijing the voice that it thinks it is entitled to. China has been critical of its underrepresentation in the World Bank and other international institutions (Humphrey 2015; Vestergaard and Wade 2012). In this sense, the US-dominated World Bank and its inability to reform can be considered as an expression of Washington seeking to maintain the upper hand in its geopolitical competition with Beijing.

Issues Confronting Non-traditional MDBs

Considering that the AIIB and NDB have been established due to the perceived inadequacies of existing MDBs, it is not surprising that they have raised a number of practical issues that China needs to address. These issues relate to the type of relationship that the new MDBs will have with their decades-old counterparts. First, there are questions about whether the world needs new MDBs. Former World Bank senior director Ravi

Kanbur (2013) has argued that from a global perspective, it is inefficient "for new institutions to be created when the old ones could in principle be reformed to reflect new realities and new economic weights". According to Beijing, reform of global institutions might have been the best option, but this has not happened (Weaver 2015).

Second, the US Treasury—among others—has expressed its concern that the AIIB will fail to meet environmental standards, procurement requirements, and other safeguards applied by the World Bank and the ADB (*New York Times* 2014). Thus, the AIIB could undermine existing practices agreed by other MDBs. This would challenge the norms currently underpinning development financing through the creation of new institutions. The Chinese government, however, has argued that the AIIB will comply with international standards. This provides support to the idea that Chinese-led MDBs have been launched due to functional needs rather than displeasure with existing institutions only—namely covering financing shortfalls and infrastructure gaps. These reassurances have probably been central to developed countries such as Australia, Germany, and South Korea becoming founding members of the AIIB.

Third, China is not a member of the OECD DAC that coordinates aid and tracks the flow of official development assistance. China stresses that it is a developing country itself and therefore defines its support for developing countries as south-south cooperation rather than development assistance; it is willing to coordinate its aid provision, but only if coordination mechanisms are reformed (*China Daily* 2015). Were this principle to be followed by the AIIB and NDB as well, new and older MDBs might end up implementing very similar projects in the same locations.

China's argument regarding aid once again points towards the potential geopolitical tension between Beijing, on the one hand, and Washington and Tokyo, on the other. Both the US and Japan are part of DAC and thus coordinate their aid, along with the other members of the committee. China, meanwhile, does not need to coordinate. Indeed, there is an ongoing competition between Beijing and Tokyo in their aid towards Southeast Asia (Pacheco Pardo 2017). And yet, this competition can be mitigated by the potential functional complementarity between Chinese and Western aid, if each of them retains its respective current focus on infrastructure and social goals.

AIIB, NDB, and "Healthy" Competition with Traditional MDBs

Considering the reasons why AIIB and NDB were set up and some practical issues regarding their operation, a key question is whether the AIIB and NDB should compete with or complement the World Bank and the ADB. A modicum of "healthy" competition would be beneficial for countries with a pipeline of infrastructure projects. The establishment of the AIIB and NDB has already started to trigger a funding race and an infrastructure investment boom. At the World Bank annual meeting in October 2015, the World Bank took initiatives to initiate a capital increase. Earlier, in March 2015, it also launched a Global Infrastructure Facility in partnership with major development partners (World Bank 2016a). The ADB has restructured its balance sheet and will increase its lending capacity from $14 billion to $20 billion by merging its Asian Development Fund lending with its ordinary capital resources (ADB 2016). Both banks have signed agreements to jointly finance infrastructure projects with the AIIB. The competitive situation could also encourage the established MDBs to streamline their operational procedures and enhance efficiency. In fact, there are signs of this happening in both the World Bank and the ADB. The G20 has also launched a Global Infrastructure Hub.

Potential for Functional Cooperation Between Traditional and Non-traditional MDBs

Beyond, "healthy" competition, both the World Bank and the ADB have shown their willingness to cooperate with the non-traditional MDBs. Beijing has reciprocated, aware of the complementarity among the different institutions in terms of functions. In order to identify possible areas for functional cooperation between the World Bank and the ADB, on the one hand, and the newly established MDBs, on the other, in Table 3.4 we review the memorandum of understanding (MoU) that have been signed between the traditional and non-traditional MDBs. The agreements show that newly launched MDBs, the World Bank, and the ADB see potential for cooperation among themselves. Six broad areas of potential cooperation can be seen from the MOU signed by the World Bank and the ADB in 2001: mutual representation and/or staff secondments, consultation, knowledge and information sharing, operational procedures and practices, country-specific, sector-specific, and theme-wise operations, and funding/co-financing arrangements. These are the areas included in

Table 3.4 World Bank and ADB agreements with AIIB and NDB

Areas	*WB-AIIB*	*WB-NDB*	*ADB-AIIB*	*ADB-NDB*
Mutual representation and/or staff secondment	–	Yes	Yes	Yes
Consultation	Yes	Yes	Yes	Yes
Knowledge and information sharing	Yes	Yes	Yes	Yes
Operational procedures and practices	–	–	–	–
Country-specific, sector-specific, and firm-wise operation	–	Yes	Yes	Yes
Funding/co-financing arrangement	Yes	Yes	Yes	Yes

Sources Co-Financing Framework Agreement between Asian Infrastructure Investment Bank and International Bank for Reconstruction and Development and International Development Association (Memorandum of Understanding between International Bank for Reconstruction and Development, International Development Association, International Finance Corporation, Multilateral Investment Guarantee Agency, and New Development Bank (2016); Memorandum of Understanding for Strengthening cooperation between Asian Development Bank and Asian Infrastructure Investment Bank (2016); Memorandum of Understanding between Asian Development Bank and New Development Bank on General Co-operation (2017)

the Table 3.4. They show that there is functional overlap between new and pre-existing MDBs, which China can address by pressing the AIIB and NDB towards functional adaptation.

Table 3.4 suggests that potential cooperation is strongest between the World Bank and NDB, and the ADB and both the AIIB and NDB, with five of the six areas included in the World Bank-ADB MOU also covered in these agreements. Cooperation in sharing "operational procedures and practices" is excluded in all four MOUs summarised in Table 3.4. "Mutual representation and/or staff secondment" and "country-specific, sector specific and firm-wise operation" are also missing in the WB-AIIB MOU. Since the traditional and non-traditional MDBs have common countries of operation in Asia, functional cooperation between them will eventually cover all six areas as they build up their capacity.

Of particular note is co-financing operations between the traditional MDBs and the AIIB. Out of 108 projects approved by the AIIB during the period 2016–2020, 55 were co-financed mostly with the World Bank (31) and the ADB (17) according to AIIB project database. Complementarity in terms of functions and geographical focus underpins cooperation. The pooling of financial resources between the older MDBs and their younger counterparts shows that states are trying to maximise membership of multiple institutions. It also shows rapid institutional adaptation from the World Bank and the ADB by signing agreements allowing for this pooling only two years after the launch of the AIIB and NDB.

An area of particular importance is collaboration in knowledge and information sharing, as this will help to address the concerns raised in some quarters regarding transparency, governance, accountability, debt sustainability, and environmental standards that will be adopted by the AIIB. It will also help build the capacity of AIIB staff, which would benefit from the expertise and experience of their World Bank and ADB counterparts. As already mentioned, as per Table 3.4, it seems that the AIIB will initially have wider links with the ADB than the World Bank. Nonetheless, the World Bank and the AIIB have already signalled their wish to cooperate beyond co-financing (World Bank 2016b). In this sense, a division of labour between the AIIB, on the one hand, and the World Bank and ADB, on the other, could emerge.

In contrast with the AIIB, the NDB has equally strong frameworks for cooperation with both the World Bank and ADB spanning five different areas, but they are yet to be put into practice. Indeed, none of the NDB projects launched at the time of writing involve the World Bank or the ADB. They are jointly financed or implemented with BRICS-country institutions or firms. This suggests that the AIIB has been more willing to embrace cooperation with traditional MDBs than the NDB.

The AIIB and NDB are likely to be under pressure to comply with DAC standards and practices. The two newly established MDBs should, therefore, seek to participate in DAC meetings even as observers—as several regional MDBs currently do (OECD Undated). China should also provide data on its official development assistance to the DAC. Likewise, China should also participate in the World Bank-IMF debt sustainability framework and other international debt monitoring mechanisms. This would be beneficial for Beijing by boosting trust on its development financing practices. It would also support capacity building of the non-traditional MDBs.

To summarise, China is pushing for cooperation between the AIIB and NDB and traditional MDBs. Beijing has expressed its displeasure with the behaviour of these MDBs and, especially, with its underrepresentation in them. But functional complementary among institutions and the need for capacity building underpin a cooperative relationship hitherto.

AIIB, NDB, and Limits to Cooperation and "Healthy" Competition with Traditional MDBs

Historically, the governance structure of the World Bank has not kept pace with the rising economic and political power of China and other emerging markets (Woods 2006). This could be a constraint to smooth cooperation between the World Bank and the new MDBs.

Arguably, however, geopolitical competition could be the biggest impediment to functional complementarity and "healthy" competition between the AIIB and NDB, on the one hand, and the World Bank and ADB, on the other. Most obviously, the US refused to join the AIIB and cannot be part of the NDB. Since the US retains veto power over World Bank decisions and continues to appoint its president (Vestergaard and Wade 2012), it could decide to block meaningful cooperation with the AIIB and NDB—particularly joint programmes if it is unhappy with it.

Similarly, the ADB has traditionally been seen as a Japan- and US-dominated institution—one in which the president has invariably been a Japanese national. It is no secret that China and Japan are engaged in a race to build infrastructure across Southeast and South Asia (Pacheco Pardo 2017). Geopolitical competition among these two Asian countries could prevent sustained cooperation between the ADB and the two newly established development banks.

Conclusions

The centralised international monetary and economic development architecture established at the Bretton Woods conference is decentralising with a number of new regional institutions being established. In Asia, we have the CMIM, AMRO, and CRA in the area of global financial safety net and the new non-traditional MDBs, namely the AIIB and NDB, in the area of economic development architecture. What type of relations should these institutions have with the traditional institutions such as the IMF and the World Bank? While a modicum of "healthy" competition between global and regional institutions would be desirable, we have argued that regional and global institutions should not—and indeed, do not—engage in "unhealthy" competition such as a race to the bottom or implement beggar thy neighbour policies. Global and regional institutions should cooperate with and complement each other. As the literature on global governance fragmentation posits, functional overlap can trigger a division of labour process leading to institutional adaptation and, ultimately, cooperation among institutions.

In the case of the global financial safety net, we have argued that the present ad hoc cooperation between the ASEAN+3 RFSN and IMF should be more structured to manage a crisis with significant contagion effects to neighbouring countries. Although it was not an ideal system and there were sometimes conflicts (Darvas et al. 2018), an arrangement worth considering is the IMF's cooperation with the European regional financial safety net to resolve the Eurozone crisis. Indeed, there is already ongoing cooperation between AMRO and the IMF in various areas of crisis prevention. Similarly, in the case of the economic development architecture, we have established how traditional MDBs—i.e. the World Bank and the ADB—cooperate with each other and suggested ways through which traditional and new non-traditional MDBs can cooperate with and complement each other.

There are, of course, limits to cooperation and "healthy" competition between East Asian and China-led institutions on the one hand and their global counterparts on the other. After all, both East Asian countries in general and China in particular have created new regimes at least in part due to displeasure with existing institutions. There is also rhetoric-reality gap regarding implementation of policies in East Asia. Geopolitical issues are also important.

Cooperation and "healthy" competition between global and regional institutions will be mutually beneficial for both. The IMF and traditional MDBs can provide knowledge and capacity building services which would be valuable to the newly established CMIM, AMRO, AIIB, and NDB. Similarly, cooperation with the new institutions would provide the IMF and MDBs with access to a larger pool of resources for liquidity provision or infrastructure financing. East Asian countries and China have chosen this path of cooperation and "healthy" competition rather than "unhealthy" competition with global institutions. But there are limits to cooperation.

References

ADB. 2016. *2015 Annual Report. Scaling Up to Meet New Development Challenges*. Manila: Asian Development Bank.

ADB. 2017. *Meeting Asia's Infrastructure Needs*. Manila: Asian Development Bank.

AMRO. 2012. "Key Points of CMIM Multilateralization Agreement." AMRO, accessed 8 December 2021. http://www.amro-asia.org/key-points-of-cmim-multilateralization-agreement/

AMRO. 2017. "AMRO, IMF Enhance Cooperation to Support Regional and Global Financial Stability." Accessed 8 December 2021. https://www.amro-asia.org/amro-imf-enhance-cooperation-to-support-regional-and-global-financial-stability/.

AMRO. 2021. "The Amended Chiang Mai Initiative Multilateralisation (CMIM) Comes Into Effect on 31 March 2021." AMRO. Accessed 8 December 2021. https://www.amro-asia.org/the-amended-chiang-mai-initiative-multilateralisation-cmim-comes-into-effect-on-31-march-2021/.

ASEAN+3 Finance Ministers. 2000. "The Joint Ministerial statement of the ASEAN+3 Finance Ministers Meeting." Accessed 8 December 2021. http://www.amro-asia.org/wp-content/uploads/2016/09/Chiang-Mai-Thailand.pdf.

ASEAN+3 Finance Ministers and Central Bank Governors. 2020. "The Joint Statement of the 23rd ASEAN+3 Finance Ministers' and Central Bank Governors' Meeting." AMRO. Accessed 8 December 2021. https://asean.org/joint-statement-23rd-asean3-finance-ministers-central-bank-governors-meeting/.

Bangko Sentral ng Pilipinas. 2020. "Chiang Mai Initiative Multilateralization." Accessed 8 December 2021. https://www.bsp.gov.ph/Media_And_Research/Primers%20Faqs/CMIM_03-2020.pdf.

Beeson, Mark, and Fujian Li. 2016. "China's Place in Regional and Global Governance: A New World Comes Into View." *Global Policy* 7 (4): 491–499.

Biermann, Frank, Philipp Pattberg, Harro van Asselt, and Fariborz Zelli. 2009. "The Fragmentation of Global Governance Architectures: A Framework for Analysis." *Global Environmental Politics* 9 (4): 14–40.

Chang, Junhong. 2016. "Keynote Speech by Dr. Junhong Chang, AMRO Director, at the 6th Asia Research Forum CMIM-Asian Multilateralism and Cooperation." AMRO. Accessed 8 December 2021. https://www.amro-asia.org/keynote-speech-by-dr-junhong-chang-amro-director-at-the-6th-asia-research-forum-cmim-asian-multilateralism-and-cooperation/.

Cheng, Gong, Dominika Miernik, Yisr Barnieh, Beomhee Han, Ika Mustika Sari, Faith Qiying Pang, Tigran Kostanyan, Alexander Efimov, Marie Houdart, Alexandrade Carvalho, Carlos Giraldo, and Viviana Monroy. 2018. "IMF-RFA Collaboration: Motives, State of Play, and Way Forward." Accessed

27 March 2021. https://amro-asia.org/wp-content/uploads/2018/10/20181010_Joint-RFA-staff-paper_final_afterHLD.pdf.

Chin, Gregory T., and Carla P. Freeman. 2016. "What Is Next? …for World Order and Global Governance." Accessed 7 December 2021. https://www.globalpolicyjournal.com/sites/default/files/pdf/Chin%20and%20Freeman%20-%20What%20is%20Next%20%E2%80%A6for%20World%20Order%20and%20Global%20Governance.pdf.

China Daily. 2015. "China Pledges $2 Billion to Support South-South Cooperation." Accessed 8 December 2021. https://www.fmprc.gov.cn/ce/ceke/eng/zfgx/t1305563.htm.

Clegg, Liam. 2013. *Controlling the World Bank and IMF: Shareholders, Stakeholders, and the Politics of Concessional Lending*. Basingstoke: Palgrave Macmillan.

Cooper, Andrew F., Christopher W. Hughes, and Philippe De Lombaerde. 2008. "Introduction: Regionalisation and the Taming of Globalisation?" In *Regionalisation and Global Governance: The Taming of Globalisation?*, edited by Andrew F. Cooper, Christopher W. Hughes and Philippe De Lombaerde. Abingdon: Routledge.

Darvas, Zsolt, Dirk Schoenmaker, and Nicolas Véron. 2018. "Reforms to the European Union Financial Supervisory and Regulatory Architecture and their Implications for Asia." In *Global Shocks and the New Global and Regional Financial Architecture: Asian Perspectives*, edited by Naoyuki Yoshino, Peter J. Morgan and Pradumna B. Rana. Tokyo & Singapore: Asian Development Bank Institute & S. Rajaratnam School of International Studies.

Desai, Raj M., and James Raymond Vreeland. 2013. "Global Governance in a Multipolar World: The Case for Regional Monetary Funds." *International Studies Review* 13 (1): 109–121.

European Stability Mechanism. 2016. "Financial Assistance." Accessed 8 December 2021. https://www.esm.europa.eu/financial-assistance.

Foot, Rosemary, S. Neil MacFarlane, and Michael Mastanduno. 2003. *US Hegemony and International Organizations: The United States and Multilateral Institutions*. Oxford: Oxford University Press.

G20. 2011. "Cannes Summit Final Declaration—Building Our Common Future: Renewed Collective Action for the Benefit of All." Accessed 8 December 2021. http://www.g20.utoronto.ca/2011/2011-cannes-declaration-111104-en.html.

Gehring, Thomas, and Benjamin Faude. 2014. "A Theory of Emerging Order Within Institutional Complexes: How Competition Among Regulatory International Institutions Leads to Institutional Adaptation and Division of Labor." *The Review of International Organizations* 9: 471–498.

Grabel, Ilene. 2018. *When Things Don't Fall Apart: Global Financial Governance and Developmental Finance in an Age of Productive Incoherence*. Cambridge: MIT Press.

Han, Beomhee, and Naoto Watanabe. 2020. "International Financial Institutions 'Response 15 Countries' Diverse Needs Amid COVID-19." AMRO. Accessed 8 December 2021. https://www.amro-asia.org/international-financial-institutions-response-to-countries-diverse-needs-amid-covid-19/.

Henning, C. Randall. 2017. "Avoiding Fragmentation of Global Financial Governance." *Global Policy* 8 (1): 101–106.

Hill, Hal, and Jayant Menon. 2014. "World Bank, Inter- American Development Bank, and Subregional Development Banks in Latin America: Dynamics of a System of Multilateral Development Banks." In *New Global Economic Architecture: The Asian Perspective*, edited by Masahiro Kawai, Peter J. Morgan and Pradumna B. Rana. Cheltenham: Edward Elgar.

Humphrey, Chris. 2015. *Developmental Revolution or Bretton Woods Revisited?* London: Overseas Development Institute.

IMF. 2013. "Stocktaking of the Fund's Engagement with Regional Financing Arrangements." Accessed 8 December 2021. https://www.imf.org/external/np/pp/eng/2013/041113b.pdf.

IMF. 2017. Collaboration Between Regional Financing Arrangement and the IMF. In *Policy Papers*. Washington, DC: International Monetary Fund.

Inderst, Georg. 2016. *Infrastructure Investment, Private Finance, and Institutional Investors: Asia from a Global Perspective*. Tokyo: Asian Development Bank Institute.

Jones, David Martin, and Michael L. R. Smith. 2007. "Making Process, Not Progress: ASEAN and the Evolving East Asian Regional Order." *International Security* 32 (1): 148–184.

Kahler, Miles. 2017. "Regional Challenges to Global Governance." *Global Policy* 8 (1): 97–100.

Kanbur, Ravi. 2013. "India, the World Bank, and the International Development Architecture." Washington, DC.

Kapur, Devesh, and Arvind Subramanian. 2013. "The G-20 and IMF Reform." Accessed 25 December 2021. https://www.business-standard.com/article/opinion/devesh-kapur-arvind-subramanian-the-g-20-and-imf-reform-109040100006_1.html.

Kawai, Masahiro, Peter A. Petri, and Elif Sisli-Ciamarra. 2009. Asia in Global Governance: A Case for Decentralized Institutions. In *ADBI Working Paper Series* Tokyo: Asian Development Bank Institute.

Kawai, Masahiro, and Pradumna B. Rana. 2009. "The Asian Financial Crisis Revisited: Lessons, Responses and New Challenges." In *Lessons from the Asian Financial Crisis*, edited by Richard Carney. New York: Routledge.

Killick, Tony. 1997. "Principals, Agents and the Failings of Conditionality." *Journal of International Development* 9 (4): 483–495.

Kindleberger, Charles. 1986. *The World in Depression, 1929–1939*. Berkeley: University of California Press.

Kragelund, Peter. 2011. "Back to BASICs? The Rejuvenation of Non-traditional Donors' Development Cooperation with Africa." *Development and Change* 42 (2): 585–607.

Morse, Julia C., and Robert O. Keohane. 2014. "Contested Multilateralism." *The Review of International Organizations* 9 (4): 385–412. https://doi.org/10.1007/s11558-014-9188-2.

Muhlich, Laurissa, and Barbara Fritz. 2021. "Borrowing Patterns in the Global Financial Safety Net: Does Governance Play a Role?" *Global Policy* 12 (4): 47–68.

New York Times. 2014. "U.S. Opposing China's Answer to World Bank." Accessed 1 December 2021. https://www.nytimes.com/2014/10/10/world/asia/chinas-plan-for-regional-development-bank-runs-into-us-opposition.html.

OECD. Undated. "OECD Partnerships with International Organisations." Accessed 1 November 2021.

Pacheco Pardo, Ramon 2017. "China, Japan, and Economic Security Competition (and Cooperation) in the Asia-Pacific." In *Chinese-Japanese Competition and the East Asian Security Complex: Vying for Influence*, edited by Jeffrey Reeves, Jeffrey Hornung and Kerry Lynn Nankivell. New York: Routledge.

Pacheco Pardo, Ramon, and Pradumna B. Rana. 2015. "Complementarity Between Regional and Global Financial Governance Institutions: The Case of ASEAN+3 and the Global Financial Safety Net." *Global Governance* 21 (3): 413–433.

Pitakdumrongkit, Kaewkamol Karen. 2016. *Negotiating Financial Agreement in East Asia: Surviving the Turbulence*. London: Routledge.

Rana, Pradumna B. 2014. "From a Centralized to a Decentralized Global Economic Architecture: An Overview." In *New Global Economic Architecture: The Asian Perspective*, edited by Masahiro Kawai, Peter J. Morgan and Pradumna B. Rana. Cheltenham & Northampton: Edward Elgar.

Reisen, Helmut. 2015. "Will the AIIB and the NDB Help Reform Multilateral Development Banking?" *Global Policy* 6 (3): 297–304.

Ren, Xiao. 2016. "China as an Institution-Builder: The Case of the AIIB." *The Pacific Review* 29 (3): 435–442.

Rhee, Changyong, Lea Sumulong, and Shahin Vallée. 2013. "Global and Regional Financial Safety Nets: Lessons from Europe and Asia." In *Responding to Financial Crisis: Lessons from Asia Then, the United States and Europe Now*, edited by Changyong Rhee and Adam S. Posen. New York: Columbia University Press.

Robles, Theresa. 2015. "Regional and Multilateral Surveillance: Normative Tensions and Implications for Cooperation in East Asia." *Global Policy* 6 (1): 34–44.

Sussangkarn, Chalongphob. 2011. "Chiang Mai Initiative Multilateralization: Origin, Development, and Outlook." *Asian Economic Policy Review* 6 (2): 203–220.

Vestergaard, Jakob, and Robert H. Wade. 2012. "Establishing a New Global Economic Council: Governance Reform at the G20, the IMF and the World Bank." *Global Policy* 3 (3): 257–269.

Wang, Hongying. 2015. The Asian Infrastructure Development Bank: A New Bretton Woods Moment? A Total Chinese Triumph? In *CIGI Policy Brief No. 59*. Waterloo: Centre for International Governance Innovation.

Weaver, Catherine. 2015. "The Rise of China: Continuity or Change in the Global Governance of Development?" *Ethics & International Affairs* 29 (4): 419–431.

Weisbrot, Mark. 2015. *Failed: What the Experts Got Wrong About the Global Economy*. Oxford: Oxford University Press.

Woods, Ngaire. 2006. *The Globalizers: The IMF, the World Bank, and Their Borrowers*. Ithaca: Cornell University Press.

World Bank. 2016a. Reflecting on the 3rd GIF Advisory Council Meeting Changsha, China: June 2016. In *GIF Briefings*. Changsha: World Bank.

World Bank. 2016b. "World Bank and AIIB Sign First Co-financing Framework Agreement." Accessed 1 November 2021. https://www.worldbank.org/en/news/press-release/2016/04/13/world-bank-and-aiib-sign-first-co-financing-framework-agreement.

Xinhua. 2014. "AIIB Complementary to Existing MDBs, Says Chinese Finance Minister." Accessed 1 December 2021. http://en.people.cn/business/n/2014/1024/c90778-8799685.html.

Zürn, Michael, and Benjamin Faude. 2013. "Commentary: On Fragmentation, Differentiation, and Coordination." *Global Environmental Politics* 13 (3): 119–130.

CHAPTER 4

Promoting Development Bank Complementarity in Asia

Xianbai Ji

Introduction

The centralised global economic architecture built on the foundation of the key Bretton Woods institutions is undergoing structural shifts with the emergence of new regional and non-traditional institutions (Rana 2014). In the field of international development financing, the decentralisation process manifests itself partly in the successive founding of regional multilateral development banks (MDBs), which are formed by a group of countries to stimulate economic and social progress in developing countries by mobilising international finance and developmental knowledge. For the past decades, the World Bank Group has played the leading role in fighting poverty and raising standards of living worldwide, but it is also becoming overly rigid, aloof, bureaucratic and dominated by the interests of the developed, non-borrowing shareholding countries (Wihtol 2014). By contrast, regional development banks in which developing countries

X. Ji (✉)
School of International Studies, Renmin University of China, Beijing, China
e-mail: xbji@ruc.edu.cn

P. B. Rana and X. Ji (eds.), *From Centralised to Decentralising Global Economic Architecture*, https://doi.org/10.1007/978-981-19-2041-7_4

are both clients and shareholders are trumpeted to be responsive, flexible, innovative and apolitical (Griffith-Jones et al. 2008).

While regional institutions indeed have brought relief to some of the pressing concerns afflicting countries in need of foreign development assistance, they also pose new challenges to the already complex ecosystem of development finance. For one, development solutions prescribed by regional banks should strive to be coherent globally to spur positive spillovers. For another, regional MDBs should not undercut each other by triggering off unhealthy competition. These two challenges are intimately intertwined—MDBs cannot serve as building blocks of an efficient global system unless there are sufficient synergies among themselves. Given the anarchic environment in which international bureaucracies operate (Grieco 1988) and MDB's tendency to expand mandates over time, a feature known as "mission creep" (Prada 2014), coordination and cooperation between regional banks based on such principles as additionality, complementarity and comparative advantage should be consciously promoted.

In this context, it is worthwhile to examine the increasingly crowded development finance landscape in Asia, where traditional donors have been the World Bank and its regional spinoff, the Asian Development Bank (ADB). The issue of donor coordination, or lack thereof, surfaced with the advent of the Asian Infrastructure Investment Bank (AIIB). While many efforts have been devoted to encouraging vertical collaboration between the World Bank and ADB, this chapter aims to shed light on the horizontal relationship between ADB and the AIIB and make recommendations on how the two Asian MDBs can promote coordination at the institutional level, cooperation at the portfolio level and co-optation at the project level. It argues that there are relevant lessons to be drawn by Asian institutions from their European counterparts. The European experience is relevant and informative. After all, for more than two decades, Europe was the only continent that is home to two leading regional MDBs—the Luxembourg-based European Investment Bank (EIB) and the London-headquartered European Bank for Reconstruction and Development (EBRD).

Data for this chapter were collected mainly from the four MDBs' corporate publications, press releases, project databases, websites and other publicly available literature. In terms of outline, the chapter is structured in the following manner. The next section provides an overview of the four MDBs concerned. The third section discusses how to smoothen inter-institutional coordination through tri-partite development partnership. Sections four and five elaborate on the experiences in Europe, and prospect in Asia, of nurturing complementary loan portfolios in terms of sectoral distribution and geographical coverage, respectively. Section six zooms in to the project level and explains why co-financing could be the first step towards a congenial inter-bank relationship in Asia. The last section concludes the chapter.

Overview of the Four MDBs

European Investment Bank

The EIB is the world's oldest regional MDB and the largest multilateral lending institution by volume. It was created in 1958 by the Treaty of Rome and now operates under a general mandate of supporting sound and sustainable investments within the European Union (EU) and beyond in the long-term interest of the 27-nation bloc.

Presiding over a total subscribed capital amounting to €248.8 billion ($280.6 billion), the EIB Group, consisting of the EIB and the European Investment Fund (EIF) dedicated to micro, small- and medium-sized enterprises (MSMEs), lent €66.1 billion ($74.6 billion) in 2020. To put the figures in context, the World Bank's capital base is $199.5 billion, and its disbursed loans in the fiscal year 2020 were $54.4 billion. As the EU's lending arm jointly governed by the EU's member states, the EIB's core business is to serve the EU's internal objectives including balanced growth, economic integration and social cohesion. But around 10% of its annual investment is allocated to operations outside the EU to fulfil Brussels' foreign policy and international development priorities.

To the extent that the EIB is a statutory body of the EU, its decision-making procedure follows the double majority principle instituted by the Lisbon Treaty. For a decision to be adopted at the EIB, a favourable vote of the majority of the board members and the majority of the subscribed capital are required. In certain policy areas, a qualified majority—18 votes and 68% of the capital—is mandatory. However, in practice, consensus decision-making has been the norm.

European Bank for Reconstruction and Development

The EBRD was founded in 1991 to be arguably the first post-Cold War multilateral institution. The historical mission of the EBRD was to assist former communist countries from Central and Eastern Europe and ex-Soviet Republics to transit from command to free market economies. Over the past decades, the EBRD has earned a reputation for its expertise on decentralisation, de-monopolisation, de-regulation, privatisation, legalisation and non-traditional development intervention in areas such as nuclear safety and de-commissioning (ADB 2016c; Robinson and Bain 2011). It is owned by 71 countries, the European Commission and the EIB. With an authorised capital pool of €30 billion ($33.8 billion), the EBRD's financing totalled €11 billion ($12.4 billion) in 2020. The EBRD's operation can be found in 30 economies from central Europe to central Asia and the southern and eastern Mediterranean.

The EBRD differs from other regional banks in four crucial ways. First, the EBRD has an outright political mandate to promote multi-party democracy, political pluralism and rule of law. Second, the EBRD's financial assistance is heavily skewed in favour of private sector clients and entrepreneurial initiatives, while the bulk of other MDBs' assistance is directed towards sovereign loans and government-backed operations. Third, the EBRD adopts the business model of a commercial investment bank characterised by high-risk taking appetite, rather than that of a conventional aid-oriented, not-for-profit development bank. The EBRD raises funds on international capital markets and follows a market-based pricing policy, compared to the EIB's risk-based policy. Lastly, the EBRD's ratio of paid-in capital is the highest among all major MDBs.

Asian Development Bank

The Manila-based ADB was established in 1966 under the auspice of the United Nation's Economic Commission for Asia and the Far East (Krishnamurti 1977). The plan to create an international financial institution (IFI) in East Asia was endorsed by the United States and Japan, which subsequently became the bank's largest shareholders and donors. ADB's mission is to reduce poverty in the Asia Pacific region through inclusive economic growth, environmentally sustainable growth and regional integration (ADB 2008). It is owned by 68 countries which contribute to its $151.8 billion equity pot. In 2020, ADB's operations climbed to a historic high of $48 billion, including $27.0 billion financed on COVID-19.

ADB is in many ways a regional replica of the World Bank—it is consciously modelled on the World Bank in terms of stated mission, governance and activities (Lesage 2013; Asher and Mason 1973) It is the only regional bank that shares the World Bank's mandate to end extreme poverty and has a similar weighted voting system to reflect members' capital subscriptions. ADB operates with a soft lending window of Asian Development Fund (ADF) for its poorest and most debt-stricken and a hard window of ordinary capital resources (OCR), mirroring the World Bank Group's separation of the concessional International Development Association and the non-concessional International Bank for Reconstruction and Development. In addition, both the World Bank and ADB are pioneers among international organisations of using rating system to evaluate the impact of country programmes and investment projects (Sasaki 2012).

Asian Infrastructure Investment Bank

The AIIB is the youngest MDB, having officially opened its doors in 2016 for a specific purpose: to "foster sustainable economic development, create wealth and improve infrastructure connectivity in Asia by investing in infrastructure and other productive sectors". Led by a veteran international finance technocrat Jin Liqun, the bank is headquartered in Beijing. The initial subscribed capital of $100 billion is contributed by 57 founding members. By the end of December 2020, the AIIB had collected $32 billion liabilities and members' equity.

Like the EBRD , the AIIB was launched at a historical turning point—the fall of the Berlin Wall for the former (Jakobeit 1992) and the increasing confidence of China as it rises to become the second largest economy in the world for the latter—against the headwinds of American oppositions. The United States boycotted the establishment of the AIIB (Tang 2015) and gave the bank a wide berth after failing to convince others to turn down Beijing's invitations. Following the lead of the United Kingdom, key American transatlantic and trans-Pacific allies, except Japan and Canada, had all flocked to sign on to the AIIB, ignoring repeated diktats from Washington.

More significantly, the pace at which the AIIB gathers momentum indicates that China may have gained an upper hand in the competition against the United States over how best to address the world's development bottleneck in the twenty-first century. Once spearheading two mega-regional free trade agreements—the Trans-Pacific Partnership and the Transatlantic Trade and Investment Partnership—the American prescription was to lower behind-the-border trade barriers through reciprocal free trade agreements (Ji 2021; Ji and Rana 2019). China, alternatively, believes in slashing logistic impediments and creating new trade routes through infrastructure development to prop up the low-flying world economy. As AIIB President Jin had put it, establishing the AIIB is not about "the amount of assets we can build up" but "the new approach we would like to try" (Jin 2015). The successful launch of the AIIB can be understood as a vote of confidence in China's more broad-based agenda.

A comparison of the four MDBs is summarised in Table 4.1.

Tri-Partite Coordination

In line with the legalistic European approach, European development banks have a tradition of formalised cooperation. In March 2011, the EIB and the EBRD set out their latest framework for effective cooperation outside the EU to govern their relations. The rationale for opting for a tri-partite memorandum of understanding (MOU)—as opposed to traditional bi-partite ones—by inviting the participation of the European Commission (EC) is manifold.

First, the triangular partnership with EC chairmanship introduces a hierarchical dimension into an otherwise horizontal relationship, thereby reinforcing equality between the EIB and the EBRD. The three parties created a steering committee with EC chairmanship to oversee "the overall coordination and supervision of institutional and operational cooperation, to share experience and to maximise synergies in policy support, financing, and grant funding". The partnership also entrusts the EC to serve as an impartial arbiter should misunderstandings arise or aggressive competitions for EU resources occur. The interlocutor in Brussels is the Director for Finance and Coordination with EIB Group, EBRD and IFIs under the Directorate-General for Economic and Financial Affairs.

Table 4.1 Comparisons of properties of EIB, EBRD, ADB and AIIB

	EIB	*EBRD*	*ADB*	*AIIB*
Year established	1958	1991	1966	2016
Headquarters	Luxembourg	London	Manila	Beijing
Head	Werner Hoyer	Odile Renaud-Basso	Masatsugu Asakawa	Jin Liqun
Membership	27 EU member states	73 (including the EU and EIB)	68	104 (57 founding members)
Capital subscription	$280.6 billion (€248.8 billion)	$33.8 billion (€30 billion)	$151.8 billion	$100 billion
Paid-in capital ratio	9%	21%	5%	20%
Financing sources	Mainly international capital market borrowing through bond issuance	Subscribed capital, market borrowing and net income	Market borrowing, special funds and subscribed capital, theme bonds	Subscribed capital and borrowing through securities issuance
Standard & poor's credit rating	AAA	AAA	AAA	AAA
Main instruments	Loans, guarantees, micro-finance, equity investment and blended finance	Loans, equity investments, guarantees, co-financing, and syndicated loans	Loans, equity investments, co-financing, guarantees, grants, and technical assistance	Equity investments, guarantees, technical assistance and others
Top shareholders	Germany (18.8%), France (18.8%), Italy (18.8%), Spain (11.3%), Netherlands (5.2%), Belgium (5.2%)	United States (10.1%), France (8.6%), Germany (8.6%), Italy (8.6%), Japan (8.6%), United Kingdom (8.6%)	Japan (15.6%), United States (15.6%), China (6.4%), India (6.3%), Australia (5.8)	China (30.8%), India (8.6%), Russia (6.8%), Germany (4.6%), Korea (3.9%)
Developing/borrowing countries voting share	–	13.8%	33.2%	Regional = 76.3%
Key decisions	Double majority	80% majority	75% majority	75% majority

(continued)

Table 4.1 (continued)

	EIB	*EBRD*	*ADB*	*AIIB*
Board of directors	Non-resident	Resident	Resident	Non-resident
Mandate and mission statement	Contribute to the balanced and steady development of the internal market in the interest of the European Union	To promote transition to open, market-based economies in our countries of operation	To help our developing member countries reduce poverty and improve quality of life	Foster sustainable economic development, create wealth and improve infrastructure connectivity in Asia by investing in infrastructure and other productive sectors
Safeguards and procurement policies	Charter of Fundamental Rights of the European Union Environmental and Social Principles and Standards	Ten different performance requirements ranging from biodiversity conservation to cultural heritage	Environmental, involuntary resettlement and indigenous peoples' safeguards	Environmental and social assessment and management, involuntary resettlement and indigenous peoples

Source Author's compilation of website information, Kawai (2015) and Engen and Prizzon (2018)

Second, the EC, as the executive arm of the world's largest development aid donor, the EU, can help scale up the interventions of the EIB and the EBRD when needed. The European development "troika" has blended their resources in schemes such as the Western Balkan Investment Facility for pre-accession countries, the Neighbourhood Investment Facility which channels aids to Southern and Eastern European countries and the Investment Facility for Central Asia (European Commission 2016). A related benefit is that the presence of the EC in the donor cooperation framework leads to a more optimal configuration of risk-sharing, boosting the EIB's and the EBRD's creditworthiness while reducing their fund-raising cost on international capital markets. For instance, pursuant to the External Lending Mandate of the EIB, the EU budget will provide guarantees against non-performing loans outside the EU (European Commission 2016).

In addition to leaning on the political authority and financial clout of "senior" institutions, the EIB and the EBRD have adopted the triangular mechanism for strategic purposes to ensure that their operations bolster the interests of, and the values espoused by, the EU. The majority of the EIB's external activity is conditioned by the region-specific mandates mapped out by the Council of the European Union and the European Parliament. Although the EU cannot control the EBRD directly, the EBRD enjoys close links to Brussels and has shown strong desires to deliver on EU priorities (Robinson and Bain 2011). A case in point is that the EBRD announced cessation of new investment activity in Russia shortly after Brussels imposed sanctions on Moscow, amidst escalating crisis in Ukraine in July 2014. Following Russia's "special military operation" in Ukraine in 2022, the EBRD swiftly offered financial resources to Ukraine for possible reconstruction and to countries affected by inflows of Ukrainian refugees.

The tri-partite framework has served European banks well, and there are good reasons for ADB and the AIIB to institutionalise a similar mechanism as well. The necessity of forging an Asian equivalent of European development troika could be better understood if one takes the volatile political dynamics in the Asia Pacific into account. It is no overstatement to assert that the relationship between the EIB and the EBRD is naturally amicable, whereas that between ADB and the AIIB is contentious from the outset. The EIB is wholly owned by the EU; the Commission, the EIB and the EU member states collectively own approximately two-thirds of the EBRD's capital. All presidents of the EIB and the EBRD have been EU citizens. In contrast, there is no cross-shareholding between ADB and the AIIB, and the largest shareholders of ADB—the United States and Japan—are the notable absentees from the AIIB's roster. In addition, each of the United States and Japanese voting shares at ADB is more than twice that of China, despite that China is the largest economy in the region and the American contributions to ADB are passive and diminishing (Okano-Heijmans 2015). Hence, the immense political needs to diffuse tensions between ADB and the AIIB—which encapsulate the underlying Sino-American/Japanese rivalry—call for constructive participation of neutral third-party international organisation, to play the role of the EC as leader (or an equal partner), for smoother donors' coordination. ADB and the AIIB should explore the possibility of entering into formal tri-partite MOUs with the World Bank, International Finance Corporation (IFC), the International Monetary Fund or United Nations Economic and Social Commission for Asia and the Pacific to coordinate their investment in countries and themes/sectors of common interest.

Besides global institutions, another set of candidates that could form one pole of the triangular partnership are regional institutions despite the observation that there is no overarching institutional equivalent to the EU in Asia, not least in terms of legitimacy, resource, authority and normative power. But the successful experiences of the Association of Southeast Asian Nations (ASEAN), as the lynchpin of East Asia regionalism and security architecture, prove that regional institutions are capable (and have a track record) of turning weakness into strength and leadership potential (Stubbs 2014).

Regional actors' participation in donor coordination will, on the one hand, anchor aid recipients firmly in the driver's seat, making sure that the loans and grants dispersed by ADB and the AIIB are demand-driven instead of supply-driven. They add value by adapting MDBs' "one-size-fits-all", prescriptive development approach to local realities as well. On the other hand, regional entities, which are charged to uphold the interest of the region as a whole, tend to have stronger incentives to minimise the negative cross-border or regional externalities of MDB's essentially country-focused development interventions. At its best, regional authorities could also help to check against the inherent political risk of development banks' investment and interventions, which cannot be adequately hedged by legal contracts, insurance or other financial instruments (Henisz and Zelner 2010).

Tri-partite partnerships are already taking shape, especially in South Asia. A consortium of the AIIB, the IFC and ADB was conceived to finance Pakistan's Diamer-Bhasha Dam. The South Asian Association for Regional Cooperation (SAARC), through the SAARC Development Fund (SDF), is also keen to form a Consortium of Financial Institutions for the Strategic Growth of South Asia involving ADB and the AIIB.

Sectoral Complementarities

There are a number of economic sectors in which both the EIB and the EBRD invest. Their sectoral division of labour is guided by the compartmentalisation of "areas of separate activity" and "areas of differentiated emphasis". In the first instances, the two banks are encouraged to monopolise certain sectors and thematic groups, while giving up other less core or competitive ones, on a path towards greater specialisation and strengthened organisational identity.

After years of interactions, conscious planning and institutional soul-searching, the EIB and the EBRD have developed complementary portfolios that reflect their core competencies and development priorities. The EIB has allocated more resources, in terms of the share in the overall portfolio, to credit lines, health and education, energy and natural resources and transport sector through on-lending, equity, guarantees and risk-sharing. The EBRD, on the other hand, ranks agribusiness including fishery and forestry, industry and information and communication technologies, services such as property and tourism and municipal infrastructure relatively higher on their agenda. In general, the EIB assumes greater responsibility in larger-scale projects as an institution that specialises in volume lending; the EBRD, in contrast, has a strong focus on smaller scale sub-sovereign investment, municipal infrastructure and trade facilitation often in secondary cities (European Commission 2016; Robinson and Bain 2011).[1]

When it comes to the areas of common interest, the emphasis is placed on differentiated intervention approaches and cooperation at the intersection of their operational strategies. In the financial sphere, for example, the EBRD provides support to SMEs directly, while the EIB focuses on providing support to the real economy through financial intermediaries.

[1] During 2010–2014, the average loan size of the EIB was €66 million per operation, while the figure for the EBRD was just €19 million (European Commission 2016).

In post-project evaluation, the EIB's key performance indicators prioritise quantifiable economic impact such as the number of jobs created by its interventions, whereas the EBRD continuously monitors the so-called second-order development effects such as skill-upgrading, gender equality, corporate governance and private fund mobilisation. As such, developing countries where the EIB's and the EBRD's operations overlap and complement benefit from both the quantity and the quality of economic growth.

ADB and the AIIB should follow suit and formulate differentiated yet complementary portfolios in line with their distinct mandates. ADB's goal is to work for an "Asia and Pacific free of poverty". The AIIB, which does not have the word "development" in its name, states in its Statute that its raison d'être is to promote infrastructure development. Hence, ADB and the AIIB could consider functional niching along the following three lines.

First, ADB should continue to take care of the social needs of developing Asia as the AIIB has no intention to do so (Kawai 2015). The AIIB's sectoral focus thus far is on energy, financial institutions and economic resilience. By comparison, ADB's internationally renowned expertise in social sector financing is one of the bank's most important strategic assets. It is telling that when ADB and the EBRD cooperated in Central Asian republics, their MOU specified that "ADB will cover social sector needs" while "the EBRD will take the overall lead in private sector activities". To tackle the demographic cliff that beleaguers many Asian economies in middle income traps, ADB is slated to double its assistance in education and health. ADB was quick to respond to the Coronavirus (COVID-19) pandemic. It announced a $20 billion comprehensive COVID-19 response package in 2020, mobilising $10.9 billion through co-financing arrangements from development partners and commercial sources in the same year. Besides, ADB takes to heart seven of the 17 Sustainable Development Goals adopted by the United Nations General Assembly by aligning policies and strategies with them. They are "addressing remaining poverty and reducing inequality"; "accelerating progress in gender equality"; "tackling climate change, building climate and disaster resilience, and enhancing environmental sustainability"; "making cities more liveable"; "promoting rural development and food security"; "strengthening governance and institutional capacity"; and "fostering regional cooperation and integration".

Second, given the AIIB's exclusive focus on physical infrastructure, ADB could bring about complementarities by leveraging its in-depth expertise on non-physical infrastructure investment, making sure that the policy environment in aid-receiving countries supports the optimal functioning of the hard infrastructure structures including those financed by the AIIB. In this regard, strengthening borrowing countries' national capacity, through policy dialogues and other up-stream investment, is of particular relevance. ADB currently deploys around 10% of its loans to promote good governance by assisting developing country governments in policy areas like fiscal management, state-owned enterprises reform, fighting corruption and e-governance. In addition, ADB could facilitate the formation of a development-oriented, self-sufficient finance ecosystem to mobilise domestic savings in borrowing countries as "market-maker" and sow the seeds of local epistemic communities to take on country-specific development challenges as a "knowledge broker". In a nutshell, ADB's interventions should be done with the understanding that government is no substitute for market and public financing ought not to crowd out private investment and entrepreneurship. Aside from these elements, ADB has an indispensable role to play in building shock resistance infrastructure, disaster mitigation and social protection systems—which all fall out of the AIIB's business purview—for at-risk communities in the Asia Pacific. For example, ADB was held at high esteem by regional countries after it responded quickly to the Nepal earthquake and the Vanuatu cyclone in 2015.

Lastly, the two banks can specialise in projects of different scale, just as their European counterparts have done. Early signs suggest that the AIIB would only target "big ticket infrastructure projects", such as toll roads, hydropower plants, deep seaports and airports while having little appetite for irrigation systems, arterial roads or rural roads (Wall Street Journal 2015). Thus, ADB, as the region's "family doctor" (Okano-Heijmans 2015), could fill the gap via operations of smaller scale and provision of support to "bottom of the pyramid" projects (Prada 2014) in tandem with micro-finance organisations. It should be highlighted that the AIIB's pre-occupation with sophisticated infrastructure undertakings can become a potential strength of the bank as the lack of knowledge about financing and constructing complex infrastructure is a more pressing issue than just funding shortage (Xu and Carey 2015). As the AIIB gets up and running and learns by doing, its accumulated expertise and hands-on experiences are likely to help borrowers better determine which projects to fund, where to build major infrastructure and address potential risks and problems upfront. The AIIB could be further incentivised to disseminate its knowledge on platforms such as the International Infrastructure Support System —an initiative piloted by ADB—to help shape international best practices. The willingness of the AIIB to share real-world solutions on a peer-to-peer basis will underscore AIIB's (and, for that matter, China's) reputation as a responsible stakeholder in the international development community.

Geographical Division of Labour

The EIB is not just a *regional* bank for Europe; it also supports investment projects in some 160 countries throughout the world stretching from South Africa to Mexico. In terms of the geographical distribution of loan stock, the EIB's non-EU exposure stood at around 16.1% as of 31 December 2020. Although the pre-accession region still stood out as the most significant recipient in terms of lending volume, the largest number of new projects was found in the Africa, Caribbean and Pacific (ACP) countries, and Asia and Latin America (ALA) regions. In contrast to the EIB's global, omni-directional coverage, the EBRD has a discernible regional orientation, and it has operations in only 38 economies so far grouped in five regions: Central Europe and the Baltic States (9), South-eastern Europe (8), Eastern Europe and the Caucasus (6), Central Asia (8) and Southern and eastern Mediterranean (7).

Figure 4.1 shows a comparison of geographical breakdown of the cumulative investment committed by the EIB and the EBRD between 1991 and 2014. A geographical division of labour is evident. The EBRD is completely absent from investing in American and Oceanian countries, whereas the EIB has major portfolios in such countries as Brazil, Argentina, Ecuador and Papua New Guinea. Dictated by its founding mandate, the EBRD allotted a greater share of its financial resources to Europe, notably Eastern Europe, Caucasus and Russia. But as the boundary of the EU moves eastwards and some peripheral European countries, such as the Czech Republic, graduate from transition assistance, Central Asia emerges as the main destination of the EBRD's aid flows. Kazakhstan is the largest aid recipient, receiving some €6.6 billion over the last two decades. In contrast, the EIB's Asian operations concentrate in a handful of neighbouring Middle East countries like Turkey, Syria and

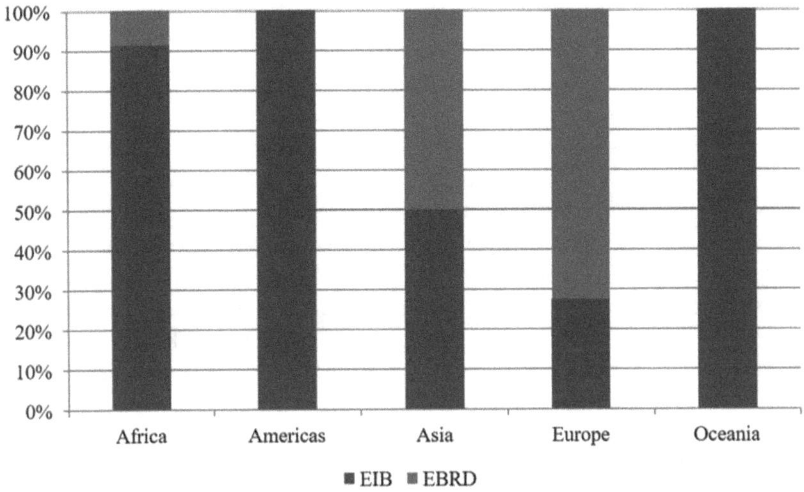

Fig. 4.1 Comparison of geographical composition of EIB's and EBRD's cumulative investment, 1991–2014. *Note* The grouping of countries is based on United Nations geoscheme (*Source* Author's calculations based on the EIB project database and EBRD's annual reports)

Lebanon.[2] In the Asia Pacific, around half of the EIB's lending operations are co-financed with ADB.

As for Asia, ADB's activities are mainly taking place in East Asia and South Asia. Although China and India started to borrow from ADB only after 1986, they quickly become the two largest borrowers. Crucially, the bottom line is this—ADB's geographical focus embodies Japan's North–South maritime understanding of the Asia Pacific as an archipelagic power (Cook 2015).

By the same token, China is likely to project its East–West continental mentality to the AIIB's operations. Conceivably, the AIIB's Eurasian and African members along the New Silk Road Economic Belt and the Twenty-first Century Maritime Silk Road (collectively known as the "Belt and Road Initiative (BRI)") will feature prominently on its agenda (Rana and Ji 2020). Since the inception of the AIIB, Chinese Premier

[2] The EIB also has relatively large investment in India, China and Sri Lanka, while the EBRD does not.

Li Keqiang had instructed the Beijing-based bank to align development strategies it devises for potential clients with the priorities of the grand scheme of the BRI. A sensible strategy for the AIIB to begin with therefore would be to concentrate its firepower on bankable infrastructure projects in some 40 countries along the BRI routes that either are non-member of or do not borrow from ADB, such as Iran, Turkey and Saudi Arabia. Investing in those countries would also boost China's energy security, promote regional stability and spur economic development in its land-locked western provinces (Ekman 2015). ADB, on its part, should commit itself more to the development needs of its members who are not eligible to borrow from the AIIB. A welcome step taken is that ADB is establishing extended missions in the Pacific region (ADB 2016a) as none of these small and micro island states—which make up 13 of the 48 regional members of ADB —is founding member of the AIIB. In the longer term, however, it is paramount that ADB and the AIIB should cooperate with a view to integrate the "Chinese made" and "Japanese made" infrastructural networks to connect the whole of Asia Pacific.

Furthermore, there seems to be scope for the AIIB to strengthen pan- and inter-regional connectivity, in the light of ADB's ongoing efforts in facilitating intra- and sub-regional integration. Due to financing constraints and the perceived uneven distribution of benefits, cross-border infrastructures are usually not provided for by national governments (ADB 2006). In the past decades, ADB has been a key advocate, monitor and administrator of a plethora of cross-border infrastructure and institution-building initiatives in several sub-regions of Asia. It serves as the Secretariat for Greater Mekong Sub-region, Central Asia Regional Economic Cooperation and South Asia Sub-regional Economic Cooperation and as development partner/technical advisor for Bay of Bengal Initiative for Multi-Sectoral Technical and Economic Cooperation, Indonesia-Malaysia-Thailand Growth Triangle and Brunei Darussalam-Indonesia-Malaysia-The Philippines East ASEAN Growth Area. Adding to these, ADB has since 2011 run a dedicated ASEAN Infrastructure Fund, with total equity contributions of $485.3 million, to enhance intra-ASEAN connectivity and facilitate the launch of the ASEAN Economic Community.

Not unlike their cross-national-border counterparts, cross-regional-border and pan-continental infrastructural networks tend to be under-developed, not least because they necessitate inter-governmental coordination and cooperation on a massive scale. However, with inter-regional trade on the rise and globalisation steadily marching forward, there is an urgent need to upgrade and build internationally integrated, inter-continental, intermodal transport and logistic networks (ESCAP 2013). It is, therefore, natural for the AIIB to take a leading and catalytic role in financing the six economic corridors that form part of the inter-continental BRI's overland route: New Eurasian Land Bridge, China-Mongolia-Russia Economic Corridor, China-Central Asia-West Asia Economic Corridor, China-Indochina Peninsula Economic Corridor, China-Pakistan Economic Corridor and Bangladesh-China-India-Myanmar Economic Corridor (CBBC 2015). Thanks to Russia's status as the AIIB's third largest shareholder, the AIIB is in a better position than ADB to finance the modernisation of the Trans-Siberian Railway and the construction of inter-continental proposals such as the Trans-Eurasian Belt.

Against this backdrop, Europe located at the other end of the Silk Road should take concrete steps to seize the opportunities offered by the AIIB and the BRI (Arduino 2016). There is a growing awareness in Europe that the new terrestrial and maritime links between Asia and Europe, planned, constructed and paid for in part by the AIIB, are conducive to Europe's search for new markets and trading partners. More profoundly, the AIIB's vision of an ever-closer Eurasia allows Europe to re-examine its relationship with Asia and decide—should Europe perpetuate its long-standing "generous but disengaged" attitudes towards the rapidly growing Asia (Okano-Heijmans and Waardenburg 2014), or ride on the wave of Asia's economic prosperity and political ascendance? European policymakers need to recognise that a strategically aligned and commercially inter-connected Eurasia has the potential to transform itself from the famous "missing link" in the triadic international economic structure to the core of the global financial and geo-economic map that is being redrawn. The successive adoptions of the "Connecting Europe & Asia: The EU Strategy" in 2018 and the Global Gateway in 2021, two Europe-centric infrastructure investment schemes, suggest that the EU might be interested in the great power competition in supplying the world with much needed infrastructure and connectivity.

Project Co-Financing

The main modality for operationalising cooperation at the project level between the EIB and the EBRD is co-financing. The EC-EBRD-EIB Tri-partite MoU articulates that, to identify co-investment opportunities at the earliest possible stage, the EIB and the EBRD are obliged to exchange information on their pipelines of potential operations every 2 months. When implementing co-investment, the EBRD—staffed mainly by economists and financial experts—relies on the strong engineering and technical capacity of the EIB during joint appraisal missions, and the latter often authorises the former to follow up with municipalities on project proposals and monitor the progress of co-financed projects due to a shortage of local representatives (European Commission 2016). Mutual recognition of procedures and standards and development of shared diagnostic tools are also consciously pursued to streamline administrative procedures, speed up loan disbursement, reduce transaction costs and avoid duplications for clients.

Over the period 1996–2015, the EIB and the EBRD co-financed more than 80 projects on a project-by-project basis or under joint facilities. The EIB and the EBRD tend to co-fund large projects where the costs and risks are high and operations where the two institutions' policy objectives converge (European Commission 2016). Their first co-financing was to help Romania rehabilitate 224 km of national roads and commercialise national road administration in 1996. Country coverage has since then been expanded to more than 20 countries in Eurasia and North Africa. The war-torn Serbia, involved in 24 joint aid programmes, was the biggest recipient of co-financing from the EIB and the EBRD. Other notable beneficiaries include Albania, Moldova, Ukraine, Armenia, Bulgaria and Bosnia and Herzegovina. Close to half of the co-financed projects were found in the transport sector, and the rest of fund went to municipal infrastructure; leasing finance, financial intermediary deposits and other credit lines; energy and natural resources; information and communication technology; and manufacturing and service industry. The scope of co-investment is now broadened to reach projects that have climate change and environmental impacts.

In addition to co-funding, the EIB and the EBRD provide technical assistance to beneficiary countries together. An example is the Joint Assistance to Support Projects in European Regions programme, under which the EIB and the EBRD offer free specialist advice to European countries to help them prepare high-quality projects to be financed by EU structural funds. Each of the banks brings their own perspectives to the table, thus consolidating the common pools of intellectual resources. The cross-fertilisations of ideas and knowledge transfer that take place during joint provisions of technical assistance also spur policy innovations and promote mutual learning between the EIB and the EBRD.

Co-financing was identified by ADB and the AIIB as a step-stone towards an in-depth and all-round donor partnership in Asia. The AIIB has started searching for co-funding opportunities with ADB in such sectors as transport, renewable energy, urban infrastructure and water supply. The first ADB-AIIB co-financed project will be the $273 million worth motorway project—the 64-km-long Shorkot-Khanewal section of the M4 motor way in Pakistan—that runs close to the China-Pakistan Economic Corridor (Reuters 2016). Between 2016 and 2020, the AIIB and ADB co-financed 11 physical infrastructure projects (not counting COVID-19 related liquidity provision schemes) mainly in South Asia (see Table 4.2).

The attractiveness of co-financing in Asia can be ascribed to a host of intertwining factors. At the strategic level, co-investment could engender a political rapprochement between China and the countries that still have reservations against Beijing's leadership and the AIIB's standards. It is widely known that the US Congress would veto any attempt that tries to channel US taxpayers' money to a Beijing-led bank, but United States could still participate indirectly in the AIIB's corporate governance and investment activities through projects that the AIIB co-finances with ADB (or the World Bank). After gaining first-hand insights into how this new bank operates and what kind of project it lends to, the United States and other outliers could eventually embrace the AIIB and become full members in the long run.

At the policy level, co-financing helps align the safeguard policies, financial discipline and operational practices of the AIIB with international standards across the project cycle. Since 2009, ADB's Safeguard and Accountability Mechanism has provided that all co-financing partners have to honour its rules concerning safeguard, transparency, bankability and procurement. Similarly, the Co-Financing Framework Agreement between the World Bank and the AIIB requires the global institution to prepare and supervise the co-financed projects in keeping with its stringent policies and procedures. In a sense, co-financing is an instrument for existing MDBs to socialise the nascent AIIB. At the transaction level,

Table 4.2 Selected projects co-financed by AIIB and ADB

Country of operation	*Project*	*Sector*	*Co-financing arrangement*			*Financing type*	*Approved year*
			AIIB ($ million)	*ADB ($ million)*	*Other institutions ($ million)*		
Pakistan	National Motorway M-4 (Shorkot-Khanewal Section)	Transport	100	278	126	Sovereign	2016
Myanmar	Myingyan 225 MW Combined Cycle Gas Turbine Power Plant	Energy	20	152.2	90	Non-sovereign	2016
Azerbaijan	Trans Anatolian Natural Gas Pipeline	Energy	600	500	7500	Sovereign	2016
India	Transmission System Strengthening (Tamil Nadu)	Energy	100	50	153.5	Sovereign	2017
Georgia	Batumi Bypass Road	Transport	114	114	87.2	Sovereign	2017
Bangladesh	Natural Gas Infrastructure and Efficiency Improvement	Energy	60	167	226	Sovereign	2017
India	National Investment and Infrastructure Fund (I)	Multi-sector	6.87	7.61	32.5	Non-sovereign	2017
Pakistan	Karachi Bus Rapid Transit	Transport	71.81	235.00	196.52	Sovereign	2018

Country of operation	*Project*	*Sector*	*Co-financing arrangement*			*Financing type*	*Approved year*
			AIIB ($ million)	*ADB ($ million)*	*Other institutions ($ million)*		
Bangladesh	Dhaka and West Zone Transmission Grid Expansion	Energy	200	300	250	Sovereign	2019
Maldives	Greater Malé Waste-to-Energy Project	Urban	40	73.39	37.74	Sovereign	2020
India	Delhi-Meerut Regional Rapid Transit System	Transport	500	1048	1900.7	Sovereign	2020

Source Author's compilation based on AIIB and ADB project databases co-financing accelerates initial phases of the AIIB's projects and reduces administrative costs in case the AIIB is induced to use existing, off-the-shelf financial products, which both existing donors and borrowers are familiar with.

Meanwhile, ADB counts on the AIIB to realise its ambitious co-financing target. ADB in its 2006 Financing Partnership Strategy made a promise that the growth of co-financing commitments would outpace that of ADB's own financing (ADB 2016b). The proportion of co-financing in ADB loans and grants approved annually more than tripled from 11% in 2007 to an average of 37% between 2012 and 2015. Adverse developments that limit ADB's co-financing capacity with other aid agencies in the future include banking culture differences (in the case of co-financing with the EBRD), non-existence or expiry of formal cooperation framework (e.g. the EIB), foreign aid budget cuts (e.g. the Australian Department of Foreign Affairs and Trade), shifting country priorities away from Asia (e.g. the British Department for International Development) and others (ADB 2016b). In this context, teaming up with the AIIB seems to be a natural choice to make. Nevertheless, it is important to note that joint financing should not be treated as an objective per se. Instead, a strategic understanding between ADB and the AIIB on how co-financing projects could serve as the nucleus for other areas of donor coordination and cooperation to maximise and aggregate the effectiveness and efficiency of their respective financing is of greater significance.

Concluding Remarks

With the AIIB maturing into a full-fledged multilateral bank, developing Asia will soon have two engines to propel its socio-economic take-off. But ADB and the AIIB cannot afford to walk on their own paths because running a multilateral organisation is no cheap business (Gehring and Faude 2014). Memberships of ADB and the AIIB overlap considerably. The over 40 countries that are party to both banks cannot logically have incentives to maintain, on a long-term basis, two regional development banks if they perform essentially identical tasks and serve the same group of countries. Had the EBRD not re-invented itself, acquired new resources or shifted its geographical scope eastwards in the face of the EIB's heightened spending in the European neighbourhood, it would have been shut down as a redundant actor (Jin 2015). Viewed in this light, promoting ADB -AIIB complementarities is not only desirable for avoiding short-term operational conflicts but essential for their long-term institutional survival.

That said, a line cannot be drawn arbitrarily between ADB and the AIIB to divide the responsibilities. This chapter, drawing in part on the collaborative experiences of the EIB and the EBRD, proposes four ways to enhance coordination and cooperation between ADB and the AIIB in order to reinforce the aid effectiveness and efficiency of each other. Specifically, it argues that ADB and the AIIB should form tri-partite coordination mechanism to promote mutual accountability and facilitate high-level policy dialogue, develop complementary portfolios in terms of sectoral exposure and geographical coverage, and co-fund projects to set the ball of cooperation rolling. More importantly, the resulting synergies will stitch the two development banks into an interdependent and coherent donor structure in Asia and beyond.

The key for ADB and the AIIB to materialise the performance-enhancing potential of their complementarities is mutual accommodation. ADB may deliberately shrink or withdraw development interventions in certain issue areas and countries where it has comparative disadvantages vis-à-vis the AIIB and invite the latter to take over. The AIIB, for its part, should enter the development business in a way that takes ADB's practices, preferences and existing client base into consideration. Admittedly, iterations of reciprocal adaption will necessarily come with a price tag (e.g. erosion of institutional sovereignty and identity), but enhanced donor coordination and refined comparative advantage will benefit Asia as a whole. In this regard, AIIB must understand that the 50-year-old ADB is certainly going to suffer from some structural inertia that prevents it from optimally and swiftly adapting to the new reality. The self-claimed "lean, clean and green" AIIB without historical baggage should, therefore, take the initiative to reach out to ADB, demonstrate willingness to make necessary adjustment and prove that its pledge to "complement and cooperate with the existing MDBs" is not just rhetorical.

Last but not least, a caveat is worth highlighting. This chapter is not a call for dismissing the value of healthy inter-institutional competition, as long as they do not escalate into open confrontation. Benign competition in a controlled manner could prevent the formation of a "cartel of good intentions" (Easterly 2002), forcing ADB to lower cost and the AIIB to raise quality in a "race to the top". A balance between collaboration and competition will have to be struck by ADB and the AIIB in their search for appropriate places in the global development finance community.

References

ADB. 2006. "Cross-Border Infrastructure Development Way to Boost Trade, Poverty Reduction." Accessed 1 November 2021. http://www.adb.org/news/cross-border-infrastructure-development-way-boost-trade-poverty-reduction.

ADB. 2008. *Strategy 2020: The Long-Term Strategic Framework of the Asian Development Bank 2008–2020*. Manila: Asian Development Bank.

ADB. 2016a. "ADB President Announces $10 Billion Funding for Indonesia Over Next 5 Years." Accessed 1 November 2021. http://www.adb.org/news/adb-president-announces-10-billion-funding-indonesia-over-next-5-years.

ADB. 2016b. *Effectiveness of Asian Development Bank Partnerships*. Manila: Asian Development Bank.

ADB. 2016c. *Effectiveness of Asian Development Bank Partnerships Thematic Evaluation Study*. Manila: Asian Development Bank.

Arduino, Alessandro. 2016. China's One Belt One Road: Has the European Union Missed the Train? In *Policy Report*. Singapore: S. Rajaratnam School of International Studies.

Asher, Robert E., and Edward S. Mason. 1973. *The World Bank Since Bretton Woods*. Washington, DC: Brookings Institution Press.

CBBC. 2015. *A Role for UK Companies in Developing China's New Initiative: New Opportunities in China and Beyond*. London: China-Britain Business Council.

Cook, Malcolm. 2015. "Two Asias: AIIB v ADB." *The Straits Times*. Accessed 1 November 2021. https://www.straitstimes.com/opinion/two-asias-aiib-v-adb.

Easterly, William. 2002. "The Cartel of Good Intentions: The Problem of Bureaucracy in Foreign Aid." *The Journal of Policy Reform* 5 (4): 223–250.

Ekman, Alice. 2015. *China: Setting the Agenda(s)?* Paris: European Union Institute for Security Studies.

Engen, Lars, and Annalisa Prizzon. 2018. *A Guide to Multilateral Development Banks*. London: Overseas Development Institute.

ESCAP. 2013. *Strengthening Connectivity of Regional and Interregional Transport Networks*. Bangkok: Economic and Social Commission for Asia and the Pacific.

European Commission. 2016. *Assessment of the Effectiveness of the Existing System of European Public Financing Institutions in Promoting Investment in Europe and Its Neighbourhood*. Brussels: European Commission.

Gehring, Thomas, and Benjamin Faude. 2014. "A Theory of Emerging Order within Institutional Complexes: How Competition Among Regulatory International Institutions Leads to Institutional Adaptation and Division of Labor." *The Review of International Organizations* 9: 471–498.

Grieco, Joseph M. 1988. "Anarchy and the Limits of Cooperation: A Realist Critique of the Newest Liberal Institutionalism." *International Organization* 42 (3): 485–507.

Griffith-Jones, Stephany, David Griffith-Jones, and Dagmar Hertova. 2008. Enhancing the Role of Regional Development Banks. In *G-24 Discussion Paper Series*. New York & Geneva: United Nations.

Henisz, Witold J., and Bennet A. Zelner. 2010, April. "The Hidden Risks in Emerging Markets." *Harvard Business Review* 88 (4): 88–95.

Jakobeit, Cord. 1992. "The EBRD: Redundant, or an Important Actor in the Transformation of Eastern Europe." *Intereconomics* 27 (3): 119–123.

Ji, Xianbai. 2021. *Mega-regionalism and Great Power Geo-economic Competition, Routledge Advances in International Relations and Global Politics*. London and New York: Routledge.

Ji, Xianbai, and Pradumna B. Rana. 2019. "A Deal That Does Not Die: The United States and the Rise, Fall and Future of the (CP)TPP." *Pacific Focus* 34 (2): 230–255.

Jin, Liqun. 2015. "Building Asia's New Bank: An Address by Jin Liqun, President-Designate of the Asian Infrastructure Investment Bank." Accessed 9 October 2021. https://www.brookings.edu/events/building-asias-new-bank-an-address-by-jin-liqun-president-designate-of-the-asian-infrastructure-investment-bank/.

Kawai, Masahiro. 2015. "Asian Infrastructure Investment Bank in the Evolving International Financial Order." In *Asian Infrastructure Investment Bank: China As Responsible Stakeholder?*, edited by Daniel Bob, Tobias Harris, Masahiro Kawai and Yun Sun. Washington, DC: Sasakawa Peace Foundation USA.

Krishnamurti, R. 1977. *ADB: The Seeding Days*. Manila: Asian Development Bank.

Lesage, Dries. 2013. "The Architecture of International Monetary and Financial Governance." In *Routledge Handbook of International Organization*, edited by Bob Reinalda. Abingdon: Routledge.

Okano-Heijmans, Maaike. 2015. "Untapped Potential: Time to Rethink European Engagement with the Asian Development Bank." *Asia Europe Journal* 13: 211–221.

Okano-Heijmans, Maaike, and Duncan Waardenburg. 2014. The Asian Development Bank—What's in it for Europe? In *Clingendael Report*. The Hague: Netherlands Institute of International Relations (Clingendael).

Prada, Fernando. 2014. "World Bank, Inter- American Development Bank, and Subregional Development Banks in Latin America: Dynamics of a System of Multilateral Development Banks." In *New Global Economic Architecture: The Asian Perspective*, edited by Masahiro Kawai, Peter J. Morgan and Pradumna B. Rana. Cheltenham: Edward Elgar.

Rana, Pradumna B. 2014. "From a Centralized to a Decentralized Global Economic Architecture: An Overview." In *New Global Economic Architecture: The Asian Perspective*, edited by Masahiro Kawai, Peter J. Morgan and Pradumna B. Rana. Cheltenham & Northampton: Edward Elgar.

Rana, Pradumna B., and Xianbai Ji. 2020. *China's Belt and Road Initiative: Impacts on Asia and Policy Agenda*. Singapore: Palgrave Macmillan.

Reuters. 2016. "China's AIIB to Co-finance First Project with ADB in Pakistan." Accessed 8 December 2021. https://www.reuters.com/article/pakistan-aiib-idINKCN0XU08J?edition-redirect=in.

Robinson, Nick, and Robert Bain. 2011. *The Implications of EIB and EBRD Co-financing for the EU Budget*. Brussels: European Parliament.

Sasaki, Ryo. 2012. "An In-Depth International Comparison of Major Donor Agencies: How Do They Systematically Conduct Country Program Evaluation?" *Journal of MultiDisciplinary Evaluation* 8 (18): 29–46.

Stubbs, Richard. 2014. "ASEAN's Leadership in East Asian Region-Building: Strength in Weakness." *The Pacific Review* 27 (4): 523–541.

Tang, Siew Mun. 2015. *The Politics of the Asian Infrastructure Investment Bank (AIIB)*. Singapore: ISEAS-Yusof Ishak Institute.

Wall Street Journal. 2015. "China-Led Bank to Focus on Big-Ticket Projects, Indonesia Says." Accessed 1 November 2021. http://www.wsj.com/articles/china-led-aiib-to-focus-on-big-ticket-projects-indonesia-says-1428647276.

Wihtol, Robert. 2014. Whither Multilateral Development Finance? In *ADBI Working Paper 491*. Tokyo: Asian Development Bank Institute.

Xu, Jiajun, and Richard Carey. 2015. "The Economic and Political Geography Behind China's Emergence as an Architect of the International Development System." In *Multilateral Development Banks in the 21st Century: Three Perspectives on China and the Asian Infrastructure Investment Bank*, edited by Chris Humphrey, Stephany Griffith-Jones, Jiajun Xu, Richard Carey and Annalisa Prizzon. London: Overseas Development Institute.

CHAPTER 5

Reforming the Global Reserve System

Pradumna B. Rana and Elgin Chan

Introduction

The international monetary system established at Bretton Woods was a "gold exchange standard" with the United States (US) dollar, convertible into gold at $35 an ounce, as the global reserve asset (see Chapter 6). In August 1971, the United States unilaterally closed the gold window (Irwin 2013), and the world has had to contend with a global reserve system (GRS) based on a "fiduciary" or "fiat" dollar, that is a dollar that has no commodity backing except the trust in the sovereign government that issues it, namely the United States. Termination of gold convertibility did not reduce the role of the US dollar as a reserve and payment currency because of the safe haven status of the United States and because many commodities including oil are priced in the US dollar. As parties are compelled to deal in the US dollar for commodities, commodity exporting countries have no alternative but to reinvest their US dollar

P. B. Rana (✉) · E. Chan
S Rajaratnam School of International Studies, Nanyang Technological University, Singapore, Singapore
e-mail: prana@ntu.edu.sg

P. B. Rana and X. Ji (eds.), *From Centralised to Decentralising Global Economic Architecture*, https://doi.org/10.1007/978-981-19-2041-7_5

back into US dollar assets. These arrangements further increased the demand for the US dollar and assets denominated in the dollar.

During the period when the gold exchange standard prevailed from 1945 to 1971, the United States generally ran current account surpluses,[1] and the provision of dollar liquidity to the rest of the world was made through the capital account. In contrast, under the "fiat" dollar standard, current account deficits of the United States became the norm rather than an exception. Concerns about the dollar heightened further in the aftermath of the Global Financial Crisis (GFC) of 2008–2009. Initially the US dollar strengthened somewhat reflecting its safe haven status, but it started to weaken in early 2009. This led to fears about the stability of the world's reserve currency especially in view of the large fiscal and monetary stimuli that were required to resolve the GFC.

Then Governor of the People's Bank of China, Zhou Xiaochuan published a paper in 2009 expressing concerns about the GRS based on the "fiat" dollar (Zhou 2009). The main concern for China was the large potential loss to the country as the largest holder of US dollar and US Treasuries if there were to be a disorderly depreciation of the dollar due to monetary and fiscal stimuli in the industrial countries. At around the same time, the Stiglitz Commission (United Nations 2009) also recommended major reforms of the international monetary system including the GRS. Yet another report from the United Nations published in the same year also noted that "[t]he crisis has intensified calls by some States for reform of the current GRS to overcome its insufficiencies. We acknowledge the calls by many States for further study of the feasibility and advisability of a more efficient reserve system, including the possible function of special drawing rights (SDRs) in any such system and the complementary roles that could be played by various regional arrangements" (United Nations Department of Economic and Social Affairs 2009).

In the above context, this chapter: (i) outlines the weakness of the "fiduciary" or "fiat" dollar-based GRS and (ii) reviews the proposals that have been made for its reform including reforming the present system of issuing and allocating the Special Drawing Rights (SDRs). It argues that there are no quick fix solutions. Only incremental reforms to the present

[1] One of the exceptional situations was in the early 1980s when US net liabilities with the world increased significantly and the G5 (US, Britain, France, Germany and Japan) came up with the Plaza Accord of 1985 to manipulate exchange rates by devaluing the dollar relative to the Japanese yen and the German Deutsche Mark.

system SDR system under the International Monetary Fund (IMF) and the decentralising/multi-layered global financial safety net appear to be feasible. Both will take time, and this means that US dollar hegemony will continue for some time, and we to a certain degree concur with authors of Chapter 6 of this volume.

Problems of the Present Global Reserve System

There are several fundamental problems plaguing the current GRS. The first is the ***asymmetric adjustment*** problem under which the burden of adjustment to payment imbalance in international commercial transactions falls solely on deficit countries. These countries had to adjust, either because they lacked external financing, or if they borrowed reserves they viewed as undesirable given the associated increase in debt. This asymmetrical burden of adjustment generates, in turn, a global deflationary bias. This bias is particularly strong during economic crisis, when the threat of capital flight and/or the lack of adequate financing forces deficit countries to adjust.

One of the major differences between, the Keynes' plan and White's plan to reform the post-war international monetary system was that John Maynard Keynes of Britain wanted the IMF (or more precisely a proposed International Clearing Union, see below) to lend in bancor, a supranational currency, while Harry Dexter White of America wanted the International Stabilization Fund (which became in due course the IMF) to lend in US dollars.[2] Adjustment under the former system would be symmetric (see discussion of the bancor below in this section), while it would be asymmetric under the latter system. The conventional wisdom about the Bretton Woods is that while the British led by Keynes had the right ideas, it was the Americans who had economic power and used that power to control the outcomes (Boughton 2002).

The second problem is the ***inequity bias*** in the present system. Developing countries have to "self-insure" themselves by accumulating foreign exchange reserves to (i) defend their currencies from potential speculative attacks, (ii) deal with temporary balance of payment difficulties, and

[2] Other differences between Keynes' Plan and White's Plan were (i) White's IMF was to be smaller than Keynes' and would allocate resources selectively rather than making them generally available and (ii) White's IMF would be more of a multilateral institution rather than one dominated by two "founders", as envisaged by Keynes (Boughton 2002).

(iii) defend against the potential exodus of capital in the event of a crisis. In terms of investing these accumulated reserves, the only option that they have is to invest in low-yielding US Treasuries, which means that the process is, strictly and ironically speaking, reverse foreign aid from the developing countries to the United States, giving rise to what was referred by Joseph E. Stiglitz to as the "capital doubtful recycling". Developing country reserves, on average, have increased from 5% of GDP in 1990 to almost 30% in 2018 (Arslan and Cantú 2019). The large sum of financial resources held in reserves means that less resources are available for development finance as is the case of Malaysia (Lim et al. 2021). The persistent need to accumulate foreign exchange reserves by developing countries would also pose longer term issues to the international financial system, as it adds to global instability and imbalances. On the other hand, the United States has an unfair advantage of being able to run perpetual balance of payment deficits by "printing money" and implementing deficit spending through quantitative easing. This allows the United States to gain seigniorage, which is the difference between the face value of the currency and the cost to produce it.

The third problem is the *inflationary* and *deflationary* bias of the system that benefit the rich reserve-issuing countries at the expense of developing countries that need reserves. This problem arises because returns and valuation of a country's foreign exchange reserve holdings will be influenced by the macroeconomic policies of the reserve-issuing countries (Di, Coats, and Zhao 2017). For example, in the post-GFC and post-European debt crisis periods, governments and central banks of reserve-issuing countries implemented expansionary macroeconomic and monetary policies through the use of near zero interest rates, quantitative easing, and fiscal stimulus to bring about economic recovery. These countries were relatively more "inflation leaning" because inflation in these countries during the period 2010–2020 averaged only 1.6%. These policies of reserve-issuing countries could have had adverse impacts on the holders of the reserve currencies due to the devaluation of the reserve currency and lower returns on their investments due to low interest rates.

The fourth problem stems from the use of a national currency as a global reserve asset. This problem is known as the *"Triffin dilemma"* (Triffin 1946–1947, 1960). To provide adequate global liquidity, the country issuing the reserve currency must perpetually run a balance of payment deficit. But these deficits and growing liabilities with the rest of the world could lead to a loss of confidence in the dollar and to large swings in the value of the US dollar as witnessed in the past four decades. Such a policy may not also be suitable to the domestic policy requirements of the reserve-issuing country. Stability of the global reserve system may, therefore, be inconsistent with the monetary policy objectives of the reserve-issuing country.

During the debates that were held to establish the Bretton Woods system, Keynes had proposed to establish an International Clearing Union (ICU) to clear trade among nations. All international trade would be denominated in a supranational currency issued by the ICU called the bancor based on the value of 30 representative commodities. The bancor was to have fixed exchange rates with national currencies. Goods exported would add bancors to a country's account, while goods imported would reduce them. Trade balances would be netted out and the remaining amount would be settled using the bancor. Countries would be encouraged to keep their balances close to zero. In the case of the surplus countries, a part of the surplus would be deposited in a reserve fund. In the case of deficit countries, their currencies would be devalued and the bancor balance reduced (Keynes 1969, 1978). This system would have overcome the Triffin Dilemma, but the proposal was rejected by the other participants in favour of the gold-backed dollar.[3] The SDR, which is a global reserve asset issued by the IMF, can be regarded as successor to Keynes' idea of a bancor,

Reform Proposals

Proposals for reforming the GRS have been advanced by many policymakers (e.g. Zhou 2009) and policy analysts and academics alike (Ocampo 2009, 2007; United Nations 2009, 1999; United Nations Department of Economic and Social Affairs 2009). These proposals can be grouped into four categories: (i) Moving to a multi-currency reserve system, (ii) Strengthening the SDR-based GRS under the IMF, (iii) Strengthening the decentralising/multi-layered global financial safety net with the IMF and regional financial safety nets (discussed in Chapter 3); and (iv) Establishing new international institutions resembling the ICU

[3] Keynes' ICU and bancor proposal would have addressed the asymmetric adjustment problem as well by requiring both the deficit and surplus countries to adjust expeditiously (Bordo and James 2012).

and bancor proposed by Keynes and the Global Reserve Bank proposed by the Stiglitz Commission.

Multi-Currency Reserve System

The global reserve system is already gradually becoming a multi-currency system to some extent as countries hold reserves in different currencies. According to the latest data available, the share of the US dollar in global reserves held by countries, although declining to some extent on a trend basis, still comprises the largest share of about 60%, followed by the euro (20%), the Japanese yen (7%), and the pound sterling (5%). The Chinese renminbi currently accounts for only about 2.5% of global reserves (See Fig. 6.1 in Chapter 6). The dominance of the US dollar means that there is basically no alternative to the dollar in terms of liquidity and return, although returns on US Treasuries are generally low. BRICS is a potential game changer, however. In the face of Western financial and trade sanctions against Russia following the outbreak of the Ukraine crisis of 2022, BRICS countries are considering creating a fresh international reserve currency based on the basket of currencies of BRICS countries.

The basic advantage of a multi-currency system of reserves is that it would provide countries some opportunity for diversifying their foreign exchange reserve portfolio to reduce risk. However, none of the other problems of the "fiat" dollar system would be addressed (Ocampo 2009). The use of national currencies as reserves will not resolve the *inequity bias* as industrialised countries, the reserve-issuing countries, would continue to benefit from seigniorage while developing countries would suffer from the need to hold foreign currencies for self-insurance purposes. Also, the use of national currencies as reserves would still lead to *asymmetric adjustment* problems and the *Triffin dilemma* between developing countries and reserve currencies on a bilateral basis. To resolve these problems, a truly global reserve asset, such as the SDR, needs to be adopted.

Establish an SDR-Based GRS Under the IMF

The SDR was created as a global reserve asset by the IMF in 1969 in the context of the fixed exchange system under the Bretton Woods monetary system. The IMF's Articles of Agreement mentions the objective of "making the SDR the principal reserve asset in the international monetary system" (Article VIII, Sect. 7 and Article XXII). The collapse of the fixed exchange rate system in 1973 and the shift of major currencies to floating exchange rate regimes, however, lessened the reliance on SDR as a global reserve asset. The initial allocation made in 1970–1972 was equivalent to 10% of the world's non-gold reserves. Over time, this fell to 0.5% (Ocampo 2009). Even with the most recent and the largest allocation of $650 billion equivalent of SDRs in 2021, the ratio has come back up to only 7.65%.[4] Hence, increased supply of US dollars under the "fiat" system has been providing the largest share of global liquidity.

The interest in SDRs has been revived after the GFC because of the need to have a less erratic system of providing global liquidity to stabilise financial and commercial transactions and to provide overall stability around the world. As former Chinese central bank governor Zhou (2009) noted in the aftermath of the GFC, "an international reserve currency should first be anchored to a stable benchmark and issued according to a clear set of rules…to ensure orderly supply; second, its supply should be flexible enough to allow adjustment according to the changing demand; third, such adjustments should be disconnected from economic conditions and sovereign interests of any single country". An SDR-based system under the IMF comes closest to meeting this proposal, for several reasons. First, the SDR is the only asset outside of the national reserve currencies that has been used as a foreign exchange reserve, it is the foremost alternative to the national reserve currencies.[5] Second, the IMF has a well-established framework under its Articles of Agreement that allows the SDR to operate effectively as a global reserve asset among its 189 members. Article XIX, Sect. 4(a) states "A participant designated by the Fund under Sect. 5 of this Article shall provide on demand a freely usable currency to a participant using special drawing rights under Sect. 2(a) of this Article", thereby making the SDR readily interchangeable to other national reserve currencies. In addition, Article XVIII provides details regarding the allocation and cancellation of the SDR, while Article XIX provides in-depth details on the operations and transactions of the SDR, thereby providing the IMF with a mechanism to administer the SDR as a global reserve asset. Third, it is important to recall that the SDR was

[4] Knoema.https://knoema.com/atlas/topics/Economy/Balance-of-Payments-Reserves/Total-reserves-excludes-gold.

[5] The EUR is inferior to the SDR because it is supported by a heterogeneous group of countries with conflicting macroeconomic objectives. Also, there are no assets denominated in the euro like US Treasuries.

initially equivalent to the US dollar. After the collapse of the Bretton Woods monetary system, the SDR was redefined as a basket of currencies. In November, 2015, the Chinese yuan joined the US dollar, euro, Japanese yen, and the pound sterling in the basket. The SDR, therefore, possesses greater stability and diversification as compared to individual national reserve currencies.

The SDR, however, has several limitations. First, the use of the SDR for trade settlement, invoicing, and foreign direct investments has been limited. The total allocated amount of only SDR 660.7 billion ($943 billion) to date, of which SDR 456 billion ($650 billion) was allocated on 23 August, 2021, in response to the COVID-19 pandemic, is small compared to the world's total money supply (M2) of approximately $40 trillion.[6] There is, therefore, a need to substantially increase the allocation of SDR before it can be used meaningfully for trade settlement, invoicing, and investment purposes.

Second, the allocation of the SDR is inequitable as it is based on IMF quotas that sharply advantage high-income countries that may not need reserves and disadvantages the middle-income and low-income countries that do.[7] Table 5.1 shows that there have been four general allocations of SDRs, so far, in 1970–1972, 1979–1981, 2009 in response to the global financial crisis, and in 2021 in response to the COVID-19 pandemic. Among the four allocations, the largest allocation was during the COVID-19 pandemic (SDR 456 billion) followed by the allocation during the Global Financial Crisis (SDR 183 billion). Allocations during 1970–1972 and 1979–1981 were relatively small SDR 9 billion and SDR12 billion respectively. In all allocations, high-income countries have received the largest number of SDRs followed by the middle-income countries, and the low-income countries respectively. During the allocation in August, 2021, high-income countries received nearly SDR 280 billion (61.4%), middle-income countries received nearly SDR 161 billion (35.4%), and low-income countries received only SDR 15 billion (3.2%) of total allocation. The disparity in SDR allocation has further exacerbated the existing inequality between the high-income and low-income countries, while also preventing the funds from being allocated to

[6] RankRed. https://www.rankred.com/how-much-money-is-there-in-the-world/

[7] IMF Members' Quotas and Voting Power, and IMF Board of Governors. https://www.imf.org/en/About/executive-board/members-quotas.

Table 5.1 SDR Allocations by Level of Development

	Allocations (in millions of SDR)				*Share in total allocations (%)*			
	1970–72	1979–81	2009	2021	1970–72	1979–81	2009	2021
High-income	6,813	8,033	112,467	280,282	73.8	66.9	61.6	61.4
United States	2,294	2,606	30,416	79,546	24.8	21.7	16.6	17.4
Japan	377	514	11,393	29,540	4.1	4.3	6.2	6.5
Others	4,142	4,913	70,658	171,196	44.9	40.9	38.8	37.5
Middle-income	1,488	2,730	54,173	161,596	16.1	22.7	29.6	35.4
China	0	237	6,753	29,216	0.0	2.0	3.7	6.4
Excluding China	1,488	2,493	47,420	158,674	16.1	20.7	26.0	29.0
Low-income	933	1,254	16,095	14,608	10.1	10.4	8.8	3.2
Total allocations	9,234	12,016	182,734	456,485	100.0	100.0	100.0	100.0

Source Ocampo (2020) and IMF data

where it is most needed, the middle-income and the low-income countries. While the allocation going to middle-income countries shows an increasing trend from 16.1% in 1970–1972 to 35.4% in 2021, the share of low-income countries has been declining from 10.1% to only 3.2%.

In this context, the G20 Rome Leaders' Declaration issued on 31 October, 2021, has noted "[w]e are working on actionable options for members with strong external positions to significantly magnify its impact through the voluntary channelling of part of the allocated SDRs to help vulnerable countries, according to national laws and regulations. We welcome the recent pledges worth around USD [45] billion, as a step towards a total global ambition of USD 100 billion of voluntary contributions for countries most in need. We also welcome the ongoing work to significantly scale up the Poverty Reduction and Growth Trust's lending capacity and call for further voluntary loan and subsidy contributions from countries able to do so" (G20 2021).

The Leaders' Declaration goes on to add that "[w]e also call on the IMF to establish a new Resilience and Sustainability Trust (RST)—in line with its mandate—to provide affordable long-term financing to help low-income countries, including in the African continent, small island developing states, and vulnerable middle-income countries to reduce risks to prospective balance of payments stability, including those stemming from pandemics and climate change. The new RST will preserve the reserve asset characteristics of the SDRs channelled through the Trust".

Third, there is a lack of secondary markets—financial markets, central banks, investors, corporations—where countries and holders can trade, hedge, or invest in the SDR. Investment products denominated in SDR also do not exist. The SDR is, therefore, an illiquid reserve asset.

Fourth, the role of the IMF as an independent institution to manage the SDR is also called into question. This is because at the IMF, major decisions such as admission of new members, increases in quotas, allocations of SDRs, and amendments to the Articles of Agreement, requires an 85% majority. The United States is the only country with more than 15% of voting rights and, therefore, has a unique veto power over major policy decisions. In recent years, for example, the US Congress delayed the implementation of the 14th Quota Review which was approved by the IMF Board of Governors in 2010 for six years to 2016. This Review doubled IMF's resources and shifted 6% of IMF quota to dynamic emerging markets and developing countries. Also, the 15th Quota Review was concluded in, 2019, with no change in quotas because of objections from the then Trump Administration (Mohan 2020).

To address the problems associated with the SDRs discussed above, the IMF should consider the following policy actions to strengthen the role of the SDR-based GRS.

First, the IMF needs to increase the allocation of the SDR. Two approaches could be considered. The best option is issuing SDRs in a countercyclical way, which means that they would be issued during crisis periods rather than during boom periods. Issuing them during crisis would help revive the crisis-stricken economy (United Nations 1999; Ocampo 2002, 2009). Alternatively, there could be regular allocations of SDRs reflecting an additional global demand for reserves as the world economy grows. For example, the Stiglitz Commission has proposed new allocations equivalent to \$150 billion to \$300 billion be made annually to meet the needs of international liquidity (United Nations Department of Economic and Social Affairs 2009; Stiglitz 2006). More than three decades ago, Polak (1979) had suggested a way to match these two approaches. IMF lending during crisis would create new SDRs, but such SDRs would be automatically destroyed once such loans are paid for, thus eliminating the global monetary expansion generated during the crisis.

Second, as Zhou (2009) had pointed out, for the SDR to be used as a supranational reserve currency, its usage will have to be broadened. A settlement system between the SDR and other currencies should be set up to allow member nations to transact between the currencies more efficiently. The IMF should also encourage the use of the SDR for settlement and invoicing among its member nations, while also promoting the use of the SDR among multi-national corporations (MNCs), financial institutions, and businesses. Allowing the use of SDRs in private transactions should be considered.

Third, as mentioned above, one of the major drawbacks of the present system is that there is a lack of capital market products or secondary market liquidity that are denominated in the SDR, thereby, making its holders reluctant to transact in the SDR. The IMF should create SDR-based financial assets that allow its holders to invest in. To start with, the IMF should establish a bond yield curve, 1-year, 2-year, 5-year, 7-year, 10-year, 15-year and 30-year that allows its holders to transact and invest in. The next step would be to encourage major economies and corporations to issue debt in the SDR, further enhancing the attractiveness and usage of the SDR.

Fourth, apart from holding the SDR as a reserve asset, developing countries can also seek a return from their SDR holdings. The IMF should, therefore, come up with investment products denominated in SDR to garner demand from countries, MNCs, and financial institutions. The IMF should also put in place adequate currency swap lines and repo lines for the SDR with member nations. The currency swap facility can be used to promote wider usage for the SDR by member nations through the swapping of major currencies to SDR and vice versa to address balance of payment and reserve requirements. The repo window essentially allows member nations to pledge securities as collateral to borrow SDR to meet balance of payment and reserve requirement needs.

Fifth, reform of quotas and voting power at the IMF will be a slow and cumbersome process. The advanced countries have been effectively dragging their feet on governance reforms of the IMF over the past decades just as the weight of dynamic emerging markets in global income started to rise. The IMF Board of Governors conducts a general review of quotas at regular intervals (no more than five years apart). Redistribution of quotas can take place only when there is an overall expansion of IMF quota resources. Countries retain their existing quotas through each review, and it is only the incremental expansion that is subjected to the distribution formula that is agreed to in each review. Hence, there is a built in hysteresis in quota shares and voice, representation, and governance at the IMF (Mohan 2020).

There was no significant increase in total IMF quotas from 1998 until the 14th Quota Review, which was delayed mainly by the US Congress for five years and implemented only in January 2016. Under this Review, 6% of IMF quota was shifted to dynamic emerging markets and developing countries. Four emerging markets (Brazil, Russia, India, and China) are now among the top-10 largest shareholders of the IMF with China as the number three. The 15th Quota Review which was to be completed in 2015 was concluded only in 2019 with no change in quota because of objections from the Trump Administration. The 16th Quota Review is not slated for completion until 2023. However, based on past experience, the next round of quota redistribution is not expected to be implemented until 2027 (Mohan 2020). This means that under the present quota-based allocation system a large portion of any new SDR issue will continue to go to high-income countries that do not need them. As in the quota distribution this year, the middle-income and low-income countries, which need international reserve and liquidity, will get much smaller amounts. In such a situation, it is therefore imperative that the IMF find ways to re-channel SDRs away from high-income countries for the benefit of middle-income and low-income countries. The IMF is considering several ways to do this: (i) using SDRs to boost the resources of its Poverty Reduction and Trust Fund, the concessional lending for low-income countries; (ii) using SDR to provide initial funding to a Resilience and Trust to be established soon focusing on climate change issues; and (iii) encouraging high-income countries to on-lend their SDRs to multilateral development banks like the World Bank (IMF 2021). As mentioned above, the G20 is supporting these ongoing efforts at the IMF.

Finally, for the SDR-based GRS under the IMF to work efficiently, there must be a commitment of all IMF members to accept exchanging SDRs for national currency when asked for by another member. The IMF had requested this commitment when the SDR was created in the 1960s. But given the stigma that many countries have against the IMF, it remains to been seen whether countries will honour their commitment going forward. For example, there is a feeling among Asian countries that they were treated differently from Europe (Mohan 2020). During the Asian Financial Crisis, IMF conditionality involved tightening monetary and fiscal policies. But such conditions were not imposed in the

European countries during the eurozone crisis. Moreover, IMF packages for Asian countries were also much smaller than for Europe (Mohan 2020). The Stiglitz Commission also suggested that the IMF create an alternative credit line, with appropriate conditionality, so that countries prefer collective insurance from the IMF over self-protection (United Nations Department of Economic and Social Affairs 2009). The IMF has responded by introducing the Flexible Credit Line and the Precautionary Credit Line, although they are still work in progress.

Strengthening the Decentralising/Multi-Layered Global Financial Safety Net

Regional monetary arrangements could also play a role in reforming the GRS. Ocampo (2009) has suggested that the IMF of future should be conceived as the apex of a network of regional funds. Such a decentralised system would have many advantages including regional funds resolving regional crisis more effectively because of local knowledge and niche information that regional funds would have. A decentralised system would also be more suitable in the context of the evolving multi-polar world as it would give greater voices to small and medium-sized countries in a region.

As discussed in Chapter 3, with the establishment of regional financial safety nets, the global financial safety net is decentralising. For example, in Europe during the eurozone crisis, the IMF was supported by the European Stability Mechanism (ESM) established in 2012. The ESM is well-resourced, with a lending capacity of 500 billion euros. In fact, the IMF was the junior partner in the programmes for Europe in terms of resources. The ESM also provided funding to member countries during the COVID-19 crisis to strengthen their public health systems (Mohan 2020). In Latin America, there is the Latin American Reserve Fund (LARF) established in 1978 by the Andean countries, Costa Rica, and Uruguay. As a reserve fund, LARF can mobilise funds from international capital market. In Asia, there is the Chiang Mai Initiative Multilateralisation (CMIM) which is a \$240 billion[8] crisis fund established in 2011 by the ASEAN + 3 countries and the ASEAN + 3 Macroeconomic Research Office (AMRO) which is the surveillance unit for CMIM. In Chapter 3

[8] This fund would be larger if South Asian countries, especially India, were to be members of the CMIM sometime in future.

of this book, Rana and Pacheco Pardo have suggested, among others, that this "self-managed" pool be centralised, like the LARF, in order to enhance the effectiveness of the ASEAN + 3 regional financial safety net. In a perception survey conducted by Rana, Chia, and Jinjarak (2012), opinion leaders from ASEAN + 3 countries had noted that a weighted regional monetary unit (RMU) should be issued to serve, among others, as a new regional reserve asset to complement the SDR at the global level. The RMU could be a CMIM-weighted basket that would have various roles like a unit of account, a reserve asset, and a currency basket. These proposals should be considered in future. The BRICS Contingent Reserve Arrangement which is a framework for the provision of liquidity support in response to balance of payments pressure in Asian countries, also exists.

An alternative regional arrangement that has been proposed by the Stiglitz Commission (United Nations 2009) is to build a global reserve system using a bottom-up approach through agreements among regional arrangements. In this approach membership in regional schemes would be open to all who wish to join. Membership would thereby grow and widen in future. Regionalism could, therefore, be a stepping-stone to multilateralism as it has played in the international trade architecture (see Chapter 7 of this volume).

Establish a New International Institution to Issue Global Currency

Two proposals that are normally discussed under this heading are: (i) Keynes' International Clearing Union which would issue the bancor to settle trade imbalances among member countries (as discussed above),[9] and (ii) Stiglitz Commission's proposal to establish the Global Reserve Bank to issue a composite currency, namely the SDR, outside of the IMF (United Nations 2009). These proposals are intuitively appealing because of the difficulty of reforming the governance of the IMF to ensure a more egalitarian distribution of SDRs. Politically negotiating the establishment of a new institutions would, however, be a daunting task and will not happen any time soon.

[9] Zhou (2009) had called Keynes' bancor approach as "far-sighted".

Conclusion

The present GRS with a "fiduciary" or a "fiat" dollar has several serious problems and thus should be reformed. The calls for reform have grown stronger in the aftermath of the GFC when countries holding the US dollar as a reserve asset had been concerned about the potential instability in the value of the dollar. If Keynes' proposal to establish an ICU to issue the bancor had been considered during the debates that took place at Bretton Woods, these problems would not have occurred.

Presently, the world is gradually heading towards a multi-currency reserve system where countries are holding various major currencies as reserves. While this system allows some room for portfolio diversification and risk reduction in reserve holdings, it does not address the fundamental problems of the GRS such as asymmetric adjustment, inequity bias, and the Triffin dilemma as the foregoing discussion of the chapter lays bear.

The best solution appears to be to fulfil the promises generated by the SDR when it was created in 1969 by the IMF, transforming it into a truly major global reserve asset. But there are many challenges for that prospect to become true, including the need to reform the governance of the IMF so that middle-income and low-income countries that need reserves can get a higher allocation of SDRs. Past experience shows that governance reform of the IMF will be slow. Hence, some have made the case for establishing a new institution to issue a global currency regularly and in a fair and more equitable manner. Politically, however, negotiating the establishment of a new institution, while the IMF is still around, will be a monumental task.

Incremental changes at the IMF to overcome the flaws of the present system in, among others, issuing and allocating SDRs, and the strengthening of the decentralising/multi-layered global financial safety net as regional financial safety nets sprout in various parts of the world, appear to be the only options that are feasible at the present time in terms of reforming the GRS. Implementation of both of these approaches cannot be done overnight and will take time. Hence, the hegemony of the US dollar will continue for some time in future.

A key concern in reforming the "fiat" dollar-based GRS would be the US's fear generated by the eventual loss of the pre-eminence of the dollar. But the United States should realise that it would also gain from the reform by avoiding destabilising speculation on the dollar and by being able to conduct macroeconomic policies with greater independence and global acceptance.

References

Arslan, Yavuz, and Carlos Cantú. 2019. "The size of foreign exchange reserves." BIS Papers No 104. Bank for International Settlements, Basel.

Bordo, Michael D., and Harold James. 2012. Reserves and Baskets. *Open Economies Review* 23 (1): 113–127.

Boughton, James M. 2002. "Why White, Not Keynes? Inventing the Post-War International Monetary System." IMF Working Papers. International Monetary Fund, Washington, DC.

Di, Dongsheng, Warren Coats, and Yuxuan Zhao. 2017. Why Does the World Need a Reserve Asset with a Hard Anchor? *Frontiers of Economics in China* 12 (4): 545–570.

G20. 2021. "G20 Rome Leaders' Declaration." Accessed 27 December 2021. http://www.g20.utoronto.ca/2021/211031-declaration.html.

IMF. 2021. "Special Drawing Rights (SDR)." Accessed 18 January 2022. https://www.imf.org/en/About/Factsheets/Sheets/2016/08/01/14/51/Special-Drawing-Right-SDR.

Irwin, Douglas A. 2013. The Nixon shock after forty years: The import surcharge revisited. *World Trade Review* 12 (1): 29–56.

Keynes, John M. 1969. "Proposals for an International Currency (or Clearing) Union: fourth draft of the 'Keynes Plan'." In *The International Monetary Fund, 1945–1965: Chronicle*, edited by John K. Horsefield. Washington, DC: International Monetary Fund.

Keynes, John M. 1978. "The origins of the Clearing Union, 1940–1942." In *Shaping the Post-War World: The Clearing Union*, edited by Elizabeth Johnson and Donald Moggridge. London: Royal Economic Society.

Lim, Guanie, Chen Li, and Xianbai Ji. 2021. "Chinese financial statecraft in Southeast Asia: An analysis of China's infrastructure provision in Malaysia." *The Pacific Review*, online first, https://doi.org/10.1080/09512748.2020.1868556.

Mohan, Rakesh. 2020. "IMF Quota Reforms and Global Economic Governance: What does the Future Hold?." New Delhi: Centre for Social and Economic Progress.

Ocampo, José Antonio. 2002. "Recasting the International Financial agenda." In *International Capital Markets: Systems in Transition*, edited by John Eatwell and Lance Taylor. New York: Oxford University Press.

Ocampo, José Antonio. 2007. The Instability and Inequities of the Global Reserve System. *International Journal of Political Economy* 36 (4): 71–96.

Ocampo, José Antonio. 2009. "Reforming the global reserve system." In *Time for a Visible Hand: Lessons from the 2008 World Financial Crisis*, edited by Stephany Griffith-Jones, José Antonio Ocampo and Joseph E. Stiglitz. New York: Oxford University Press.

Ocampo, José Antonio. 2020. "Transforming Special Drawing Rights for International Cooperation." In *Building Back a Better Global Financial Safety Net*, edited by Kevin P. Gallagher and Haihong Gao. Boston: Global Development Policy Center

Polak, Jacques J. 1979. "Thoughts on an International Monetary Fund based fully on SDR." Pamphlet Series No 28: International Monetary Fund, Washington, DC

Rana, Pradumna B., Wai-Mun. Chia, and Yothin Jinjarak. 2012. Monetary integration in ASEAN+3: A perception survey of opinion leaders. *Journal of Asian Economics* 23 (1): 1–12.

Stiglitz, Joseph E. 2006. *Making Globalization Work*. New York: W.W. Norton.

Triffin, Robert. 1946–1947. "National Central Banking and the International Economy." *The Review of Economic Studies* 14 (2): 53–75.

Triffin, Robert. 1960. *Gold and the Dollar Crisis: The Future of Convertibility*. New Haven: Yale University Press.

United Nations. 1999. "Towards a New International Financial Architecture: Report of the Task Force of the Executive Committee on Economic and Social Affairs of the United Nations." Accessed 27 December 2021. https://www.un.org/esa/ffd/wp-content/uploads/2014/10/66geg_EC-ESA_FinancialArchitecture1999.pdf.

United Nations. 2009. *Report of the Commission of Experts of the President of the United Nations General Assembly on Reforms of the International Monetary and Financial System*. New York: United Nations.

United Nations Department of Economic and Social Affairs. 2009. "Outcome of the Conference on the World Financial and Economic Crisis and its Impact on Development." New York: United Nations.

Zhou, Xiaochuan. 2009. "Zhou: Reform the international monetary system." The People's Bank of China.

CHAPTER 6

The Evolving International Monetary System: Will Dollar Hegemony Outlive the Digital Revolution?

Xueying Wang, Dongsheng Di, and Ruiling Liu

Introduction

The inherent vulnerabilities and asymmetric relations in the international monetary system were exposed by the 2008 Global Financial Crisis (GFC), leading to calls for the reform of the system. When the United States (US)-induced crisis broke out, capital paradoxically flew back into the United States because it was seen still as the financial safe haven. By contrast, countries in the "global periphery" were hit hard by the GFC. This state of affairs led to a series of discussions following the GFC about the weaknesses of the international monetary system. In March 2009,

X. Wang · D. Di (✉)
School of International Studies, Renmin University of China (RUC), Beijing, China
e-mail: didongsheng@vip.sina.com

R. Liu
London School of Economics and Political Science (LSE), London, England

P. B. Rana and X. Ji (eds.), *From Centralised to Decentralising Global Economic Architecture*, https://doi.org/10.1007/978-981-19-2041-7_6

then-governor of the People's Bank of China, Zhou Xiaochuan, published an essay entitled "Reform the international monetary system" on the bank's website. He suggested that the current monetary system was defective due to an the hegemonic position of the US dollar, an arrangement which has contributed to the increasing frequency and intensity of financial crises that have followed the collapse of the Bretton Woods system (Zhou 2009).

It is important to note that, the current international monetary system goes against interests of both the United States and the peripheral countries in some important respects. In the case of the United States, the global demand for US assets has become an external driving force for the creation of toxic assets in the US financial sectors (Caballero and Krishnamurthy 2009). In addition, the external demand for US dollar liquidity requires the United States to maintain a long-term trade deficit (Rebucci and Hunt 2005). For other countries in the system, spillovers from the US monetary policy are likely to trigger fluctuations in their domestic financial markets. Specifically, when there was an easing in US monetary policy, excess capital left the United States in pursuit of high yields, increasing the possibility of financial market bubbles; in the opposite case, when the US monetary policy was tightened or "tapered", domestic liquidity shortage and thus higher interest rate occurred, resulting in capital outflows from peripheral economies, which may trigger turmoil in the financial markets of those developing economies. Historically, changes in the monetary policy of the United States have been an important reason for the outbreak of debt crises, exchange rate crises, and even financial crises in a number of peripheral economies. Notable examples include the Latin American debt crisis in the 1980s (Cardoso and Fishlow 1992), the Asian financial crisis in the 1990s (Ito 2007) and exchange rate crises in Turkey, Brazil, Argentina and, other countries in 2018 triggered by the dollar interest rate hike cycle. Furthermore, countries face the risk of their financial assets being confiscated due to US sanction,[1] a danger facilitated by the SWIFT system which makes it possible and even

[1] For example, the US sanctions against Iran prohibit foreign financial institutions that conduct major financial transactions with Iranian financial institutions from opening or maintaining accounts in the United States, cutting off Iran's financial exchanges with other countries. Another example is to freeze the US dollar accounts of sanctioned countries so that the foreign exchange reserves of these countries cannot be used. Iraq, Iran, Libya, and Russia have all been sanctioned in this way.

convenient for the United States to impose financial sanctions on other countries to achieve its political goals. As economic coercion often constitutes an adverse exogenous economic shock to the targeted country's economy, financial sanction by the United States might lead to a possible bank run or even a systematic banking crisis. Further, studies also find that financial sanctions are often associated with deterioration in human rights and democratic freedom and political stability in target countries (Hatipoglu and Peksen 2016). Hence, the threat of US sanctions is not only credible, but terrifying. Indeed, European countries tried to bypass the US sanctions on Iran by using INSTEX to construct a barter-based trading platform, but this effort proved extremely arduous (Dizard 2019).

These imbalances in the global monetary system necessitate urgent reforms. The desirable goal, therefore, is to reduce the hegemony of the US dollar in the international monetary system. The hegemony of the US dollar had begun from the Bretton Woods era of the 1940s. In the following decades, the dollar hegemony was not weakened, but strengthened, despite (or perhaps thanks to) the collapse of the Bretton Woods monetary system. The international monetary system moved from a gold exchange system to a fiduciary US dollar system after August, 1971, but this did not reduce the hegemony of the US dollar since the United States convinced the Arabs to price oil in US dollar. Dollar hegemony has brought the United States many privileges including seigniorage, capital flow gains, and financial risks offshoring (Cohen 1977; Gourinchas and Rey 2005; Norrlöf 2008). Furthermore, due to the network effects in the monetary system, the dominance of the US dollar has decreased only slightly since the turn of the century. As shown in Fig. 6.1, the share of US dollar reserves held by central banks around the world fell from about 70% in 2000 to 60% presently. The dollar's status did not decrease very much during the GFC. But with the eurozone crisis, the euro's share in global reserves fell, further consolidating the share of the dollar. During the Trump presidency, the US dollar's share of world currency reserves began to show a slightly weakening trend. This trend continued with the COVID-19 pandemic, and the share of the dollar dropped below 60%, reaching its lowest level in 25 years in the first quarter of 2021. Yet, in general, as the primary reserve currency for the global economy, the dollars' pre-eminence remains secure and unmatched.

This chapter begins by introducing the Bretton Woods system and outlining the major reasons that contributed to its collapse. It then focuses on the hegemony of the US dollar after its decoupling from

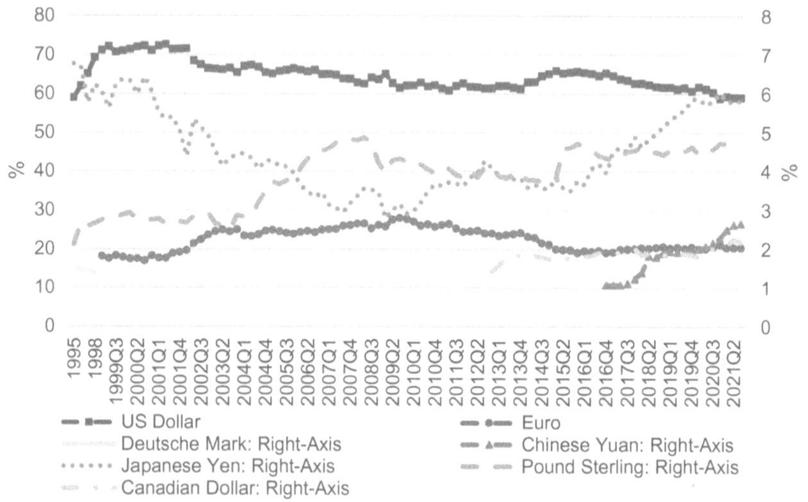

Fig. 6.1 Global share of major currencies (*Source* Author's illustration based on data from the IMF)

gold in 1971 and assesses the benefits and costs of the hegemony from the perspectives of the United States and developing countries. Next, the chapter discusses the factors that could reduce dollar hegemony in future—expansionary fiscal policy in the United States, geopolitical tensions, and efforts of Russia and China to denominate trade in alternative currencies. Finally, the chapter explores the impacts of digital currencies on the international monetary system. It finds that the convenience and support offered by digital currencies, for all their advantages, will probably not help reduce the hegemony of the US dollar, at least, in the immediate future.

The Bretton Woods System: The Last Gold-Standard System

Competing to determine the future of international monetary order, the "Keynes Plan" and the "White Plan" were respectively put forward by the United Kingdom in 1940 and the United States in 1941. The competition came to a head in July, 1944, when representatives of the 44 allied nations came together at the Bretton Woods Conference and created what is today known as the Bretton Woods system. The agreement included a series of global rules that led to the creation of the International Monetary Fund (IMF) and the World Bank.

Central to the Bretton Woods system was the establishment of a gold exchange standard based on the US dollar. At that time, the United States held about 75% of the world's gold reserves (Green 1999), hence it made sense to link the value of the US dollar to gold. The Bretton Woods system required the currencies of other countries to link to the US dollar, which in turn was convertible to gold at a fixed exchange rate of $35 an ounce. Compared with the gold specie standard and the gold bullion standard during the era of the pound sterling, the gold exchange standard system was the finale of the gold standard. Under the system, most swaps between gold and the US dollar emerged at the central bank level with gold exchanged at a fixed dollar price. Once people no longer believed in the fixed price, a gold run would be possible, which might threaten the stability of the system.

This system had an inherent flaw which had been identified by Robert Triffin, a Belgian-American economist. It was thus known as the Triffin Dilemma (Triffin 1946, 1947). He had argued that the dominant country (the US) would need to increase debt to alleviate international reserve shortages, which would gradually weaken foreigners' confidence in the dollar and cause the collapse of the system (Triffin 1961).[2] His arguments about the unsustainability of the Bretton Woods system appeared to be prescient. From this point of view, the collapse of the system was an inevitable development.

Though it had a fundamental defect, i.e. the Triffin Dilemma,[3] the Bretton Woods monetary system lingered on for nearly 30 years thanks to US monetary diplomacy that helped shore up the value and credibility of the US dollar. One such effort was the swap lines provided by the Fed to other central banks to prevent them from converting unwanted dollar reserves into gold (Ghizoni 1971). Another effort was the creation of the London Gold Pool in 1961 by the Fed and seven European central banks

[2] Having anticipated the Triffin Dilemma which occurs when the international monetary system is based on a single currency, Keynes had proposed to establish the International Clearing Union and a global reserve currency called Bancor (Steil 2013). But this proposal was rejected during the debates that preceded and during the Bretton Woods conference.

[3] The other flaws of the Bretton Woods monetary system were the asymmetric adjustment problem and the inequity bias (see Chapter 5 of this book).

to collaboratively intervene in the London gold market. These central banks sold gold when the price of gold spiked, and bought gold when the price was weak, with a view of maintaining a stable price of gold (Ghizoni 1971).

Even with the coordinated and collaborative efforts, central banks could not stop markets from worrying about the sustainability of the fixed exchange rate between the dollar and gold. The international monetary management system gradually came into paralysis. In 1967, an attack on the pound and a run on gold occurred in the pound sterling area, causing a sizeable loss for the gold pool (Bordo, Monnet, and Naef 2019). Consequently, the British government was forced to devalue the pound, dramatically damaging the credibility of the gold-dollar parity (Gavin 2004; Schenk 2010; Bordo, Monnet, and Naef 2019). In mid-March 1968, a dollar run ensued as well. After runs on pound, gold, and the dollar, France withdrew from the pool. The London Gold Pool was dissolved in March, 1968, at the request of the US government.

In 1971, the US gold reserves totalled just 25% of dollars held by foreign governments and central banks (Garten July 1, 2021) and the gold-dollar parity was crumbling. Moreover, with the high inflation rate in the United States, caused partially by the expansionary monetary policy in the United States to finance the Vietnam War, led to growing balance of payments surpluses in the European countries and Japan. As a result, they began to convert dollar reserves into gold (Bordo 2019). In response, in August, 1971, President Nixon announced an end to dollar-gold convertibility. His decision brought an abrupt end to the gold standard, creating an international monetary system of anchorless currencies. In early 1973, the US dollar depreciated again and suffered a sell-off. Consequently, many advanced countries adopted a floating rate regime and the Bretton Woods monetary system formally collapsed.

Summing up, revisiting the collapse of the Bretton Woods system, it is not hard to recognise that the problem was the unsustainability of its design. The Bretton Woods system was the product of hegemonic preference, rather than the result of prudential theoretical research. The restriction of keeping the dollar price of gold fixed had led to the Triffin Dilemma. Nonetheless, the Bretton Woods system was maintained for nearly 30 years. Sustaining its existence was the trust and cooperation between governments and central banks, but the loss of trust and cooperation was also the source of its collapse. The establishment and disintegration of the Bretton Woods monetary system tells us that any future reform of the international monetary system must be based on prudent thinking, reasonable adjustment methods, and mutual trust in international cooperation.

A System Without Hard Anchor

Since the collapse of the Bretton Woods system in the 1970s, the international monetary system has progressed into a regime without hard anchors, and where the only possible (soft) constraint is a commitment to target inflation. Currencies of the industrial countries float freely vis-a-vis the dollar, but most developing countries have preferred to keep their currencies pegged to the dollar either directly or in some sort of basket pegging arrangement. We describe this system as one characterised by the absence of hard anchors and the ever-expanding balance sheets of major central banks (Fig. 6.2). The currency system has broken out of the gilded cage of a fixed exchange rate system, resembling a large balloon that is constantly inflating. This system, despite changes, remains one of dollar domination, shown in three ways. The first one is the hegemony of the US dollar, the second is a global financial imbalance between core and

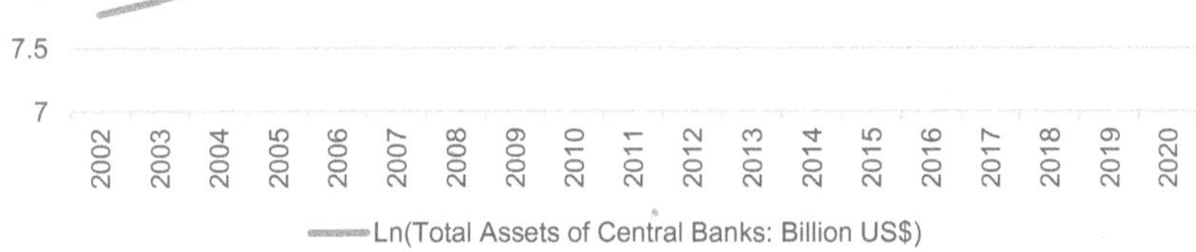

Fig. 6.2 Balance sheets of major central banks (*Note* The major central banks include the Federal Reserve, the European Central Bank, the Bank of Japan, the Bank of England, and the People's Bank of China. Total assets in the figure refers to the scale of central bank balance sheet after deducting foreign currency assets, special drawing rights, and gold. The Bank of England data was not included before 2013 due to missing data from the database. *Source* CEIC)

periphery countries, and the third is the economic symbiosis of China-US relations.

US Dollar Hegemony: Benefits, Costs, and Threats

Network effects, which refer to a phenomenon where the value of a currency to users' depends on how many other entities are also using the currency in question, are widely observed in currency markets. Network effect was modelled by Dowd and Greenaway (1993). They demonstrated that even if all currency users believe that using a certain currency is an inferior choice, the existence of network effects and conversion costs will still discourage users from choosing other currencies. McKinnon (1996) and Greenspan (2001) note that currency has the characteristics of a natural monopoly and that an incumbent currency has intrinsic advantages accorded to it. Based on the strong network effects in the monetary system, the widespread use of the US dollar produces a self-reinforcing system. This is to say that whilst the use of US dollars is not the subjective will of some countries, it is made the safest and most efficient choice for them by other market entities which generally use dollars. The dominance of the US dollar has brought the United States a broad range of privileges and benefits (Cohen 1977; Gourinchas and Rey 2005; Norrlöf 2008) as well as costs.

Benefits of Dollar Hegemony to the US

Three key benefits of dollar hegemony for the United States are seigniorage, excess returns on foreign investment and ability to maintain internal stability by transferring the costs of economic fluctuations to other countries.

First, seigniorage, the most intuitive benefit, is obtained when the United States purchases various commodities around the world at a cost of almost zero. The current account deficit can be roughly understood as seigniorage benefits to the United States. As Fig. 6.3 shows, in absolute terms, US's current account deficit has been increasing since 1980s. But the inflation rate has been falling. Hence, in real terms seigniorage benefit to the United States, by this measure, is relatively low. The US dollar current account deficit constitutes a small share of US national

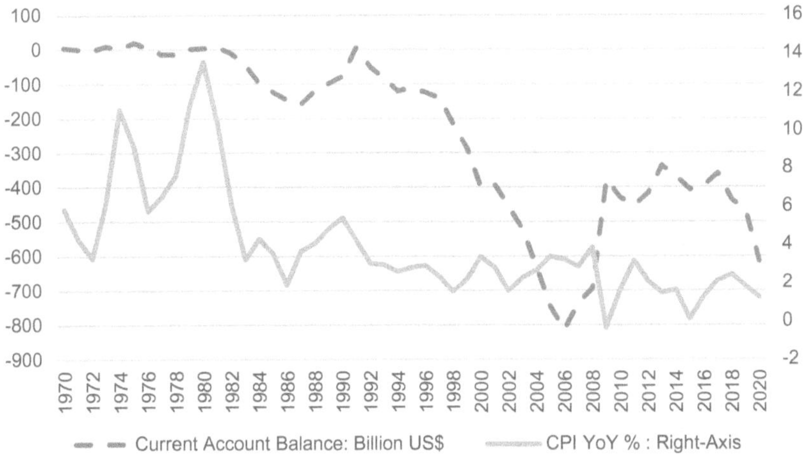

Fig. 6.3 US current account deficits and inflation rates since 1960 (*Source* US Department of Labour, US Bureau of Economic Analysis)

GDP, with an average of 2.30% from 2016 to 2020.[4] However, access to cheap industrial products overseas has helped the United States maintain long-term low domestic inflation. As shown in Fig. 6.3, in the 1980s, with the expanding current account deficit, high domestic inflation in the late 1970s and early 1980s has been eased in the United States. The United States benefited from importing large amounts of cheap industrial products to alleviate the domestic inflationary pressures.

Second, the excess return that the United States obtains on its investments is also a manifestation of dollar hegemony. The United States obtains excess investment income mainly through two channels, one is the risk channel and the other is the liquidity channel. On the one hand, the United States borrows money through low-interest and low-risk funds (such as US Treasuries) and invests it in global high-yield, high-risk assets like foreign direct investment and equity (Gourinchas and Rey 2007) to earn excess returns. On the other hand, during crisis, market actors of different countries often sell assets at low prices due to the urgent need for liquidity. US investors then provide them with liquidity and buy assets

[4] World Bank, https://data.worldbank.org/indicator/BN.CAB.XOKA.GD.ZS?end=2020&locations=US&start=2016.

at low prices. In the long run, they obtain high returns that exceed the normal rate of return ("excess returns"). Analysts such as Gourinchas and Rey (2007, 2014), Gourinchas, Rey, and Sauzet (2019), Mendoza, Quadrini, and Ríos-Rull (2009), and Forbes (2008) have argued that the US dollar occupies an asymmetrical dominant position in cross-border investment. Furthermore, they argue that such a position is a manifestation of US dollar hegemony for US investors who can invest in risky assets to obtain excess returns. Gourinchas and Rey (2007) estimate that US excess returns accounted for 2.1% of GDP from 1995 to 2004, noting that excess returns increased significantly after the collapse of the Bretton Woods monetary system. Forbes (2008) estimates that the average rate of excess returns was about 6.9% per year between 2002 and 2006. He finds that countries that invest more in US equity and bond markets are those with relatively underdeveloped domestic financial markets, weaker internal capital controls, and trading closely with the United States. Furthermore, countries that have lower returns on their domestic stock markets and those "close" to the United States in terms of language and distance are also more inclined to invest in the US stock market.

Third, dollar hegemony gives the United States the ability to transfer domestic volatility risks outwards. This makes the United States not only far richer but also far more stable than peripheral countries. For example, during the GFC, as shown in Table 6.1, the US stock market remained the most stable when compared to other economies even though the GFC originated on American soil. Given that the United States was the epicentre of the GFC, how could its financial markets be more stable than those of other countries in the system? We argue the US dollar assets' safe haven status is key to explain this phenomenon. At the beginning of the crisis, panic set in different financial markets which faced a shortage of liquidity, and global capital flowed to the United States because of the need for hedging. As a result, the US financial market gradually stabilised whilst other financial markets remained more prone to violent fluctuations due to the flight of assets. This development helped to stabilise US financial markets at the expense of capital flight from peripheral countries and violent fluctuations in their financial markets. Subsequently, the Fed's large-scale loose monetary policies[5] were put in place to mitigate domestic liquidity stress. The fall in interest rates and excess domestic liquidity in

[5] Including the rapid reduction of the policy interest rate to near zero alongside launching multiple rounds of Quantitative Easing.

Table 6.1 Volatility in the financial markets of various countries in 2008

	Volatility of Major Stock Indexes (%)	*Exchange Rate Volatility Relative to the US Dollar (%)*
US	−40.67	0.00
Germany	−41.35	7.41
Italy	−49.60	7.41
China	−61.52	−7.19
Japan	−45.55	−18.26
Korea	−41.44	46.23
India	−52.02	23.18
Brazil	−40.83	34.08
Russia	−71.65	14.57

Note The table demonstrates the trends in financial indicators throughout 2008, with December statistical data as the final period and January statistical data as the initial period. The volatility of the stock index and the exchange rate is the percentage change of the final period relative to the initial period. A negative stock index volatility represents a decline in the stock index, and vice versa; meanwhile, a negative exchange rate volatility represents an appreciation of the currency in US dollars, and vice versa. *Source* CEIC

the United States drove liquidity once again out of the United States to financial markets of other countries. Financial bubbles were created in peripheral countries with capital inflows, currency appreciation, and stock market booms, especially for some countries with relatively fragile economic and financial environments,[6] which paved the way for the next similar cycle (Bhattarai, Chatterjee, and Park 2021). The influx of excess liquidity also made peripheral countries more prone to high inflation, which could lead to political and social turmoil in countries with weaker economic results and poor governance capabilities.

Costs of Dollar Hegemony to the US and Peripheral Countries

Dollar hegemony also has a number of costs both on the United States and peripheral countries. These include rising global imbalances and deindustrialisation in the United States, rising imbalances and financial

[6] From 2015 to 2016, some resource-based emerging market countries experienced exchange rate fluctuations. In 2018, the exchange rates of Turkey, Argentina, and other countries depreciated significantly.

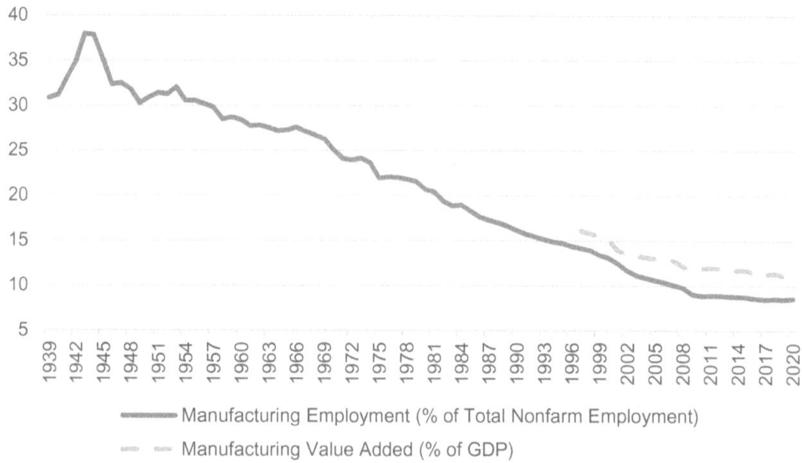

Fig. 6.4 Deindustrialisation in the US (*Source* Federal Reserve, St Louis; World Bank)

crisis in peripheral countries, and the weakening of US-China symbiotic relationship.

Global Imbalance and Deindustrialisation in the US

With the ever-increasing privileges of the US dollar, the international monetary system has experienced systemic imbalances with the United States and peripheral countries both suffering damages from this imbalance.

Global division of labour is an important driver of the deindustrialisation of developed countries (Kollmeyer 2009; Van Neuss 2018). Firms embrace outsourcing to reduce production costs, leading to the loss of manufacturing jobs within the developed world. For the United States, due to positive correlation between the globalisation and economic growth, the loss of manufacturing jobs (Fig. 6.4) was accepted by policymakers.[7] However, the loss of manufacturing employment especially

[7] In 2014, C. Fred Bergstein and others mentioned in a speech at the Peterson Institute that for every job loss in the manufacturing industry, the annual GDP of the United States increased by 1.5 million US dollars.

in the southern and Midwestern states of the country caused increasingly serious economic and political polarisation (Pierce and Schott 2016; Bloom et al. 2019; Autor et al. 2020). Since polarisation is too serious to be overlooked, both Trump and Biden promised to restore US manufacturing (Garcia and Smith 2020; Churchill 2021), although, the practical effect has been limited. For example, the trade war launched by Trump at the beginning of 2018 seems unlikely to maintain and create blue-collar employment. This is because it seems difficult for the United States to fundamentally solve the problem of the hollowing out of the US industry if the prevailing international monetary system does not undergo proper structural reform. Specifically, the current global monetary system marked by the dollar hegemony requires the United States to export currency liquidity to the rest of the world as the world's lender, which requires that the United States maintain long-term trade deficits with other countries in the system. This structural feature requires the United States to import more overseas commodities and export fewer domestic products, naturally leading to shrinking industrial sectors. If the United States with a variety of prosperous manufacturing sectors and correspondingly a satisfying level of manufacturing employment, the United States would no longer need to import a large number of manufactured products from other countries in the world, or even export more manufactured products. If that was the case, how could the United States export dollar liquidity to other countries? Hence, the global production and huge trade deficit, which have caused deindustrialisation in the United States, can hardly to be changed fundamentally under the current international monetary system.

Global Imbalances and Financial Crises in Peripheral Countries

From the perspective of peripheral countries, the international monetary system limits their ability to ensure domestic financial stability. By its nature, the goal of US monetary policy is to serve the US economy and achieve domestic objectives of "maximum employment, stable prices, and moderate long-term interest rates" as articulated by the Federal Reserve. However, the influence of the US monetary policy can reach every corner of the international monetary system dominated by the US dollar. During the dollar depreciation cycle, excess dollar liquidity enters peripheral countries, triggering financial bubbles, paving the way for an exchange rate crisis and a general financial crisis in the subsequent dollar appreciation cycle. As shown in Fig. 6.5, every dollar appreciation cycle was accompanied by a financial crisis in peripheral countries. Though the

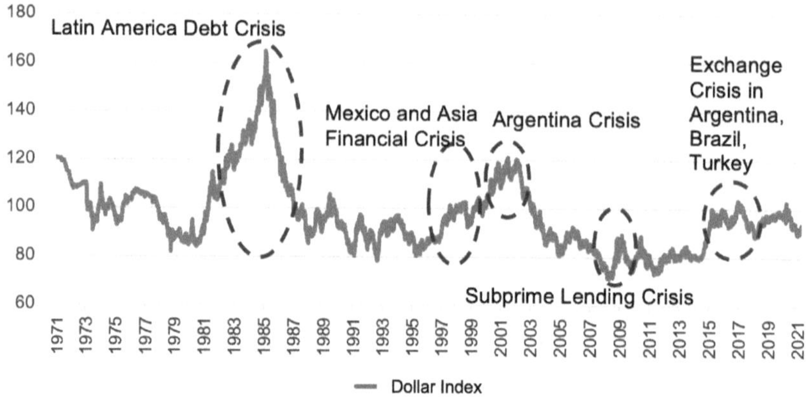

Fig. 6.5 Correlation between financial crises and dollar index (*Source* CEIC)

outbreak of the crisis was also related to the debt status and economic development of the peripheral countries, the large inflow and outflow of dollar liquidity undoubtedly magnified the problem and affected their inherently fragile financial systems.

Weakening US-China Symbiotic Co-Existence

The symbiotic relationship between China and the United States is also an important feature of the global monetary system. China has a large trade surplus, which means that it exports a large number of goods to the United States and then allocates the US dollars earned from trade surplus into US dollar assets, supporting the hegemony of the US dollar. As noted in Table 6.2, the proportions of reserve currencies do not match

Table 6.2 GDP and reserve currency shares of major regions, 2020

	GDP (% of World Total)	*Currency (% of Allocated Reserves)*
Euro Area, Switzerland, United Kingdom	19.53	28.04
United States, Canada	26.62	65.30
China, Japan	25.29 (China: 17.39)	8.90 (China: 2.45)
Others	28.56	4.82

Source World Bank, IMF

the proportion of each economy's global GDP, especially for North American and East Asian countries. North American countries' proportion of reserve currencies to their share of global GDP are significantly greater than those of the East Asian economies. Hence, it can be concluded that East Asian countries, especially China, have long supported the hegemony of the US dollar. However, for the following reasons, the symbiotic relationship between the United States and China has become increasingly difficult to maintain, shaking the foundation of the international monetary system.

The United States believes that the Sino-US trade deficit is an important contributor to its domestic deindustrialisation as noted above. It has also sparked worries that China's technological rise will weaken the American national security and international hegemony (Curran 2019; Liu and Woo 2018). This ongoing situation has caused frictions between the United States and China in trade, finance, technology, and other fields. These frictions further turned into trade war against China, especially to curb China's technological catch-up by placing sanctions on ZTE, Huawei, and other Chinese companies. The United States even sanctioned Chinese officials through the SWIFT system.[8] The sanctions imposed by the United States on China laid bare the fragility of the asymmetric and yet symbiotic relationship between China and the United States, leading to the collapse of strategic mutual trust. In October, 2019, the Politburo collectively studied blockchain technology and increased its efforts to launch the digital renminbi (RMB), a development which reflected the distrust of senior officials within the Chinese government towards the existing international monetary system (Xi 2019).

China's domestic political needs have also inspired the Chinese government to adjust the Sino-US symbiotic relationship. For a long time, China has kept its domestic labour prices down to continuously export cheap industrial products to the United States. However, as China's domestic supply of cheap labour shrinks and labour prices continue rising, this relationship has become increasingly difficult to sustain (Li et al. 2012; Wei, Xie, and Zhang 2016). In addition, as the cost of low domestic wages, China's domestic welfare has suffered greatly, many Chinese citizens cannot afford the products China exports. This situation is unsustainable

[8] Sanctions were applied in August, 2020, on eleven Chinese officials following the promulgation of the National Security Act of Hong Kong (Churchill and Fromer 2020).

and not in accordance with the ruling party's people-oriented concept of governance.

Therefore, under the impact of collapsing Sino-US mutual trust and Chinese domestic political pressure and economic transformation, China has promoted RMB internationalisation and the construction of digital yuan, accelerated the process of capital account opening, striven to build a financial sector independent of the United States, and proposed the "dual circulation" growth model based on domestic circulation (Yao 2020). As shown in Fig. 6.6, the RMB internationalisation index has shown an upward trend in general. During 2015–2016, China experienced a "double decline" in the stock market and the foreign exchange market. Therefore, Chinese policymakers focused more on the structural reforms of the domestic financial system, rather than on enhancing the position of the RMB in the international monetary system. Many financial reform measures have been implemented to improve and consolidate the domestic financial system. For example, the Financial Stability

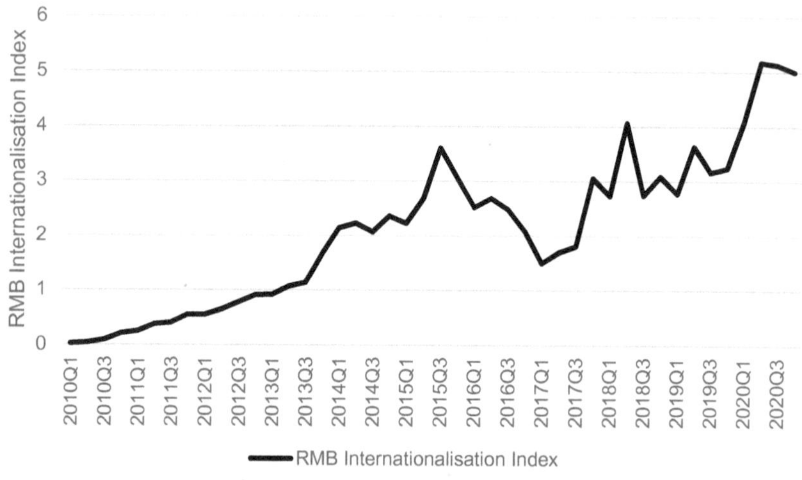

Fig. 6.6 RMB Internationalisation Index (*Note* The RMB Internationalisation Index is a comprehensive and quantitative indicator developed by International Monetary Institute that objectively describes the development of RMB's dynamics as an international currency in trade settlement, financial transactions, and official reserves. *Source* International Monetary Institute of Renmin University of China)

and Development Committee under the State Council was established in 2017. In other words, China moved away from the previous model, and adopted a more cautious, multi-pronged approach after 2015 and promoted the internationalisation of the RMB whilst ensuring the stability of the domestic financial system. This led to a brief decline in the RMB internationalisation index from 2016 to 2017, but it also made the subsequent RMB internationalisation process more stable. The Chinese government has promoted the inclusion of the renminbi into the IMF's special drawing right (SDR) basket (see Chapter 5 of this book), given over 10 central banks the right to use trillions of RMB through currency swap agreements, built the two-step rollout of The Cross-Border Interbank Payment System (CIPS)[9] project which has equipped the renminbi with a global payment platform, advocated for the establishment of multilateral international financial and monetary cooperation platforms such as the Asian Infrastructure Investment Bank (AIIB), the New Development Bank (NDB), and the BRICS Contingent Reserve Agreement (CRA) (see Chapters 3 and 4 of this book), established several open commodity exchanges and corresponding derivatives, especially the launch of gold and oil futures, to help form a crude oil-renminbi-gold triangle cycle, and endeavoured to position Shanghai as a global financial centre.

Potential Factors that Could Undermine Dollar Hegemony

As both the United States and peripheral countries are "suffering" from the deficiencies of the international monetary system to varying degree and the Sino-US symbiotic relationship is weakening, the international monetary system urgently needs reform. Though the hegemony of the US dollar is difficult to end in the short run, certain long-term latent dangers have already been evident. Some threats include the unsustainability of domestic US fiscal policy, China's transformation from "world factory" to "world market", and geopolitical undercurrents.

First, expansionary US fiscal policies may threaten the US dollar's hegemony by reducing the attractiveness of holding US treasuries. As shown in Fig. 6.7, although the US federal fiscal deficit has been rising, thanks to the long-term low-interest-rate environment, interest payments have remained stable. Facing the outbreak of the COVID-19 epidemic,

[9] It is a payment system which offers clearing and settlement services for its participants in cross-border RMB payments and trade.

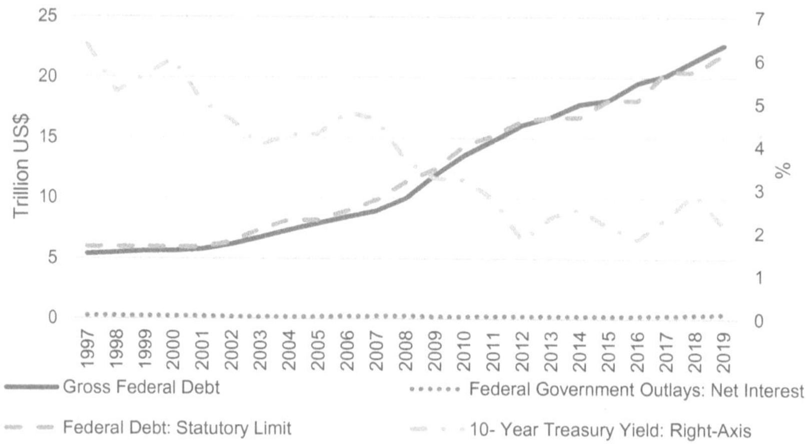

Fig. 6.7 Federal debt and interest payments (*Source* Federal Reserve)

the Federal Reserve launched an unlimited quantitative easing policy in March, 2020, and lowered interest rates to near zero, keeping interest payments of federal government low. However, the rapid rise of inflation, which was partly induced by the breakdown of the supply chains, the spikes of commodity prices and the extremely loose monetary policy, has forced the Federal Reserve to consider raising interest rates (Milstein, Powell, and Wessel 2021; Smialek 2021). If the Federal Reserve indeed raises the policy interest rate to tame inflation, the interest rate of US treasury will rise significantly as well. Moreover, in the long run, with domestic inequality, ageing, political polarisation, and other destabilising phenomena fermenting in the United States, Democrats and Republicans will likely converge towards more similar views on alleviating inequality, improving ageing, confronting China, and reducing cheap industrial product imports to increase employment in US manufacturing. Such efforts can stimulate domestic demands and increase the prices of industrial products. Consequently, the high inflation environment may last for a long period and further push up the policy rate. Therefore, whether in the short or long term, the high inflation may force the Federal Reserve to raise the policy interest rate and keep it at a relatively high level, though the Federal Reserve is not willing to raise the policy rate, since a hike in rates will raise the borrowing costs for the US government.

However, in terms of fiscal structure, the US government debt can hardly be reduced. There is currently no sign of a jump in US fiscal revenues; meanwhile, US fiscal expenditures are difficult to cut or even maintain at a steady level. For example, President Joe Biden proposed the three-part "Build back better" agenda[10] which indicates that the federal fiscal deficit will possibly continue to rise in future.[11] The rising nominal interest rate and the expanding size of the federal deficit will jointly push up interest payments on federal fiscal debt. If fiscal revenues fail to maintain interest payments, the credibility of US Treasury bonds will be shaken. Furthermore, if peripheral economies no longer recognise US Treasury bonds and stop buying or even selling them on a large scale, the US dollar's hegemony will be weakened.

Second, China's ongoing economic transition may pose another risk to the US dollar hegemony. For China, the transformation from the "world factory" to the "world market" means China would no longer maintain a surplus trade balance which would be converted to trade deficit. In that case, it will be difficult for the United States to continue to obtain cheap industrial products from China, and domestic inflation in the United States may rise as a result. As noted above, high inflation is not conducive to the maintenance of the dollar hegemony. Furthermore, as the "world market", China may proactively provide RMB liquidity to other major exporting countries, reduce foreign exchange reserves, and cut down its holdings of US Treasury bonds, lessening the Sino-US symbiotic relationship. As the second largest foreign holder of US Treasury bonds, China's insistence on reducing its holdings of US Treasury bonds will greatly destroy the international credit of the US dollar and raise the interest rate of US Treasury bonds, making it even more difficult for the United States to repay the interest on Treasury bonds.

Third, geopolitical conflicts could be another potential threat to the US dollar's dominance. The US's use of the SWIFT system to impose economic sanctions on other countries to achieve political goals, a tactic

[10] President Biden proposed a three-part "Build back better" agenda, which included signing a $1.9 trillion stimulus bill, the American Rescue Plan, alongside the American Jobs Plan and American Families Plan.

[11] On 15 November, 2021, Biden signed the bipartisan $1.2 trillion "once-in-a-generation" infrastructure bill into law at the White House, dealing with rebuilding America's roads and bridges and spreading broadband internet. It was the largest federal investment in the country's infrastructure for decades.

that has weakened the appeal of the US dollar. Notably, Russia and Iran have struggled to switch to other currencies for payments to bypass the continuous sanctions imposed by the United States. In the fourth quarter of 2020, US dollar-denominated Russian exports fell by more than 50% for the first time. The ongoing denomination of the oil trade between Russia and China in euro is an important reason for the decline in the use of the US dollar in Russia's foreign trade (Doff and Quinn 2021). In addition, Russia has also removed $186 billion in assets from its National Wealth Fund and increased its investments into euro assets, RMB assets and gold (Shead 2021). Russian President Vladimir Putin once stated that Russia did not intend to abandon the use of the US dollar as a reserve currency or payment currency altogether, but the pressure of the US sanctions forced Russia to adopt other currencies for settlement (Tass 2021). Iran has also tried to use euro instead of dollar given the US sanctions, through the INSTEX system between Iran and the European Union to bypass the SWIFT system; the first such transaction was completed in March 2020 (Brzozowski 2020). Moreover, to circumvent US sanctions, China has also been working on reducing its dependence on the US dollar gradually but firmly, launched the CIPS cross-border payment project and actively promoted the development of digital RMB. Data from SWIFT show that the euro has surpassed the US dollar twice as the most important payment currency, in October 2020 and May 2021 (Fig. 6.8). As such, it can be argued that geopolitical conflict is an important consideration for countries to reduce the use of the US dollar as a payment currency. With the improvement of competing payment systems, the decline of the US dollar's status as a payment currency will continue.

To sum up, the unsustainability of US fiscal policies alongside China's economic transformation and deepening geopolitical conflicts are the main threats to the US dollar's international predominance. Notably, the three interwoven factors may further intensify each other. Firstly, should the domestic fiscal environment of the United States deteriorate in a fundamental way, a lot of countries will accelerate their divestment of the US dollar. This will reduce the international use of the US dollar, as intensifying geopolitical tensions would likewise lead to reduced use of the US dollar. Secondly, if the geopolitical conflicts escalate, the United States will strengthen its sanctions, China can be one of the sanction targets, leading to increased disapproval of the US dollar by sanctioned parties and a reduction in the purchases of US Treasury bonds, which will also further deteriorate fiscal sustainability within the United States.

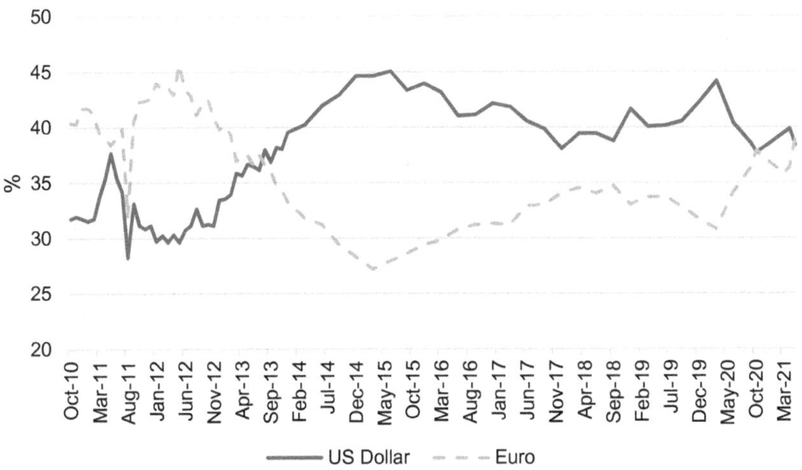

Fig. 6.8 Comparison of US dollar and euro uses as worldwide payment currency (*Source* SWIFT)

Thirdly, should China reduce exports to the United States as well as the holding of US treasuries during economic transformation, the treasury interest rate will soar due to the possible plunge in global US treasuries demand, intensifying the unsustainability of US expansionary fiscal policy and weakening the US dollar's international credibility. As a result, the Sino-US strategic conflict would get worse, and China will further promote economic transformation and decouple from the United States.

Towards the Era of Digital Currencies

In this section, we mainly focus on the impact of central bank digital currencies (CBDCs) on the international monetary system. Technological changes are creating new strategic opportunities for the internationalisation of the RMB which may contribute to the reform and improvement of the international monetary system (Huang 2020; Peters, Green, and Yang 2020).

To start with, the adoption of CBDC can transform macroeconomic management. In China for example, through CBDCs, the People's Bank of China, China's central bank, can theoretically obtain all transaction information nationwide, helping to formulate and implement monetary and other economic policies more accurately and more effectively. Moreover, CBDCs can also help to improve and modernise the governance capabilities of governments. Through CBDCs, governments can effectively suppress corruption and other illegal activities, as well as more accurately implement income and wealth redistribution to promote targeted welfare policies, improving the efficiency of the existing welfare system. For instance, with the assistance of CBDCs, government can directly deliver a certain amount of money to the elderly, the jobless, and the disabled through digital currency payment system rather than distributing the money through the administrative staff. For now, the digital RMB is still characterised as M0 (cash in circulation). When digital RMB starts to play the role of M1 (narrow money supply) and M2 (broader money supply, M1 plus "near money"), reforms to the current monetary system will be more revolutionary.

China's accelerated test of digital currencies is closely related to its concerns about US-China decoupling. Facing extreme pressure imposed by the Trump and Biden administrations, China has had to develop adequate plans and responses to possible financial sanction risks. In other words, it was not the intention for China to develop a digital RMB to replace the US dollar's dominant status; but digital RMB constitutes a preventive measure to help China mitigate potential risks brought by the US dollar.

In future, the potential widespread use of digital RMB can provide alternatives to market players, especially for those developing countries who have suffered from the volatility of the US dollar. According to Zhou Xiaochuan (2021), the former governor of the People's Bank of China, China's digital yuan is not designed to replace the US dollar's status, but to serve its original purpose to promote international economic efficiency. With efforts to modernise and digitalise the RMB payment system, the Digital Currency/Electronic Payment (DC/EP) project enables the RMB to be used for cross-border settlement more safely, efficiently, and conveniently. Those technical means can help to increase the international usage of China's sovereign currency, which may in effect weakens US dollar hegemony.

Having said this, at present, digital sovereign currencies are still in their infancy. Though the People's Bank of China is the first central bank to issue a cryptocurrency (Peters, Green, and Yang 2020), the scale of use of the digital RMB is still limited. It is still difficult for the digital

RMB to significantly influence the international pricing, settlement, and reserve functions of the US dollar (Peters, Green, and Yang 2020). The People's Bank of China officially launched a study on the DC/EP in 2014 and a small-scale test of digital renminbi began at the end of 2019. According to a white paper released by People's Bank of China, by the end of 2021, the total number of transactions in digital yuan was 70.75 million including about 20.87 million personal wallets and 3.51 enterprise wallets. Digital yuan trials have reached 34.5 billion yuan ($5.34 billion) which is insignificant compared to China's total social retail sales of 3758.6 billion yuan in June 2021. As people have become accustomed to WeChat Pay and Alipay, the digital RMB has missed the golden period of 2013–2015 to develop. Unless the government actively and forcefully promote it in future,[12] the development of DC/EP will still face considerable resistance. The Bank of England, the Federal Reserve, the Bank of Japan, the European Central Bank, and other major central banks around the world have also started the currency digitisation process,[13] but they not unlike the digital RMB are still in their infancies as well.

We emphasise that even if the use of CBDC increase further in future, there is still a strong uncertainty about the extent to which digital currencies will change the current currency system. The political will of countries, rather than the specific form of currency, remains the most essential determinant in remaking and remoulding the international monetary system. As stated above, the development of the digital RMB is not intended to influence the international status of the US dollar.

[12] For instance, the government could provide more incentives for users of digital renminbi, stipulate that all salaries of national civil servants are paid in the form of digital renminbi and cannot be converted into other forms or make it cheaper to use digital RMB to buy goods.

[13] In October 2020, the Bank for International Settlements (BIS) released a report entitled "Central Bank Digital Currency: Basic Guidelines and Core Features", trying to gain an advantage in international competition by collectively formulating central bank digital currency technical standards. In the same month, the European Central Bank (ECB) published the "Digital Euro Report", which opened a public consultation on the digital euro. In April 2021, the Bank of Japan, which previously claimed that it did not plan to issue a central bank digital currency, began a one-year digital yen test. The Federal Reserve is also actively participating in digital dollar research and development projects, assessing the technical, policy, and legal feasibility of digital dollar implementation. Obviously, as major countries and currency areas in the world are accelerating the pace of local currency digitalisation, the global competition for central bank digital currencies has become increasingly obvious and fierce.

The future of the international yuan mainly depends on policy choices of Beijing and the direction and process of domestic reform and opening up.

It is unclear how the pricing model of exchange rate in the era of digital currency is to be structured. Should it operate without hard anchor? Or should it peg to precious metal like gold, or to the price of a basket of commodities, or to the price of a certain currency basket? If the pricing of digital currencies continues to follow current rules without hard anchors, then who will provide liquidity and meanwhile bear the trade deficit? If the United States continues to shoulder the responsibility, then digital currencies will only change the current international monetary system in form, not in substance. However, if the United States no longer plays the role, which country or organisation will provide liquidity and act as the lender of last resort to the entire system? How can the country avoid the hollowing out of its industry, which may result from providing liquidity and bearing a deficit? If the digital currency returns to the era of hard anchors, then the expansion of the central bank's balance sheet will be restricted by the anchor target, will it trigger deflation and economic depression?

Digital currencies, which are mainly intended to provide more efficient and convenient technical solutions to the entire system, could not provide any satisfying answers to the above questions. Therefore, the reform of the international monetary system depends on the aggregate political will and policy coordination of major economies such as China, the United States, Europe, Japan, and India, especially China and the United States. Like the Bretton Woods Conference in 1944, the necessity of the gathering to conduct another negotiation is becoming more and more obvious. We argue that China has the political determination to gradually reform the international monetary system. Chinese scholars Jia (2020), Di (2020) and others have advocated that China should take the initiative to decouple from US finance, maintaining either a balanced trade structure, or a slight trade deficit. In that way, China will no longer be a supporter of US dollar hegemony; instead, becoming a competitor of the United States. This change of China's identity can help the United States to relieve the pressure of deindustrialisation whilst weakening the US dollar's hegemony accordingly. A series of China's actions indicate that the government indeed determined to change its position in the current monetary system. Specifically, China has unveiled a "dual circulation" strategy, which focuses on domestic consumption, to cut its dependence on overseas markets and technology in its former developmental trajectory. In addition, more importance has been attached to the imports, which can be found from the successful hosting of the China International Import Expo. Besides, the trade surplus as a proportion of China's GDP has shown an overall downward trend since the financial crisis. Moreover, the promotion of RMB internationalisation and digital yuan also indicates that China has firm determination to gradually reduce its dependence on the United States.

Conclusions

The hegemony of the US dollar has continued after the decoupling of the US dollar from gold in 1971. The dollar plays an important role in the present day international monetary system. Dollar hegemony benefits the United States by bringing seigniorage, generating an excess return on foreign investments, and maintaining a stable financial system. But it has also led to costs including deindustrialisation in the United States and financial crisis in peripheral countries that are crisis prone. As the largest buyer of the US dollars, China has also gradually lost its trust in the United States. Hence, the reform of the international monetary system is an inevitable trend. Network benefits of dollar hegemony notwithstanding, going forward, three factors could undermine the US dollar hegemony. The first is rising fiscal deficit in the United States which could lead to higher interest rates and difficulties in servicing debt and keeping it sustainable. The second is China becoming a "world market". The third is the escalation of geopolitical conflicts which could reduce overseas usage of the US dollar.

The United States has been wary about the development of digital currencies, which poses a potential threat to the Fed's monetary control and the effectiveness of US monetary policy (Michaels and Vigna 2019). However, even the digital RMB, which is at the forefront of the development of CBDCs, is still at its infancy (Michaels and Vigna 2019). It is unclear whether CBDCs can revolutionise the international monetary system. If CBDCs can find a reasonable anchor relying on technology and curtail the disorderly expansion of major central banks' balance sheets, then the digital currencies could have a significant impact. If, however, digital currencies merely replace legal currencies in technical form with the United States continuing to incur balance of payment deficit and provide liquidity to the world, the effect of digital currencies in reforming the international monetary system will be minimal and decorative.

References

Autor, David, David Dorn, Gordon Hanson, and Kaveh Majlesi. 2020. "Importing Political Polarization? The Electoral Consequences of Rising Trade Exposure." *American Economic Review* 110 (10): 3139–3183. https://doi.org/10.1257/aer.20170011.

Bhattarai, Saroj, Arpita Chatterjee, and Woong Yong Park. 2021. "Effects of US Quantitative Easing on Emerging Market Economies." *Journal of Economic Dynamics and Control* 122: 104031. https://doi.org/10.1016/j.jedc.2020.104031.

Bloom, Nicholas, Kyle Handley, Andre Kurmann, and Philip Luck. 2019. The Impact of Chinese Trade on U.S. Employment: The Good, The Bad, and The Apocryphal. Society for Economic Dynamics.

Bordo, Michael D. 2019. "The Operation and Demise of the Bretton Woods System, 1958–1971." In *Bretton Woods Agreements: Together with Scholarly Commentaries and Essential Historical Documents*, edited by Naomi Lamoreaux and Ian Shapiro. New Haven: Yale University Press.

Bordo, Michael D., Eric Monnet, and Alain Naef. 2019. "The Gold Pool (1961–1968) and the Fall of the Bretton Woods System. Lessons for Central Bank Cooperation." *The Journal of Economic History* 79 (4): 1027–1059.

Brzozowski, A. 2020. "EU's INSTEX mechanism facilitates first transaction with pandemic-hit Iran." *EURACTIV.com*, April 1. https://www.euractiv.com/section/global-europe/news/eus-instex-mechanism-facilitates-first-transaction-with-pandemic-hit-iran/.

Caballero, Ricardo J., and Arvind Krishnamurthy. 2009. "Global Imbalances and Financial Fragility." *National Bureau of Economic Research Working Paper Series* No. 14688. https://doi.org/10.3386/w14688.

Cardoso, Eliana, and Albert Fishlow. 1992. "Latin American Economic Development: 1950–1980." *Journal of Latin American Studies* 24 (S1): 197–218.

Churchill, O., & Fromer, J. 2021. "Moser 2021 Biden vs. Trump on Reshoring: A Review, and a Critique." *Industry Week*, February 9. https://www.industryweek.com/the-economy/trade/article/21154656/biden-vs-trump-on-reshoring-a-review-and-a-critique.

Cohen, B. J. 1977. *Organizing the World's Money: The Political Economy of International Monetary Relations*. Palgrave Macmillan.

Curran, E. 2019. "How the U.S.-China Trade War Got to This Point. Bloomberg." *How the U.S.-China trade war got to this point. Blooming point.* https://www.bloomberg.com/professional/blog/how-the-u-s-china-trade-war-got-to-this-point/.

Di, Dongsheng. 2020. "Ten Judgment on the Current Situation." Guan Cha, Last Modified Mar 167. https://www.guancha.cn/DiDongSheng/2020_03_17_542061.shtml.

Dizard, John. 2019. "Trying to Bypass US Sanctions on Iran is Futile." *Financial Times*, August 7. https://www.ft.com/content/d227f7b3-468c-3608-ab02-3e1ea6dd0c04.

Doff, Natasha, and Áine Quinn. 2021. "Putin's Bid to Ditch Dollar Picks Up as Exports Move to Euro." *International Trade* Apr 27. https://ajot.com/news/article/putinas-bid-to-ditch-dollar-picks-up-as-exports-move-to-euro.

Dowd, Kevin, and David Greenaway. 1993. "Currency Competition, Network Externalities and Switching Costs: Towards an Alternative View of Optimum Currency Areas." *The Economic Journal* 103 (420): 1180–1189. https://doi.org/10.2307/2234244.

Forbes, Kristin J. 2008. "Why do Foreigners Invest in the United States?" *National Bureau of Economic Research Working Paper Series* No. 13908. https://doi.org/10.3386/w13908.

Garcia, Cardiff, and Stacey Vanek Smith. 2020. "How Biden and Trump Plan to Reshore Jobs." *The Indicator From Planet Money*, November 3. https://www.npr.org/2020/11/03/930906829/how-biden-and-trump-plan-to-reshore-jobs.

Garten, Jeffrey E. 2021, July 1. "When the U.S. Gave Up Gold." The Wall Street Journal. Accessed 20 November 2021. https://www.wsj.com/articles/when-the-u-s-gave-up-gold-11625148788.

Gavin, Francis. J. 2004. *Gold, Dollars, and Power: The Politics of International Monetary Relations, 1958–1971*. UNC Press Books.

Ghizoni, Sandra Kollen. 1971. "Nixon Ends Convertibility of U.S. Dollars to Gold and Announces Wage/Price Controls." Federal Reserve History. Accessed 20 November 2021. https://www.federalreservehistory.org/essays/gold-convertibility-ends.

Gourinchas, Pierre-Olivier, and Hélène Rey. 2005. "From World Banker to World Venture Capitalist: US External Adjustment and the Exorbitant Privilege." *National Bureau of Economic Research Working Paper Series* No. 11563. https://doi.org/10.3386/w11563.

Gourinchas, Pierre-Olivier, and Hélène Rey. 2007. "From World Banker to World Venture Capitalist: U.S. External Adjustment and the Exorbitant Privilege." In, 11–66. National Bureau of Economic Research, Inc.

Gourinchas, Pierre-Olivier, and Hélène Rey. 2014. "Chapter 10 - External Adjustment, Global Imbalances, Valuation Effects." In *Handbook of International Economics*, edited by Gita Gopinath, Elhanan Helpman and Kenneth Rogoff, 585–645. Elsevier.

Gourinchas, Pierre-Olivier., Hélène. Rey, and Maxime Sauzet. 2019. "The International Monetary and Financial System." *Annual Review of Economics*

11 (1): 859–893. https://doi.org/10.1146/annurev-economics-080217-053518.

Green, T. S. 1999. "Central Bank Gold Reserves: An Historical Perspective Since 1845." *World Gold Council.*

Greenspan, Alan. 2001. "The Euro as an International Currency." The Federal Reserve Board, Last Modified November 30. https://www.federalreserve.gov/boarddocs/speeches/2001/200111302/default.htm.

Hatipoglu, Emre, and Dursun Peksen. 2016. "Economic Sanctions and Banking Crises in Target Economies." *Defence and Peace Economics* 29 (2): 171–189. https://doi.org/10.1080/10242694.2016.1245811.

Huang, Roger. 2020. China Will Use Its Digital Currency To Compete With The USD. Forbes.

Ito, Takatoshi. 2007. "Asian Currency Crisis and the International Monetary Fund, 10 Years Later: Overview." *Asian Economic Policy Review* 2 (1): 16–49.

Jia, Genliang. 2020. "Application of domestic large circulation, which popular opinion to break?". Guan Cha, Last Modified September 14. https://www.observersnews.com/JiaGenLiang/2020_09_14_565010_s.shtml.

Kollmeyer, Christopher. 2009. "Explaining Deindustrialization: How Affluence, Productivity Growth, and Globalization Diminish Manufacturing Employment." *American Journal of Sociology* 114 (6): 1644–1674. https://doi.org/10.1086/597176.

Li, Hongbin, Lei Li, Binzhen Wu, and Yanyan Xiong. 2012. "The End of Cheap Chinese Labor." *Journal of Economic Perspectives* 26 (4): 57–74. https://doi.org/10.1257/jep.26.4.57.

Liu, Tao, and Wing Thye Woo. 2018. "Understanding the U.S.-China Trade War." *China Economic Journal* 11: 319–340.

McKinnon, Ronald I. 1996. *The Rules of the Game: International Money and Exchange Rates*, vol. 1. MIT Press Books: The MIT Press.

Mendoza, Enrique G., Vincenzo Quadrini, and José Víctor. Ríos-Rull. 2009. "Financial Integration, Financial Development, and Global Imbalances." *Journal of Political Economy* 117 (3): 371–416. https://doi.org/10.1086/599706.

Michaels, D., and P. Vigna. 2019. "The Coming Currency War: Digital Money vs. the Dollar." *The Wall Street Journal.*

Milstein, E., T. Powell, and E. Wessel. 2021. "What Does the Federal Reserve Mean When it Talks About Tapering? Brookings." *What does the Federal Reserve mean when it talks about tapering? Brookings.* https://www.brookings.edu/blog/up-front/2021/07/15/what-does-the-federal-reserve-mean-when-it-talks-about-tapering/.

Norrlöf, Carla. 2008. "Strategic Debt." *Canadian Journal of Political Science* 41 (2): 411–435. https://doi.org/10.1017/S0008423908080475.

Peters, Michael A., Benjamin Green, and Haiyang Yang. 2020. "Cryptocurrencies, China's Sovereign Digital Currency (DCEP) and the US Dollar System." *Educational Philosophy and Theory*, 1–7. https://doi.org/10.1080/00131857.2020.1801146.

Pierce, Justin R., and Peter K. Schott. 2016. "The Surprisingly Swift Decline of US Manufacturing Employment." *American Economic Review* 106 (7): 1632–1662. https://doi.org/10.1257/aer.20131578.

Rebucci, Alessandro, and Benjamin Hunt. 2005. "The US Dollar and the Trade Deficit: What Accounts for the Late 1990s?" *International Finance* 8: 399–434. https://doi.org/10.1111/j.1468-2362.2005.00165.x.

Schenk, Catherine R. 2010. *The Decline of Sterling: Managing the Retreat of an International Currency, 1945–1992*. Cambridge: Cambridge University Press.

Schumacher, E.F. 1943. "Multilateral Clearing." *Economica* 10 (38): 150–165. https://doi.org/10.2307/2549461.

Shead, S. 2021. "Russia Says it will Remove Dollar Assets from its Wealth Fund." *CNBC*, June 3. https://www.cnbc.com/2021/06/03/russia-to-remove-dollar-assets-from-national-wealth-fund.html.

Smialek, J. 2021. "Jumping Prices and the Ghost of 2013's Market Meltdown Loom Over the Fed." *The New York Times*, July 28. https://www.nytimes.com/2021/07/28/business/economy/fed-taper-questions.html.

Steil, Benn. 2013. *The Battle of Bretton Woods: John Maynard Keynes, Harry Dexter White, and the Making of a New World Order*. Princeton: Princeton University Press.

Tass. 2021. "Russia Does Not Want to Give Up Dollar as Reserve Currency or Means of Payment—Putin." *Tass*, June 5. https://tass.com/economy/1299253.

Triffin, Robert. 1946–1947. "National Central Banking and the International Economy." *The Review of Economic Studies* 14 (2):53–75.

Triffin, Robert. 1961. "Gold and Dollar Crisis: The Future of Convertibility." *International Affairs* 37 (1): 81–81. https://doi.org/10.2307/2611532.

Van Neuss, Leif. 2018. "Globalization and Deindustrialization in Advanced Countries." *Structural Change and Economic Dynamics* 45:49–63.https://doi.org/10.1016/j.strueco.2018.02.002

Wei, Shang-Jin, Zhuan Xie, and Xiaobo Zhang. 2016. "From "Made in China" to "Innovated in China": Necessity, Prospect, and Challenges." *National Bureau of Economic Research Working Paper Series* No. 22854. https://doi.org/10.3386/w22854.

Xi, Jinping. 2019. Xi Stresses Development, Application of Blockchain Technology. Xinhua.

Yao, K. 2020. What We Know About China's 'Dual Circulation' Economic Strategy. Edited by Reuters: Reuters.

Zhou, Xiaochuan. 2009. Zhou: Reform the International Monetary System. The People's Bank of China.

Zhou, Xiaochuan. 2021. "Digital Yuan Not Designed to Replace US Dollar's Dominance: Former PBC Governor." *Global Times*, May 23. https://www.globaltimes.cn/page/202105/1224228.shtml.

CHAPTER 7

Managing the Decentralising International Trade Architecture

Pradumna B. Rana, Wai-Mun Chia, and Xianbai Ji

Introduction

Global economic governance—broadly defined as the act of governing economic relationship that transcends national boundaries in the absence of sovereign authority (Madhur 2012)—is in flux. The centralised governance architecture established at Bretton Woods is decentralising with the co-existence of "senior" global economic institutions and a plethora of

P. B. Rana
S. Rajaratnam School of International Studies, Nanyang Technological University, Singapore, Singapore
e-mail: prana@ntu.edu.sg

X. Ji (✉)
School of International Studies, Renmin University of China, Beijing, China
e-mail: xbji@ruc.edu.cn

W.-M. Chia
School of Social Sciences, Nanyang Technological University, Singapore, Singapore

P. B. Rana and X. Ji (eds.), *From Centralised to Decentralising Global Economic Architecture*, https://doi.org/10.1007/978-981-19-2041-7_7

newly established regional institutions (Rana 2014). A mere increase in the number of regional institutions per se is neither good nor bad from the perspective of the delivery of public goods. The outcome is contingent on the nature of the working relationship between new regional and existing global institutions. The quality of global economic governance improves with "healthy" competition and functional complementarity and deteriorates when "unhealthy" competition that encourages forum shopping, resource duplication and race to the bottom practices prevails between the more established global institutions and their newer regional counterparts. This inherent indeterminacy leads to an analytical conundrum for academics and policymakers alike. That is, have the benefits of institutional decentralisation outweighed the risks across the financial, development and trade pillars of the global economic governance architecture?

In a series of papers, Rana and Pacheco Pardo (2015, 2018), Pacheco Pardo and Rana (2015, 2018) and Rana (2019) have argued that, in the realm of financial stability and development finance, the benefits of new regional institutions and decentralisation appear to have exceeded the risks. For instance, they find that the relationship between the International Monetary Fund (IMF), the pre-eminent global financial safety net (GFSN), and the Chiang Mai Initiative Multilateralisation (CMIM), a major regional financial safety net (RFSN) in East Asia, is characterised by "healthy" competition (and resource additionality) and close inter-institutional functional cooperation and division of labour in various tasks of crisis prevention and crisis management. In the economic development architecture, they argue that the establishment of the Asian Infrastructure Investment Bank (AIIB) and New Development Bank (NDB) has triggered "an infrastructure investment boom" that helps fill the infrastructure financing gaps in developing countries. The memorandums of understanding (MOUs) that have been signed between these institutions and the World Bank and Asian Development Bank (ADB) promote functional cooperation in the areas of knowledge and information sharing, country-specific and sector-specific cooperation, and co-financing. The MOUs also contribute to the ratcheting up of the governance and operational standards of the newly founded AIIB and NDB. Likewise, Wang (2017) also asserts that as long as China refrains from abusing its leading position in the AIIB and NDB, the two regional institutions will "complement the World Bank in supporting different dimensions of development".

Do the above arguments and findings in favour of new institutions and the decentralisation process also apply to international trade? In other words, does global trade governance also benefit from the decentralisation process whereby regional trade agreements (RTAs) proliferate (Fig. 7.1) in the presence of the World Trade Organisation (WTO)? In this chapter, we attempt to provide answers to the question by employing the "benefit-risk" analysis or the "complementarity-competitiveness" framework as outlined in Kahler et al. (2016). This policy-oriented method begins with listing "benefits" or "complementarities" and "risks" or "competitiveness" of the subject matter before proposing policy recommendations

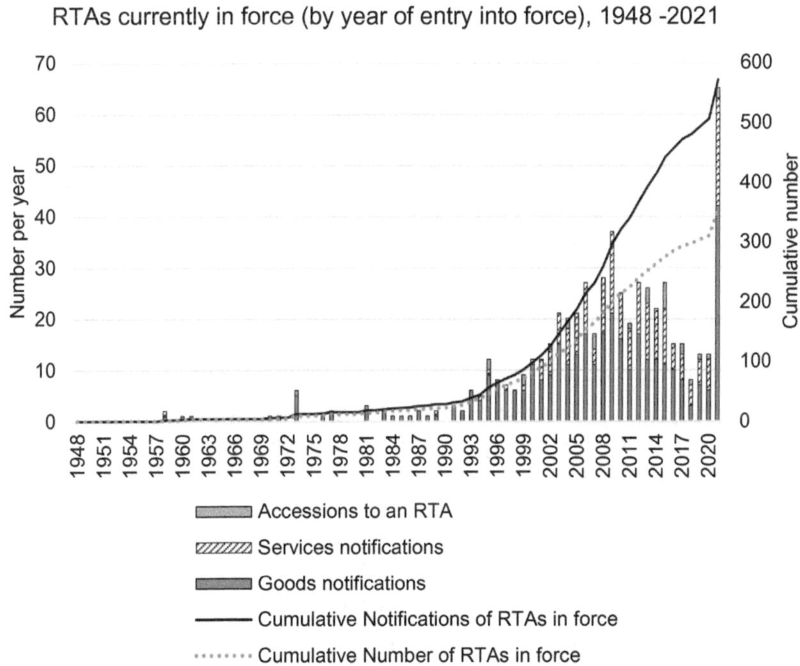

Fig. 7.1 Rising popularity of RTAs (*Note* Notifications of RTAs: goods, services and accessions to an RTA are counted separately. Physical RTAs: goods, services and accessions to an RTA are counted together. The cumulative lines show the number of notifications/physical RTAs currently in force)
(*Source* WTO Secretariat, as of 11 December 2021)

geared towards managing the process or "increasing the benefits and decreasing the risks".

More specifically, the analytical framework of this chapter is to partly rebut the "contested multilateralism" approach which defines the idea that emerging powers dissatisfied with existing institutions create new institutions to challenge the older ones leading to a decentralised architecture (Morse and Keohane 2014).[1] A priori decentralisation would have negative connotations because it would lead to forum shopping and race to the bottom (Zürn and Faude 2013). This is the case where benefits of decentralisation are lower than risks. However, decentralisation could also have positive impacts on global governance if there is functional complementarity in policy domains and financing between global and regional institutions as noted. This is the case where the benefits of decentralisation outweigh the costs. Therefore, "contested multilateralism" is not only related to contestation per se but can also result in improved governance.

This chapter is structured as follows. The next section briefly reviews the history of trade regionalism. Section 7.3 discusses the key "benefits" and "risks" that emerge as the architecture of global trade governance decentralises. We do so in part by drawing from existing literature on the pros and cons of regionalism. It should also be emphasised that the "benefits" and "risks" to be discussed are framed from a global economic governance point of view. Section 7.4 proposes policy actions that should be taken by the WTO to manage the decentralisation process. The reasons for highlighting the WTO are threefold. First, the WTO is the incumbent global trade governance body which is ultimately responsible for the coherence of the decentralising trade "regime complex" (Abbott, Green, and Keohane 2016) should regionalism come into conflict with multilateralism. Second, the WTO used to adopt a passive stance towards RTAs, assuming them to be expedient interim arrangements that would be obviated by a big-bang multilateral liberalisation round. The enduring popularity of RTAs, however, is prompting deep think on the part of the WTO to reposition itself in a new environment where regionalism accounts for an ever-growing part of the global trade regime. Third, unlike the IMF and World Bank which have gone through successive phases of institutional reforms, the WTO is in a relatively unreformed

[1] "Contested multilateralism" could also be regime shifting where states and/or non-stare actors shift their focus from one existing institution to another (Morse and Keohane 2014).

state, in view of the continual negotiation deadlocks and the possible dysfunction of the appellate body. Thus, the WTO has a stronger impetus to manage trade decentralisation in ways that allow it to stay at the centre of international governance. Otherwise, the WTO could be on the path of redundancy.

Asia is at the forefront of trade regionalism. Its role in the decentralising trade architecture, therefore, warrants special examination in Sect. 7.5. We argue that Asian countries, especially the "Asia 5 + 1" countries namely China, Japan, India, South Korea and Indonesia plus Australia, should play a leading role to shape trade decentralisation and lobby for WTO reform. This is because "Asia 5 + 1" are currently participating in global governance through the Group of Twenty (G20) and, importantly, because they are leading some of the world's most ambitious regional undertakings like mega-regional trade agreements and the Belt and Road Initiative (BRI). That said, by prescribing a role for a loosely defined "Asia", we do not posit that Asia is a homogenous group free from internal conflicts. For sure, there are and will be conflicts of interest within "Asia 5 + 1" and the group may not have a common "Asian approach" on how the WTO reform ought to proceed. Yet, the countries are structurally similar outward-oriented economies which depend on a robust global trading system for economic prosperity. Meanwhile, they represent a group of predominantly non-Western powers seeking to claim a greater say in global trade governance; therefore, there is sufficient common ground for them to work side by side to make the multilateral trading system more effective and less Western-centric.

From Centralised to Decentralising Trade Architecture

The Bretton Woods conference of 1944 had recognised the need for a comparable institution for trade to complement the IMF and the World Bank. But the United States (US) did not ratify the Havana Charter to establish the proposed International Trade Organisation; countries had to fall back to the General Agreement on Tariffs and Trade (GATT) to provide a temporary structure to assist in and regulate the rapid expansion of global trade (Bronz 1956; Toye 2003). From the late 1970s, the Group of Seven (G7) of industrialised countries, and in particular the "Quad" consisting of the US, Canada, Japan and Europe, acted as the informal oversight body of GATT. Meeting three to four times a year,

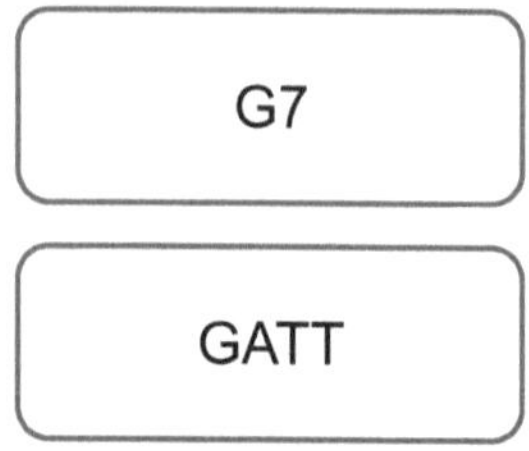

Fig. 7.2 Pre-WTO centralised international trade architecture

the G7 and Quad exercised decisive leadership at GATT via calling for the (re)launch of trade rounds, shaping negotiating agenda, bridging differences in national negotiation positions, setting deadline for conclusion and laying out the rudimentary dispute settlement mechanisms (Ullrich 2006; Sherifis and Astraldi 2001). Together, the G7 and GATT made up a two-level global trade governance architecture (Fig. 7.2). Eight rounds of multilateral trade liberalisation took place under the auspice of GATT between 1947 and 1994, reducing tariffs (on trade in manufactures) from an average level of 40% in 1947 (World Bank 1987) to around 15% (simple average for all products) in 1995, when the WTO was established. Successful trade liberalisation ushered in a sustained period of economic growth and social development across the world. Over the past decades, however, this centralised architecture has also been decentralising (WTO 2011).

Growing Popularity of "New Regionalism" in the 1990s

The first round of regionalism, known as "old regionalism", occurred soon after World War II in the 1950s and 1960s. In Europe, the European Coal and Steel Community (ECSC) and the European Economic Community (EEC) were established in 1952 and 1958, respectively. The EEC prompted several European countries that chose to stay outside of it to form a rival bloc, the European Free Trade Association, in 1960 and served as the template for pursuing regional integration for the then-newly independent countries in Africa, Latin America and the Caribbean. A common feature of the early-stage regional arrangements was that they were formed primarily among geographically neighbouring developing countries for the purposes of either supporting import substitution industrialization (ISI) policies or pooling resources to augment collective bargaining power (Langhammer and Hiemenz 1990) vis-à-vis the developed countries in the North. This "old" model of regionalism quickly fell out of favour by the end of 1970s (de Melo and Panagariya 1993) in part because of the autarkic nature of ISI policies and the closing power disparity between the developing and the developed countries in conducting international economic relations.

The rise of second wave of regionalism, or "new regionalism" (Ethier 1998), occurred in the 1990s. In 1991, Argentina, Brazil, Paraguay and Uruguay created the MERCOSUR. In 1992, the Association of Southeast Asian Nations (ASEAN) transformed itself from an anti-communism political-security alliance to an economic community by adopting the ASEAN Free Trade Area. With the 1993 passage of Maastricht Treaty, the EU was officially born. North American countries joined the race by launching the North American Free Trade Agreement (NAFTA, now known as the US-Mexico-Canada Agreement after treaty revision) in 1994. By the end of the same year, the Common Market for Eastern and Southern Africa was founded, marking a step towards the realisation of an envisaged African Economic Community.

The first factor that led to this phase of regionalism was the end of the Cold War. On one track, former Soviet republics struck trade agreements with each other and with Russia to cope with trade disruptions arising from the dissolution of the Council for Mutual Economic Assistance in 1991. On the other track, the Baltics edged towards the EU membership by entering into Association Agreements with the EU. Both dynamics led to a large number of RTAs in Eurasia. The second factor that drove "new regionalism" was a shift in the trade policy of the US. For some four decades after World War II, the US was the champion of the multilateral approach to trade governance. This pro-multilateralism policy stance took shape initially because the US believed that it had been the victim of exclusive European colonial blocs and that the absence of globally coordinated trade policy cooperation had aggravated the Great Depression in the 1930s. But as the European integration project steadily enlarged and the frustrations over the long-drawn-out Uruguay Round negotiations mounted, the US turned to regionalism in the mid-1980s to promote free trade while advancing its geopolitical interest (Fiorentino et al. 2007). It signed its first RTA with Israel in 1985. In the early 2000s, the US rolled out a "Competitive Regionalism" strategy, resulting in trade pacts with countries like Peru and Oman. The demonstration effect of the US trade

Table 7.1 Rising regionalism in Asia

Year	*Framework agreement signed*	*Negotiations launched*	*Signed but not yet in effect*	*Signed and in effect*	*Total*	*Proposed*
1986	0	0	1	3	4	0
1991	0	0	2	5	7	1
1996	0	0	7	31	38	1
2001	0	8	5	42	55	2
2006	15	37	8	80	140	42
2011	12	46	9	118	185	58
2016	5	74	5	148	232	76
2018	4	79	13	156	252	91

Source Asia Regional Integration Centre, ADB

policy paradigm shift was enormous, and many countries followed suit to pursue regionalism.

The third factor that led to the popularity of "new regionalism" was the frustration with difficulties in negotiating global agreements. GATT began as a relatively small international institution dominated by the Western countries. As GATT/WTO membership expanded steadily from 23 to 164, the complication of reaching multilateral agreements among an increasingly diverse group on an agenda that was becoming more complex became more difficult. Thus, when the Uruguay Round of GATT negotiations stalled, many governments turned to RTAs under the Article XXIV of GATT (as well as Enabling Clause of the Generalised System of Preference and Article V of General Agreement on Trade in Services). Similarly, the slow progress of the negotiations of the Doha Development Agenda (DDA) has also led to the proliferation of RTAs worldwide (Fig. 7.1).

Gradually, Asia also emerged at the forefront of regionalism (see Table 7.1). In 1991, there were only five in-effect RTAs involving ADB's regional members. In 2001, the count grew by more than eight-fold to 42. In 2018, there were 156 RTAs in force, 13 RTAs are pending enactment and 79 RTAs are under negotiations.

Regionalism did not play a central role in East Asia's dynamic growth story until the 1990s.[2] Countries living through colonialism and the

[2] For reviews of Asian regionalism in the 1990s and 2000s, see Urata (2019).

Cold War jealously guarded their hard-won sovereignty and found it less desirable to strike transnational economic arrangements like RTAs that might infringe on their commercial policy autonomy. Also, economic interdependence in East Asia was low as countries traded more with developed country markets outside Asia than with each other. Therefore, apart from the Asia–Pacific Trade Agreement (APTA) in existence since 1975, there were just a few RTAs in East Asia prior to the 1990s and countries adopted export-oriented development strategies to drive economic growth. In the 1990s, regionalism gradually took hold in East Asia. AFTA was implemented as noted.[3] East Asian countries also became more interwoven on the back of sprawling regional supply chains that held regional countries economically close together (Dent 2016). Against this backdrop, governments became receptive to RTAs as a policy instrument to facilitate market-led de facto economic integration. Towards the end of the last century, two trajectory-altering economic shocks—one negative, one positive—fully unleashed the regionalism potential of East Asia. The negative shock was the Asian Financial Crisis (AFC) of 1997–1998 which not only exposed the region's interconnectedness and shared vulnerabilities but also laid bare the urgency of regional cooperation on trade and investment (Chia 2010, ADB 2008). Therefore, once the AFC subsided, Singapore quickly signed an RTA with New Zealand in 2000 and another one with Japan in 2002. The positive shock, on the other hand, concerned China's entry into the WTO in 2001. To allay ASEAN's fear that China's WTO membership would drain trade and inward investment flows from Southeast Asia, China proposed a China-ASEAN Free Trade Area (CAFTA) in 2000. In the following years, Japan, South Korea, Australia and New Zealand and India all courted ASEAN with similar trade accords. CAFTA set in motion a domino effect.

Beginning of Mega-FTA Negotiations Post-Global Economic Crisis

At the dawn of the twenty-first century after the global economic crisis, the world's major powers pivoted towards three mega-RTAs. Defined as "deep integration partnerships in the form of RTAs between countries or regions with a major share of world trade and FDI and in which two or more of the parties are in a paramount driver position, or serve as hubs,

[3] AFTA was subsumed by a more ambitious ASEAN Trade in Goods Agreement (ATIGA) in 2008.

in global value chains (i.e. the US, the EU, Japan, China)" (Meléndez-Ortiz 2014), mega-RTAs included the Trans-Pacific Partnership (TPP) comprising 12 Pacific Rim countries (Australia, Brunei, Canada, Chile, Japan, Malaysia, Mexico, New Zealand, Peru, Singapore, Vietnam and the US), the EU-US Transatlantic Trade and Investment Partnership (TTIP) and the Regional Comprehensive Economic Partnership (RCEP) bringing together sixteen countries (Brunei, Cambodia, Indonesia, Laos, Malaysia, Myanmar, Philippines, Singapore, Thailand and Vietnam plus China, Japan, South Korea, India, Australia and New Zealand) (Ji 2021).

Mega-regionalism can be distinguished from previous waves for three reasons, first of which was the fact that they each drew on a much wider network of participating countries. Barring TTIP which could still be categorised as a "North–North" framework, the TPP and RCEP exhibited great heterogeneity with respect to membership composition, linking together a large number of countries of different sizes, development levels, economic structures, political systems and socio-cultural traditions. Second, mega-RTAs were truly gigantic trading blocs. For instance, RCEP (with India) covered 47% of global population, 32% of the global output, 29% of global trade and 32% of global investment flows (2018 figures). Third, the scope (i.e. the number of issue areas covered) and depth (i.e. the degree of market integration) of trade liberalisation under the mega-RTAs in the making were remarkably high. The TPP sought to eliminate 75% of tariff lines upon entry into force and 99% at the end of transition period (Freund et al. 2016). The tariff liberalisation target for RCEP is to reduce customs duties on around 90% of tradable goods after country-specific transition periods of varying lengths. More importantly, unlike conventional RTAs that were mainly tariff-cutting exercises, mega-RTAs were poised to be landmark twenty-first-century trade agreements collectively setting a new high standard for global trade. They were to contain deep commitments governing "behind the border" issues such as rules for protecting investments, intellectual property, environment and labour rights, and regulations on product standards. Though also motivated by gains from ambitious tariff reductions as the average tariff levels among its members remained relatively high, RCEP represents the most ambitious trading arrangement that many participants have ever negotiated.

The TPP agreement was signed amidst much fanfare on 4 February 2016. However, as Japan and New Zealand moved swiftly to ratify the agreement, the Trump administration pulled the US out of the pact.

Ji and Rana (2019) argue that the failure of the TPP in the US was due to a confluence of "bad timing" (2016 presidential election), "bad politics" (Trump's problematic worldviews and unsympathetic attitudes on trade) and "bad context" (public backlash against US trade policy). But the remaining 11 countries carried on with the deal and signed a trimmed-down agreement, called Comprehensive and Progressive Agreement for Trans-Pacific Partnership (CPTPP), in March 2018 without the US. Starting from 30 December 2018, the CPTPP has taken effect in Australia, Canada, Japan, Mexico, New Zealand, Singapore and Vietnam. As of this writing, all members except for Malaysia and Chile have ratified the deal. In Malaysia, the ratification process is pending and in Chile, the Senate has suspended deliberation on the matter. Nevertheless, a few economies including China, Taiwan (China), Ecuador, South Korea, Britain, Thailand, the Philippines, Indonesia and Colombia have either started formal acccession process or announced interest to join. Among all potential entrants, Britain has been the closest to the CPTPP membership.

RCEP witnessed a comparable withdrawal by India which was turning protectionist and autarkic given the professed goal of achieving self-reliant India (Atmanirbhar Bharat Abhiyaan). Since India's trade ties with the rest of the RCEP membership are not strong, its existence is unlikely to dent the economic gains from RCEP for other members. Even without India, RCEP will still be the world's largest free trade agreement. RCEP has been ratified by Australia, New Zealand, Brunei Darussalam, Cambodia, China, Japan, Indonesia, Laos, South Korea, Singapore, Thailand and Vietnam. RCEP entered into force on 1 January 2022. The Philippines and Myanmar have not yet ratified the agreement. Bangladesh and Hong Kong (China) have applied for accession into the partnership.

TTIP negotiations were launched in July 2013. The two sides had exchanged offers to eliminate duties on 97% of all tariff lines. But formal negotiations were "suspended" in early 2017 when Trump took office. Despite calls to resume TTIP negotiations not least to form a united North Atlantic front against China's allegedly unfair and predatory trading practices, TTIP was not resuscitated. Prompted by the US' withdrawal from the Paris Agreement, the European Council adopted a decision in April 2019 to terminate the TTIP negotiating directives that it had granted to the European Commission. To cope with the rise of China, the US and the EU established a Trade and Technology

Council (TTC) in 2021. The TTC's mandate is twofold: to (i) "coordinate approaches to key global technology, economic, and trade issues"; (ii) and to "deepen transatlantic trade and economic relations, basing policies on shared democratic values" (European Commission 2021).

Global Responses to Trump's Protectionist Trade Agenda

Lately, in response to former US President Trump's "America First" and his emphasis on "bilateral and reciprocal trade", the rest of the world led by the EU, Japan and China are standing up for open trade and rules-based economic freedom.

Shortly after Trump was sworn in as the 45th US president and promulgated a message in his inauguration address of making trade decisions solely to "to benefit American workers and American families", the European Parliament gave its consent to the Canada-EU Comprehensive Economic and Trade Agreement (CETA) in February 2017, allowing CETA to be implemented provisionally. Four months later, before the G20 summit in Hamburg, the EU announced the conclusion of the Japan-EU Economic Partnership Agreement (JEEPA) at the political level, sending a strong signal in support of economic cooperation and free trade (Jungbluth et al. 2017). JEEPA, which was fast tracked in the face of pressure from Trump protectionism, entered into force on 1 February 2019. It is estimated that the deal would increase the GDP of the EU and Japan by €11 billion and €9 billion per year, respectively (Felbermayr et al. 2017). Elsewhere in the Asia–Pacific, the EU approved the EU-Singapore trade pact in February 2019, signed the agreement with Vietnam in June 2019 and is negotiating with Indonesia, Australia and New Zealand. Negotiation with ASEAN on a region-to-region FTA was technically resumed. The EU reached a Comprehensive Agreement on Investment with China although the passage of the deal was derailed by political row. The EU is also making headway in Latin America. Most notably, an agreement was reached on an EU-MERCOSUR bloc-to-bloc FTA in June 2019.

Once described as an "unlikely pivotal state" in regionalism hampered by "dysfunctional trade politics" (Solís and Katada 2015), Japan is taking on the leadership mantle as US-led trade liberalisation is on the retreat. First, Japan moved ahead with an 11-country CPTPP as noted and is backing the membership bids of Thailand, Colombia and the United Kingdom in an attempt to spread the momentum of anti-protectionism.

Second, Japan has worked with China and ASEAN to conclude and ratify RCEP. Third, despite internal divisions like the most recent Japan-Korea trade row,[4] economic trilateralism is taking hold in Northeast Asia thanks to Tokyo's persistent push for the realisation of a China-Japan-Korea (CJK) trade pact. Last but not least, a Trade Agreement on Goods (TAG) is put into effect with the US. Collectively, the CPTPP, RCEP, CJK and TAG have placed Japan in the linchpin role of Asia–Pacific trade liberalisation efforts.

China has taken a complimentary approach to regionalism, by focusing on infrastructure development and physical connectivity (i.e. the "hardware" component of the international trade). In this regard, President Xi Jinping's signature scheme, the BRI, inaugurated in 2013, is the main game in town (Rimmer 2018; Rana and Ji 2020). China reportedly plans to invest between 1 to 8 trillion dollars (Hillman 2018) into BRI-related infrastructure projects to connect diverse parts across the Eurasian and African continents.

The developments discussed above have led to a multi-layered and decentralised international trade architecture as depicted in Fig. 7.3. The G20 Finance Ministers process was elevated to the G20 Summits and rose to prominence during the 2008 Global Financial Crisis (GFC) (Schmucker and Gnath 2011). It took the place of G7 as a macroprudential body overseeing global cooperation issues including international trade. The strength of the decentralising architecture is that it pulls together the oversight function of the G20, the technical capabilities and legitimacy of the WTO and the rule-making endeavour and agility of RTAs.

[4] In 2018, the South Korean Supreme Court issued a ruling asking Japanese companies to pay compensation to Koreans over forced wartime labour. The decision drew harsh condemnation from Japan which announced in early July 2019 that it would impose export restrictions of chemicals vital for South Korea's semiconductor industry. South Korea retaliated by fining several Japanese companies. Japan subsequently escalated trade sanctions by removing South Korea from the "white list" of trusted trading partners. In response, South Korea decided to not to renew the bilateral intelligence-sharing pact. The two countries have brought the case to the WTO. This acrimonious episode of trade disputes has deep historical roots and by itself does not signal that Japan is backpedalling on its presently pro-trade liberalisation trade policy to embrace protectionism.

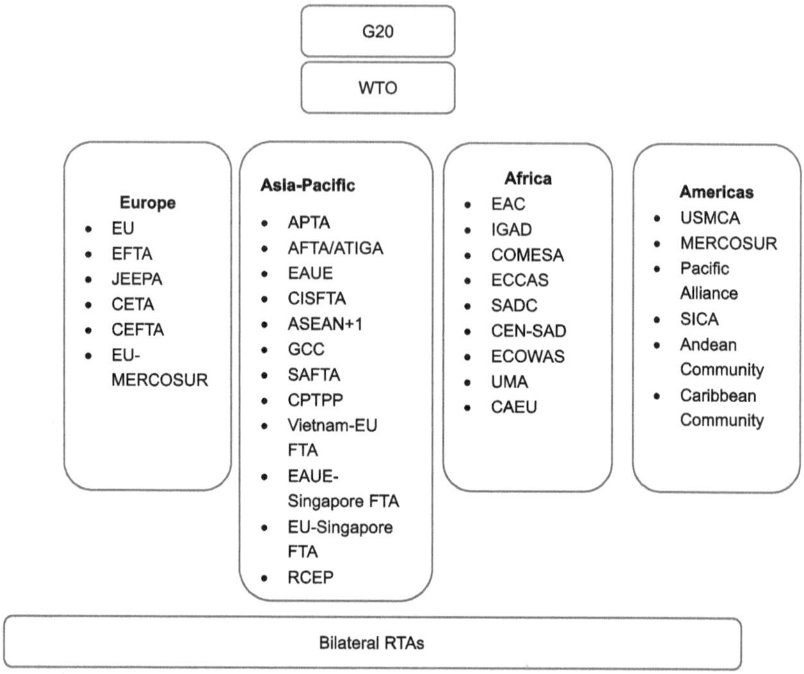

Fig. 7.3 The decentralising international trade architecture post-GFC (*Note*: APTA = Asia-Pacific Trade Agreement; AFTA = ASEAN Free Trade Area; ATIGA = ASEAN Trade in Goods Agreement; CAEU = Council of Arab Economic Unity; CEFTA = Central European Free Trade Agreement; CEN-SAD = Community of Sahel–Saharan States; CISFTA = Commonwealth of Independent States Free Trade Area; COMESA = Common Market for Eastern and Southern Africa; EAC = East African Community; EAEU = Eurasian Economic Union; ECCAS = Economic Community of Central African States; ECOWAS = Economic Community of West African States; GAFTA = Greater Arab Free Trade Area; GCC = Gulf Cooperation Council; IGAD = Intergovernmental Authority on Development; PACER-plus = Pacific Agreement on Closer Economic Relations Plus; SADC = Southern African Development Community; SAFTA = South Asian Free Trade Area; SICA = Central American Integration System; UMA = Arab Maghreb Union)

Benefits and Risks

The establishment of new regional institutions leading to the decentralising trade architecture has benefits ("healthy" competition and functional complementarity) as well as risks ("unhealthy" competition).

Benefits of Regionalism and Decentralisation

A number of benefits of RTAs can be highlighted. First, RTAs provide for an alternative approach to liberalising trade in addition to the WTO-centric multilateralism. In the event of stalling WTO negotiations, as is the case at the present, RTAs lock in existing commitments, permit the continuation of the trade liberalisation process and put pressure on the global process. As C. Fred Bergsten's famous "bicycle theory" goes, if you do not pedal forward, you slip backward (Bergsten 1996). And with fewer countries involved, finding a compromise is relatively more achievable in an RTA context; hence, it is easier to reach a reciprocal agreement to swap trade preferences and concessions. By contrast, the DDA launched in 2001 has been stuck for a long time and sharp North–South divisions over non-agricultural market access, trade in services, intellectual property rights and trade rules remain as key obstacles in the path towards the successful conclusion of the round. After the contentious December 2015 Nairobi WTO ministerial conference, the DDA had been proclaimed dead by analysts (Wilkinson et al. 2016). As such, WTO members have shifted trade negotiating emphasis towards mega-regionals and other RTAs. This trend broadly fits with what Desker (2004) has described as a move "from purity to pragmatism" against the background of multilateralism standstill.

There are tangible economic benefits for countries to do so. Petri and Plummer (2016) estimate that the TPP would promise substantial benefits for Japan, Malaysia and Vietnam; annual real income gains by 2030 would be $492 billion for the world as a whole. Building on their analysis, the World Bank (2016) simulations suggest that the TPP would raise member country GDP by an average of 1.1% and intra-TPP trade by as high as 11% by 2030, although benefits are likely be back-loaded. With the US withdrawal, the benefits of CPTPP are comparatively more modest. But it would still generate real GDP gains of about 0.075% or economic welfare benefits of about $13.5 billion by 2035 (Ciuriak et al. 2017).The projected gains from RCEP agreement are high, too. For instance, the latest estimate by Itakura (2019) using a dynamic computable general equilibrium model projects that the agreement's GDP impacts on ASEAN countries are in the range between 0.2% (for tariff liberalisation only) and 4.7% (reflecting additional services liberalisation and foreign direct investment enhancement effects) by 2035; the agreement could also raise global GDP in a range of 0.1%–0.3% over the long run.

Second, modern RTAs typically permit deeper integration as compared to the shallower integration of the WTO which mainly tackles "on-the-border" barriers. The five GATT rounds from the 1940s to the 1960s focused mainly on tariff reductions. Negotiations on reducing non-tariff measures (NTMs) were included in the agenda of Tokyo round (1973–1979) and Uruguay round (1986–1993), but the mandates of negotiation only covered a few issue areas largely of technical nature including customs valuation, import licensing, export restrictions, public procurement, technical barriers to trade, and antidumping and countervailing procedures, among others (Oxley 1994). In this regard, RTAs play an indispensable positive role in terms of broadening the scope of international trade negotiations via incorporating ground-breaking new disciplines that are known as WTO-plus or WTO-extra provisions. The former deepens commitments already undertaken multilaterally with enhanced import duties liberalisation as the best example. Countries agree to a certain maximum upper limit for most-favoured-nation (MFN) tariffs, but they extend further tariff cuts through regionalism to selected free trade partners. WTO-extra commitments, on the other hand, are RTA provisions for which there is no WTO counterpart. Examples include mega-RTA's rules on labour and environmental standards, transparency, competition, state owned enterprises, small and medium sized enterprises (SMEs) and regulatory coherence.

Third, the importance of WTO-extra and WTO-plus trade disciplines can be best understood with reference to what Baldwin (2014) calls the "differences between twentieth and twenty-first century trade". The twentieth-century trade is marked by cross-border flow of finished products (e.g. manufactures and farm produces). Therefore, the basic GATT rules focusing on removing border taxes and limited instances of NTMs liberalisation were enough to promote international trade. In the twenty-first century, however, in part due to advances in information and communications technologies, intermediate and supply-chain trade, services trade, international movement of labour and capital flows come to define interlocking international trade relations and policy agenda (Baldwin 2014; WEF 2016). As such, there have been calls for deeper economic integration rules that would reflect the growing complexity of international trade patterns. However, GATT/WTO has been proven slow in responding to such demand (Lester et al. 2008) and the three mega-RTAs and other deep RTAs are filling the gap to craft and experiment with new rules governing many "behind-the-border" issues.

Risks of Regionalism and Decentralisation

Regionalism and the decentralising trade governance structure also pose a number of risks. The first is that regionalism is seen as "discriminatory" in nature. Granting preferences to some countries effectively discriminates against trade with others which could be more efficient trading partners, resulting in potentially costly trade diversion. That said, problems with trade diversion are more serious at the theoretical level than in practice. Often the growth impetus from RTAs yields trade creation, positive externality and reversal of trade diversion over time. In comprehensive surveys of the theoretical and empirical regionalism literature, Schott (2008) and Freund and Ornelas (2010) find strong evidence of the primacy of trade creation over trade diversion. Specifically, Freund (2010) investigates the third-country economic impacts of NAFTA, MERCOSUR, Andean Community and three waves of EU accession, concluding that "there is no evidence of trade diversion" in any of the six cases. In fact, she goes on to argue that the perceived risk of trade diversion represents a strong incentive for "for external trade liberalization [by excluded parties] to prevent trade diversion". With particular reference to Asian regionalism, Lee and Shin (2006) find that East Asian RTAs, both "in effect" and proposed, "create more trade among members without diverting trade from non-members".

The second category of risks conventionally associated with RTAs is the so-called spaghetti bowl phenomenon (Bhagwati 1995). It arises when overlapping RTAs create a web of trade agreements with different documentation rules, inspection procedures, rules of origin (Cadot and Ing 2019), tariff schedules and institutional arrangements, in effect raising the transaction and compliance costs for the business community in their day-to-day trading activities. Less-than-full utilisation of preferential tariff margins is often the symptom of the problem (Gretton 2017). While there is some element of truth to this argument, this risk also seems to be overstated. First, an ADB Asia-wide, firm-level survey finds that "the view that the Asian noodle bowl has severely harmed the region's business activity over the last eight years [2001–2008] receives little support from the firm surveys" (Kawai and Wignaraja 2011). A similar survey conducted in Latin American countries by Estevadeordal et al. (2009) finds similar results, dismissing the "spaghetti bowl" argument. Second, RTAs are becoming increasingly alike in terms of substance. This is because the process of negotiating an RTA is exceedingly complex and there are obvious benefits of recycling the text from one model agreement to another (Ilott et al. 2017). Over time, the substantive variations across RTAs actually decrease, thereby reducing the trade dampening effect of the "spaghetti bowl". Third, the negative aspects of overlapping RTAs can be mitigated if appropriate public advice and well-designed capacity-building programmes are offered to targeted business communities. The Asia–Pacific Economic Cooperation (APEC), for instance, regularly organises capacity-building workshops on RTA utilisation.

A third and potentially much more critical risk of regionalism is that it could undercut the WTO (Bhagwati 2008). But the possibility of such risk is not high as regionalism has actually cemented the centrality of the WTO's adjudicational arm. It was feared by the advocates of multilateralism that RTAs would predispose participating countries to litigating trade disputes in venues different to the WTO. This is not happening in actuality. For one, the dispute settlement procedures contained in RTAs have not introduced direct competition with the WTO. The CPTPP, for instance, concedes most traditional, market-access-related issues to the WTO process while focusing on those historically not taken up by the WTO. For another, the WTO has institutional comparative advantage in resolving state-on-state commercial disputes. Bown (2016) notes that "[d]espite many RTAs having their own dispute settlement mechanism provisions, most formal disputes arising since 1995 between RTA partners have been adjudicated at the WTO. Canada, Mexico, and the US, for example, routinely file disputes against one another in Geneva, even though in-house NAFTA provisions exist to adjudicate their potential grievances. They are not alone: roughly 15% of all WTO disputes have involved members of an existing RTA using WTO to resolve their bilateral disagreements". The reason is that, unlike the WTO, there is no possibility of appeal for any dispute rulings made under RTAs, and there is no RTA secretariat that would provide the same sort of support that are of service to WTO jurists and arbitrators (Bown 2016). In the

WTO, appeals and secretariat staff help contribute to the stability of the system by ensuring that consistent legal decisions are made over time. Dispute settlement mechanisms in RTAs, by contrast, are less transparent, less legitimate, more costly and largely untested.[5]As a result, it remains unclear whether members will adhere to their rulings.

Managing Trade Decentralisation

The full consequences of trade decentralisation remain largely unknown. Yet, from the discussions above, on the whole, it can be argued that the benefits of new regional institutions and the decentralising trade architecture are likely to outweigh the risks mainly because the risks are overstated. In other words, RTAs could be "stepping stones" rather than "stumbling blocks" to multilateralism. This point is also supported by an opinion survey of Asian policymakers and experts conducted by the authors with regards to the relationship between mega-RTAs and multilateralism (Ji et al. 2016). The survey found that 62% of the respondents felt that mega-RTAs contributed to global trade liberalisation in the long term. Nevertheless, what more should be done to maximise the benefits while minimising the risks of the decentralising architecture or, to use the term promoted by Baldwin and Low (2009), "multilateralise regionalism"? The following policy actions could be considered by the WTO. Where possible we justify the rationale for these recommendations with reference efforts by other Bretton Woods institution to strengthen engagement with their regional counterparts.

1. WTO should further enhance its collaboration with RTA member countries by creating a principled multilateralism-regionalism interface. Of particular importance to the functionality of such interaction is transparency. In 2006, the WTO General Council adopted an enhanced transparency mechanism for RTAs (Crawford 2007). The mechanism requires WTO members to inform the WTO secretariat about the initiation, conclusion, substance and implementation of RTAs on a timely basis so that the WTO's Committee on Regional

[5] Discussion with Pasha Hsieh at the Singapore Trade Policy Forum on 24–25 October 2018.

Trade Agreements (CRTA) can verify the compliance of the notified RTAs with WTO regulations and circulate relevant information to other WTO members. This was a good first step because it signalled the WTO's intention to monitor regional processes from a position of authority. A robust transparency mechanism would also better protect WTO members by allowing them to keep an eye on RTAs from which they are excluded. Developing countries could hone their trade negotiation skills by tapping into the rich technical resources that would be generated by the transparency mechanism (Panezi 2016). But for it not to be merely symbolic "due diligence", the transparency mechanism needs to be strengthened. The WTO should put in place a right mix of incentives and disincentives to ensure that, as former European Commissioner for Trade Cecilia Malmström (2018) has put it, "there should be rewards for following the rules and there should be penalties for breaking them". Making access to a variety of WTO-specific services, WTO-administered global trade infrastructure and confidential institutional memory of GATT/WTO conditional on RTA members' conformity to the regulations put forth by the WTO is one possibility. Such idea is not wholly unprecedented as a similar arrangement can be found in the decentralising financial architecture. For instance, for Asian countries to apply for short-term liquidity support that goes over 40% of their total allotment under the CMIM, an agreement with the IMF is necessary. This link between IMF consent and CMIM disbursement serves as an effective multilateralism-regionalism interface. Additionally, MOUs between the WTO and RTA members and/or secretariats[6] could also be considered. In the field of development assistance, the World

[6] We acknowledge that creating a centralised administrative body to support the implementation of an FTA is not a common practice at the moment, as borne out by the failed attempt to establish a North American Trade Secretariat with permanent location and staff under the NAFTA agreement (Bélanger 2007). But since new RTAs like the CPTPP and RCEP are typically structured to cover deep integration and highly complex to implement, there is a need for a stronger institutional foundation to strengthen internal management (with respect to periodic amendment, ROOs and dispute settlement mechanism etc.) and coordinate external relations for example with the WTO and other trading blocs. Establishing secretariats for mega-FTAs in the making should be on the table. For the CPTPP, the potential secretariat could be located in New Zealand, the Depositary of the agreement. As for RCEP, the ASEAN Secretariat could perhaps be in a position to function as an RCEP secretariat.

Bank, ADB, AIIB, and NDB have also signed formal MOUs with each other (Ji 2017; Rana and Pacheco Pardo 2015).

2. It is essential for the WTO to have meaningful oversight over the substances of the RTAs being negotiated. This entails the WTO to prepare a high quality "model RTA" for prospective RTA members to work on as their common negotiation baseline. The availability of such a template with WTO-sanctioned provisions has enormous benefits. It allows the WTO to maintain its relevance as the traditional "rule-writer" while creating approvable legal precedents around which potential multilateral disciplines could emerge. The "spaghetti bowl" problem could also be eased as a result. The CPTPP is one such potential template for future RTA to emulate. Alternatively, the WTO may opt to develop one of its own from scratch. The economic research staff from the CRTA and other divisions have undertaken rigorous analytical work to characterise and categorise different kinds of provisions arising from notified RTAs (Bown 2016) and they should be tasked to come up with an RTA template on the basis of their research.

   To maximise the benefits of the WTO as a knowledge centre, there is also a case for the WTO to establish regional advisory centres to help countries to design and implement "multilateralisable" and WTO-consistent RTAs. This is a common practice for other Bretton Woods institutions like the IMF which has dedicated Regional Advisory Groups for Asia and Pacific, Caucasus and Central Asia, Europe, Sub-Saharan Africa and Western Hemisphere.

3. The WTO should also encourage RTA members to make their RTAs as open as possible. Ji et al. (2018) empirically find that a hypothetical transition from RCEP to an expanded Free Trade Area of the Asia–Pacific (FTAAP +), one including mega-RTA countries which are currently not party to Asia–Pacific Economic Cooperation (APEC) forum such as India, would significantly increase gains from trade. Real GDP gains would be even higher should regional countries implement mega-RTAs and FTAAP + on an "open regionalism" basis. The notion of open regionalism championed by APEC refers to a practice of RTA signatories voluntarily extending negotiated concessions and market opening to non-members. Since the approach is more acceptable politically than unilateral trade liberalisation and more rewarding economically than the traditionally "closed" and selective trade deals, the WTO should

actively promote this liberalisation modality alongside with APEC. Unfortunately, the emphasis of Trump administration on "fair and reciprocal" trade (Gibbon and Vestergaard 2017) may run counter to the WTO's and regional countries' potential efforts to anchor inter-state trading relationship in an open regional trading system.

4. In terms of the configuration of RTAs, the WTO should encourage countries to pursue "regional" agreements with as broad country participation as possible instead of signing scattered "bilateral" treaties. As Schott (2017) succinctly argues, when it comes to regional trade arrangements, "bigger is better". For instance, the economic benefits increased as the EU enlarged and the gains from trade reduced as the US withdrew from the TPP. In areas beyond trade such as financial regionalism, the benefits of consolidating smaller arrangements into bigger regional ones are recognised. The evolution of the CMIM illustrates this point particularly well. The CMIM initially emerged as a loose network of bilateral currency swaps and repurchase agreement facilities among members. It was subsequently consolidated into a regional facility in 2010 in the aftermath of the global financial crisis for wider benefits.
5. Many large developing countries including China, India and South Africa are not willing to abandon the DDA as yet because issues like agriculture trade is still important to them. Hence, it would be difficult to walk away from the Doha agenda and focus on the so-called WTO 2.0 as proposed by Baldwin (2012). One way out of the impasse is for the WTO to plurilateralise RTAs. Annex 4 of the Agreement Establishing the WTO allows four sectoral "Plurilateral Trade Agreements" (PAs): the Agreement on Government Procurement and the Agreement on Trade in Civil Aircraft and two others that were terminated in 1997 (the International Dairy Agreement and the International Bovine Meat Agreement). These PAs are closed agreements in terms of accruing benefits and obligations only for contracting parties. The WTO also recognises a set of open PAs, also known as "critical mass" agreements, including Information Technology Agreement (1996) and Trade Facilitation Agreement (2017) that are implemented on an MFN basis. The Trade in Services Agreement is under negotiation. A wider application of such sectoral and plurilateral approaches to trade and services liberalisation, once criticised for undermining multilateralism (Oyane 2001), could open up an escape route for the WTO in the era of

(mega)regionalism. As noted, both CPTPP and RCEP strive to write new trade rules on a host of WTO-extra policy areas. If and when the two mega-RTAs' provisions on a certain issue (e.g. SME) the skeleton of a PA (on SME) involving all CPTPP and RCEP countries could emerge. This mega-regionalism-to-plurilateralism (M2P) process may not happen on its own particularly given the difficulties plaguing the negotiations for RCEP and TTIP. The WTO can therefore play an active role to facilitate the process of M2P. Of particular importance for the WTO is to quickly determine which WTO-plus commitments arising from mega-RTAs and other innovative RTAs can be used to update existing PAs and which WTO-extra regional disciplines have the potential to be plurilateralised under the WTO (Bown 2016).

Role of Asia

Since it is the global leader of regionalism and concurrently a fast-growing constituency in the WTO with growing trade shares, Asia should exercise front-line leadership in reforming the WTO. However, it is doubtful whether Asia could act on the proposals sketched out in the preceding section under the present WTO governance system. To understand the root cause of the WTO stasis and map possible routes for reform, it is useful to bring in the "governance trilemma" conceptualised among others by Kawai et al. (2010) and Baldwin (2018). The theory posits that the requirements for international economic institutions to be "democratic" in terms of institutional governance, "universal" in terms of member coverage and policy ownership, and "effective" in timely delivering on the public goods sought after by its member governments, add up to a trilemma (or an "impossible trinity"): achieving any two makes the attainment of the third objective difficult. The WTO as it stands is democratic (consensus-based) and (nearly) universal (in terms of membership), but falling short on the score of effectiveness. Any in-depth analysis of the WTO's governance reform[7] is beyond the scope of this chapter, and we concede that there are no easy and quick solutions to the WTO's woes, but the trilemma in Fig. 7.4 points to two basic yet meaningful ways to

[7] Interested readers can find useful materials in Jones (2015, 2010).

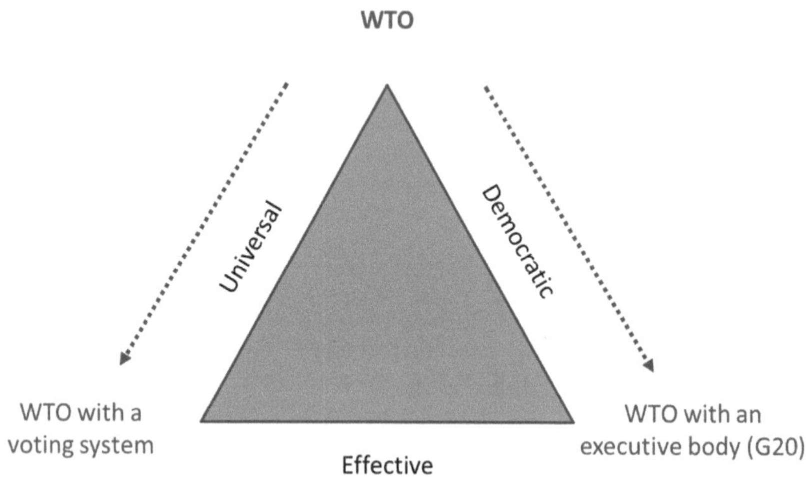

Fig. 7.4 The governance trilemma and two plausible ways to reform the WTO

make the WTO more effective, malleable and adaptable to the rapidly changing global economy.

One possible strategy is to move the WTO to the left-hand side triangle corner to become an institution that is effective and universal but comparatively less democratic. This entails fundamental reforms to the WTO's prevailing consensus-driven legislative tradition for decision-making by instituting some majority voting procedures. An useful and balanced proposal of institutionalising a voting system in the WTO comes from Narlikar (2011) who advocates a two-threshold voting system akin to the EU's "qualified majority" rule.[8] Under such a system, for a WTO-wide decision to go through, a double-majority in an un-weighted vote (i.e. one country, one vote) and a weighted vote must both be reached. The advantage is that a majority in the former honours sovereign equality to protect smaller economies from disenfranchisement, and a majority in the latter secures the buy-in of major stakeholders in the multilateral trading system (who are investing in mega-regional alternatives to the WTO). While the exact threshold for a weighted vote would (and should) be

[8] At the EU, a decision is normally adopted if 55% of the EU members, representing at least 65% of the population of the EU, vote in favour.

debated and even a blocking minority could be explicitly allowed in exceptional circumstances, the formulae proposed by Cottier and Takenoshita (2003) allocating voting rights based on considerations of trade share, economic size, market openness and population seems acceptable to many in principle. The Warwick Commission (2007) used to argue against voting for an important reason that the practice violates the institution's consensus principle and egalitarian culture. Yet, voting is a legitimate fall-back option for arriving at decisions under GATT/WTO (Hoekman and Kostecki 2001). And it should be recalled that voting was a regular legal instrument for decision-making in the early days of GATT (before being phased out in the 1950s) and was resorted to in the case of Ecuador's accession to the WTO. Perhaps it is time for voting to come back in vogue as the beleaguered WTO fights for self-perseveration.

A second plausible strategy of addressing the WTO's effectiveness deficit is to push the organisation to the right-hand side corner. Retaining its essential democratic characteristics, the WTO could increase flexibility in decision-making by compromising on the principle of universality. Delegating some powers to an executive board where unanimity is the norm could be a viable proposition in this genre of solutions. Proposals centred on forming a "WTO executive committee" are in fact one of the most commonly discussed reform options and have found favour among some members like the EU (Dube 2012). The precedent for this can be found in the informal "Green Room" format of decision-making in GATT/WTO. A typical Green Room process begins by a small group of self-selected developed countries in consultation with a set of invited developing countries broking breakthroughs before presenting their decisions to the GATT/WTO membership for formal, multilateral adoption. Historically, this inner circle of decision-makers and agenda-setters in the WTO had, depending on the issue at hand and the number of countries involved, taken many forms, such as the "Consultative Group of Eighteen" in the Tokyo Round, the Quad in the Uruguay Round and the Group of 4, Five Interested Parties, Group of 6 and Group of 7 in the Doha Round (Vickers 2012; Dube 2012). These various "G" groups customarily faced considerable apathy, if not resentment, in the WTO due to their self-serving nature, legitimacy deficit, and the bullying tactics of imposing decisions on the rest of the WTO members on a take-it-or-leave-it basis (VanGrasstek 2013). Therefore, the WTO is left in a situation where decision-making is proceeding at glacial speed without an executive body, but existing and historical intra-GATT/WTO coalitions are not up to the task of facilitating decision-making and building preliminary consensus on global trade matters.

Against this background, the G20, the so-called premier forum for international economic cooperation and the de facto global steering committee for macroeconomic coordination, could provide part of the answer. G20 also consists of countries and "guests" invited without transparent and well-established membership rules (Slaughter 2013), but the grouping's economic size, demographic weight,[9] geographical representativeness and institutional status bestow upon on it a significantly higher degree of legitimacy and influence in comparison with the past and existing country constellations in the GATT/WTO. The G20's greater and more direct participation in the global trade decision-making process should be welcomed by G20 members and cautiously tolerated by countries external to it if the mini-ministerial level forum proves able to get the WTO out of the current deadlock.

The Buenos Aires G20 Summit in 2019 elevated the subject of WTO reforms as an agenda item for the G20 for the first time. With Asia's strong presence in G20 in mind, it would be best if the "Asia 5 + 1" (already defined above) despite their varied positions on specific issues, could follow up by fleshing out concrete Asian ideas and perspectives about the future of multilateralism at relevant G20 meetings such as the G20 Trade and Investment Ministers meetings and the G20 summits.[10] In the area of finance, the G20 had come up with six broad principles for cooperation between the IMF and RFSNs; further to this, the Fund proposed specifically 7 lessons and 4 modalities to operationalise IMF-RFSN cooperation. Based on these activities, encouraging progress is being made in the cooperation between the IMF and CMIM (Rana 2019).The G20 should also develop similar principles for WTO-RTA cooperation which the WTO could implement.

[9] Countries participating in 2018 G20 Summit made up 85% of global economic output, 66% of global population, 75% of international trade and 80% of global investment.

[10] For an account of the relationship between the WTO and G20, see Hoekman (2016). Additionally, it should be recalled that the establishment of the global financial safety net and promoting complementarity between the IMF and RFSNs was an agenda item of the Seoul G20 Summit of 2010. This action has resulted in encouraging progress in promoting collaboration between the IMF and RFSNs (Rana and Pardo 2018).

Apart from seeking to engineer adaptive governance reforms in the WTO, Asia can take actions to improve the decentralising trading architecture in three other ways. First, with the US abdicating its long-standing leadership role in the liberal, rules-based trade order and Europe being consumed by domestic policy objectives, the leadership task falls to Asia. And, it is incumbent upon Asian policymakers to seize the historic opportunity to play a much bigger role in shaping the evolution of global trade system in an era of great policy uncertainty. Implementing the RCEP agreement will be a natural litmus test of the potential, seriousness and credibility of Asia's global trade leadership role. After all, how can Asia play a constructive leading role on trade governance if it cannot enact its own flagship trade initiative?

Second, Asian countries should eventually promote the convergence of RCEP and CPTPP (Ji and Rana 2018). The convergence between the two mega-regional trade undertaking can be realised through a dual-track approach (Ji et al. 2018) or a multi-tier approach (Petri and Abdul-Raheem 2014; Scollay 2016). Under the former option, the process starts by Asian countries securing dual membership. CPTPP-only countries should sign up to RCEP when possible (for greater export opportunities for companies to China and India), and RCEP track-only signatories should reciprocate the move by seeking accession into the CPTPP (not least to gain valuable exposure to CPTPP rules). Then, there would be impetus to rationalise redundancy arising from the co-existence of the CPTPP and RCEP by merging the two into one agreement. The multi-tier option, for its part, envisages the installation of an "umbrella agreement" from day one. Within this overarching agreement, the CPTPP and RCEP members each adhere to their own rules, and the two groups of countries are glued together by a common set of intermediate obligations achievable in the short term. The expectation is that RCEP countries would voluntarily ratchet up their commitments towards CPTPP standards in the end. A streamlined agreement integrating the RCEP and CPTPP would provide sizable economic gains and a better and more inclusive institutional base for Asian economic integration, fortifying the region's leading position in the global trade landscape.

Third, Asia should promote cooperation between RCEP and China's BRI, considering that the potential for complementarity and functional cooperation between the tariff-cutting RCEP and the infrastructure-enhancing BRI is striking (Intal 2018). But unlike with the proposed membership convergence between the CPTPP and RCEP, there will not be greater membership overlap between the BRI and RCEP in the medium term. Three key RCEP negotiating parties (Japan, India and Australia) are unlikely to join the BRI in the foreseeable future for geopolitical reasons, and non-RCEP BRI countries like Pakistan and Mongolia cannot accede to RCEP due to the absence of a separate trade deal with ASEAN. To realise complementarity between the BRI and RCEP, what needs to be done first is to sign a BRI-RCEP MOU to lay the foundation of formal cooperation between the two initiatives. With the MOU, BRI countries currently not participating in RCEP could be allowed to benefit from the trade and investment agenda of the planned RCEP (Vines 2018) and accorded priority status when RCEP is ready for expansion. On the other hand, the MOU could provide the extra incentive for Japan, India and Australia to take part in the BRI to provide cheques and balances from within it given their shared concerns about an unconstrained China allegedly wielding "debt-trap diplomacy" to gain geopolitical advantages.

Conclusion

This chapter has traced the evolution of the international trade architecture from a centralised to a decentralised one because of the establishment of new regional institutions. We argue that the drivers of this phenomenon include the rising popularity of "new regionalism" in the aftermath of Cold War, the negotiations for mega-RTAs in the post-GFC period, the protectionist trade policies of the Trump administration in recent years, and disappointments with the progress of WTO negotiations. The establishment of new regional institutions that have led to decentralisation have a number of benefits such as "healthy" competition and functional cooperation between the WTO and RTAs. At the same time, it also has the risks such as "unhealthy" competition. We argue that the benefits appear to have outweighed the costs and that the global governance of trade has probably improved. Looking ahead, a number of policy actions have to be taken to manage the trade decentralisation process or "multilateralise regionalism" and to improve the governance of the WTO. Asian countries, especially the "Asia 5 + 1" countries, whose footprints in the global economic and political system are increasing have an important role to play in this regard.

References

Abbott, Kenneth W., Jessica F. Green, and Robert O. Keohane. 2016. Organizational Ecology and Institutional Change in Global Governance. *International Organization* 70 (2): 247–277.

ADB. 2008. "Asian Regionalism: Context and Scope." In *Emerging Asian Regionalism: A Partnership for Shared Prosperity*. Mandaluyong: Asian Development Bank.

Baldwin, Richard. 2012. WTO 2.0: Global Governance of Supply-Chain Trade. In *CEPR Policy Insight*. London: Centre for Economic Policy Research.

Baldwin, Richard. 2014. "Multilateralising 21st Centry Regionalism." *Global Forum on Trade: Reconciling Regionalism and Multilateralism in a Post-Bali World*. Paris.

Baldwin, Richard. 2018. *Sources of the WTO's Woes: Decision-Making's Impossible Trinity*. VoxEU.

Baldwin, Richard, and Patrick Low. 2009. *Multilateralizing Regionalism: Challenges for the Global Trading System*. Cambridge: Cambridge University Press.

Bélanger, Louis. 2007. "Diverging Preferences: The Impact of NAFTA on the Member States' Trade Policies." In *Regionalism and the State: NAFTA and Foreign Policy Convergence*, edited by Gordon Mace. Hampshire: Ashgate.

Bergsten, C. Fred. 1996. Globalizing Free Trade. *Foreign Affairs* 75 (3): 105–120.

Bhagwati, Jagdish. 1995. "US Trade Policy: The Infatuation with FT As." In *The Dangerous Obsession with Free Trade Areas*, edited by Claude Barfield. Washington, DC: American Enterprise Institute.

Bhagwati, Jagdish. 2008. *Termites in the Trading System: How Preferential Agreements Undermine Free Trade*. New York: Oxford University Press.

Bown, Chad P. 2016. "Mega-Regional Trade Agreements and the Future of the WTO." In *Global Order and the New Regionalism*. New York: Council on Foreign Relations.

Bronz, George. 1956. An International Trade Organization: The Second Attempt. *Harvard Law Review* 69 (3): 440–482.

Cadot, Olivier, and Lili Yan Ing. 2019. "How restrictive are ASEANs Rules of Origin?" In *East Asian Integration: Goods, Services and Investment*, edited by Lili Yan Ing, Martin Richardson and Shujiro Urata. Abingdon and New York: Routledge.

Chia, Siow Yue. 2010. Regional Trade Policy Cooperation and Architecture in East Asia. In *ADBI Working Paper*. Tokyo: Asian Development Bank Institute.

Ciuriak, Dan, Jingliang Xiao, and Ali Dadkhah. 2017. Quantifying the Comprehensive and Progressive Agreement for Trans-Pacific Partnership. *East Asian Economic Review* 21 (4): 343–384.

Cottier, Thomas, and Satoko Takenoshita. 2003. The Balance of Power in WTO Decision-Making: Towards Weighted Voting in Legislative Response. *Aussenwirtschaft* 58 (2): 169–214.

Crawford, Jo-Ann. 2007. A New Transparency Mechanism for Regional Trade Agreements. *Singapore Year Book of International Law* 11: 133–140.

de Melo, Jaime, and Arvind Panagariya, eds. 1993. *New Dimensions in Regional Integration*. London: Centre for Economic Policy Research.

Dent, Christopher M. 2016. *East Asian Regionalism*, 2nd ed. Abingdon and New York: Routledge.

Desker, Barry. 2004. In Defence of FTAs: From Purity to Pragmatism in East Asia. *Pacific Review* 17 (1): 3–26.

Dube, Memory. 2012. The Way Forward for the WTO: Reforming the Decision-Making Process. In *Economic Diplomacy Programme Occasional Paper*. Johannesburg: South African Institute of International Affairs.

Estevadeordal, Antoni, Jeremy Harris, and Kati Suominen. 2009. Multilateralising Preferential Rules of Origin around the World. In *IDB Working Paper*. Washington, DC: Inter-American Development Bank.

Ethier, Wilfred J. 1998. The New Regionalism. *The Economic Journal* 108 (3): 1149–1161.

European Commission. 2021. "EU-US Trade and Technology Council Inaugural Joint Statement." Accessed 1 December 2021. https://ec.europa.eu/commission/presscorner/detail/en/STATEMENT_21_4951.

Felbermayr, Gabriel, Fukunari Kimura, Toshihiro Okubo, Marina Steininger, and Erdal Yalcin. 2017. On the Economics of an EU-Japan Free Trade Agreement In *GED Study*. Gütersloh: Bertelsmann Stiftung.

Fiorentino, Roberto V., Luis Verdeja, and Christelle Toqueboeuf. 2007. The Changing Landscape of Regional Trade Agreements: 2006 Update. In *WTO Discussion Paper*. Geneva: World Trade Organization.

Freund, Caroline. 2010. Third-Country Effects of Regional Trade Agreements. *World Economy* 33 (11): 1589–1605.

Freund, Caroline, Tyler Moran, and Sarah Oliver. 2016. "Tariff Liberalization." In *Trans-Pacific Partnership: An Assessment*, edited by Cathleen Cimino-Isaacs and Jeffrey J. Schott. Washington, DC: Peterson Institute for International Economics.

Freund, Caroline, and Emanuel Ornelas. 2010. Regional Trade Agreements. *Annual Review of Economics* 2: 139–167.

Gibbon, Peter, and Jakob Vestergaard. 2017. *US Trade Policy Under Trump: Assessing the Unilateralist Turn*. Copenhagen: Danish Institute for International Studies.

Gretton, Paul. 2017. Bilateral and Regional Trade Agreements: Detangling the Noodle/Spaghetti Bowl. In *EABER Working Paper 130*. Canberra: East Asian Bureau of Economic Research.

Hillman, Jonathan E. 2018. How Big Is China's Belt and Road? In *CSIS Commentary*. Washington, DC: Center for Strategic and International Studies.

Hoekman, Bernard. 2016. Revitalizing the Global Trading System: What Could the G20 Do? *China & World Economy* 24 (4): 34–54.

Hoekman, Bernard, and Michel Kostecki. 2001. *The Political Economy of the World Trading System: The WTO and Beyond*. Oxford: Oxford University Press.

Ilott, Oliver, Ines Stelk, and Jill Rutter. 2017. *Taking Back Control of Trade Policy*. London: Institute for Government.

Intal, Ponciano S. 2018. "East Asia's Transformation and Regional Architecture." In *Asian Economic Integration in an Era of Global Uncertainty*, edited by Shiro Armstrong and Tom Westland. Canberra: ANU Press.

Itakura, Ken. 2019. "Economic Effects of East Asian Integration on Southeast Asia." In *East Asian Integration: Goods, Services and Investment*, edited by Lili Yan Ing, Martin Richardson and Shujiro Urata. Abingdon and New York: Routledge.

Ji, Xianbai. 2017. Promoting Regional Development Bank Complementarity: Challenges to Asia and Lessons from Europe. *Asia Europe Journal* 15 (3): 261–281.

Ji, Xianbai. 2021. *Mega-Regionalism and Great Power Geo-economic Competition*. London & New York: Routledge.

Ji, Xianbai, and Pradumna B. Rana. 2018. "The United States and the Rise, Fall and Future Prospects of the (Comprehensive and Progressive Agreement for) Trans-Pacific Partnership." 12th Berlin Conference on Asian Security, Berlin.

Ji, Xianbai, and Pradumna B. 2019. ""A Deal that Does Not Die: The United States and the Rise, Fall and Future of the (CP)TPP." *Pacific Focus* 34 (2): 230–255.

Ji, Xianbai, Pradumna B. Rana, Wai-Mun Chia, and Changtai Li. 2016. Economic and Strategic Dimensions of Mega-FTAs: A Perception Survey of Asian Opinion Leaders. In *RSIS Working Paper*. Singapore: S. Rajaratnam School of International Studies.

Ji, Xianbai, Pradumna B. Rana, Chia Wai-Mun, and Changtai Li. 2018. "Post-TPP Trade Policy Options for ASEAN and its Dialogue Partners: "Preference Ordering" Using CGE Analysis." *East Asian Economic Review* 22 (2): 177–215.

Jones, Kent. 2010. *The Doha Blues: Institutional Crisis and Reform in the WTO*. New York. Oxford University Press.

Jones, Kent. 2015. *Reconstructing the World Trade Organization for the 21st Century: An Institutional Approach*. New York: Oxford University Press.

Jungbluth, Cora, Gabriel Felbermayr, Fukunari Kimura, Toshihiro Okubo, Marina Steininger, and Erdal Yalcin. 2017. "EU-Japan: Free Trade Agreement a Sign of Commitment to Economic Cooperation." In *Future Social Market Economy Policy Brief*. Gütersloh: Bertelsmann Stiftung.

Kahler, Miles, C. Randall Henning, Chad P. Bown, Hongying Wang, Erik Voeten, and Paul D. Williams. 2016. "Global Order and the New Regionalism."" In *Discussion Paper Series on Global and Regional Governance*. New York: Council on Foreign Relations.

Kawai, Masahiro, Peter A. Petri, and Elif Sisli Ciamarra. 2010. "Asia in global economic governance: a case for decentralized institutions." In *Asian Regionalism in the World Economy: Engine for Dynamism and Stability*, edited by Masahiro Kawai, Jong-Wha Lee, Peter A. Petri and Giovanni Capanelli. Cheltenham: Edward Elgar.

Kawai, Masahiro, and Ganeshan Wignaraja, eds. 2011. *Asia's Free Trade Agreements: How Is Business Responding?* Cheltenham and Northampton: Edward Elgar.

Langhammer, R. J., and U. Hiemenz. 1990. *Regional Integration Among Developing Countries: Opportunities, Obstacles and Options*. Tübingen: JCB Mohr.

Lee, Jong-Wha, and Kwanho Shin. 2006. "Does Regionalism Lead to More Global Trade Integration in East Asia?" *The North American Journal of Economics and Finance* 17 (3): 283–301.

Lester, Simon, Bryan Mercurio, and Arwel Davies, eds. 2008. *World Trade Law: Text, Materials and Commentary*. Oxford, UK: Hart Publishing.

Madhur, Srinivasa. 2012. "Asia's Role in Twenty-First-Century Global Economic Governance."" *Internationl Affairs* 88 (4): 817–833.

Malmström, Cecilia. 2018. EU–U.S. *Trade and the Future of the WTO: A Conversation with Commissioner Malmström*. Edited by Rod Hunter. Washington, DC: The German Marshall Fund of the United States.

Meléndez-Ortiz, Ricardo. 2014. "Mega-regionals: What Is Going on?" In *Mega-regional Trade Agreements: Game-Changers or Costly Distractions for the World Trading System?*, edited by Global Agenda Council on Trade & Foreign Direct Investment. Geneva: World Economic Forum.

Morse, Julia C., and Robert O. Keohane. 2014. Contested Multilateralism. *The Review of International Organizations* 9 (4): 385–412.

Narlikar, Amrita. 2011. "Adapting to new power balances: institutional reform in the WTO." In *Governing the World Trade Organization: Past, Present and Beyond Doha*, edited by Thomas Cottier and Manfred Elsig. Cambridge: Cambridge University Press.

Oxley, Alan. 1994. "The Achievements of the GATT Uruguay Round." *Agenda: A Journal of Policy Analysis and Reform* 1 (1): 45–53.

Oyane, Satoshi. 2001. ""Plurilateralism" of the United States and its APEC Policies." In *IDE APEC Study Center Working Paper*. Chiba: Institute of Developing Economies.

Panezi, Maria. 2016. "The WTO and the Spaghetti Bowl of Free Trade Agreements." In *Policy Brief No.87*. Waterloo: Centre for International Governance Innovation.

Pardo, Ramon Pacheco, and Pradumna B. Rana. 2015. ""Complementarity between Regional and Global Financial Governance Institutions: The Case of ASEAN+3 and Global Financial Safety Net." *Global Governance* 21 (3): 413–433.

Pardo, Ramon Pacheco, and Pradumna B. Rana. 2018. "Cooperation not Threat: The New Multilateral Development Banks and Old." *Global Asia* 13 (1): 72–77.

Petri, Peter A., and Ali Abdul-Raheem. 2014. "Can RCEP and the TPP be Pathways to FTAAP?" In *State of the Region*. Singapore: Pacific Economic Cooperation Council.

Petri, Peter A., and Michael G. Plummer. 2016. "*The Economic Effects of the Trans-Pacific Partnership: New Estimates*."" In PIIE Working Paper. Washington, DC: Peterson Institute for International Economics.

Rana, Pradumna B. 2014. "From a Centralized to a Decentralized Global Economic Architecture: An Overview." In *New Global Economic Architecture: The Asian Perspective*, edited by Masahiro Kawai, Peter J. Morgan and Pradumna B. Rana. Cheltenham & Northampton: Edward Elgar.

Rana, Pradumna B. 2019. "The ASEAN+3 Regional Financial Safety Net 20 Years On." In *Financial Cooperation in East Asia*, edited by Tomoo Kikuchi and Masaya Sakuragawa. Singapore: S. Rajaratnam School of International Studies.

Rana, Pradumna B., and Xianbai Ji. 2020. *China's Belt and Road Initiative: Impacts on Asia and Policy Agenda*. Singapore: Palgrave Macmillan.

Rana, Pradumna B., and Ramon Pacheco Pardo. 2015. "ASEAN+3 and the IMF: The Need for a Marriage of Convenience." *Global Asia* 10 (1): 64–71.

Rana, Pradumna B., and Ramon Pacheco Pardo. 2018. "Rise of Complementarity between Global and Regional Financial Institutions: Perspectives from Asia." *Global Policy* 9 (2): 231–243.

Rimmer, Peter J. 2018. "China's Belt and Road Initiative: Underlying Economic and International Relations Dimensions." *Asia-Pacific Economic Literature* 32 (2): 3–26.

Schmucker, Claudia, and Katharina Gnath. 2011. "From the G8 to the G-20: Reforming the Global Economic Governance System." In *European Yearbook of International Economic Law 2011*, edited by Christoph Herrmann and Jörg Philipp Terhechte. Berlin and Heidelberg: Springer.

Schott, Jeffrey. 2008. *The Future of the Multilateral Trading System in a Multipolar World*. In Discussion Paper. Bonn: German Development Institute.

Schott, Jeffrey J. 2017. *US Trade Policy Options in the Pacific Basin: Bigger Is Better*. In Policy Brief. Washington, DC: Peterson Institute for International Economics.

Scollay, Robert. 2016. "APEC, TPP, and RCEP: Towards an FTAAP." In *Trade Regionalism in the Asia-Pacific: Developments and Future Challenges*, edited by Sanchita Basu Das and Masahiro Kawai. Singapore: ISEAS-Yusof Ishak Institute.

Sherifis, Rossella Franchini, and Valerio Astraldi. 2001. *G7/G8: From Rambouillet to Genoa*. Milan: FrancoAngeli.

Slaughter, Steven. 2013. "Debating the International Legitimacy of the G20: Global Policymaking and Contemporary International Society." *Global Policy* 4 (1): 43–52.

Solís, Mireya, and Saori N. Katada. 2015. "Unlikely Pivotal States in Competitive Free Trade Agreement Diffusion: The Effect of Japan's Trans-Pacific Partnership Participation on Asia-Pacific Regional Integration." *New Political Economy* 20 (2): 155–177.

Toye, Richard. 2003. "Developing Multilateralism: The Havana Charter and the Fight for the International Trade Organization, 1947–1948." *International History Review* 25 (2): 282–305.

Ullrich, Heidi. 2006. "Explaining G7/8 Multilateral Trade Commitments: Is the G7/8 still relevant?" Annual Meeting of the International Studies Association, San Diego, CA, 22–25 March.

Urata, Shujiro. 2019. "Trends of FTAs in East Asia from the 1990s to the 2010s: Defensive and Competitive Regionalism." In *East Asian Integration: Goods, Services and Investment*, edited by Lili Yan Ing, Martin Richardson and Shujiro Urata. Abingdon and New York: Routledge.

VanGrasstek, Craig. 2013. "The future of the WTO." In *The History and Future of the World Trade Organization*. Geneva: World Trade Organization.

Vickers, Brendan. 2012. "The Role of the B(R)ICS: System supporters or Change agents in the WTO?" In *The Oxford Handbook on The World Trade Organization*, edited by Amrita Narlikar, Martin Daunton and Robert M. Stern. Oxford: Oxford University Press.

Vines, David. 2018. "The BRI and RCEP: Ensuring Cooperation in the Liberalisation of Trade in Asia." *Economic and Political Studies* 6 (3): 338–348.

Wang, Hongying. 2017. "New Multilateral Development Banks: Opportunities and Challenges for Global Governance." *Global Policy* 8 (1): 113–118.

Commission, Warwick. 2007. *The Multilateral Trade Regime: Which Way Forward?* Coventry: University of Warwick.

WEF. 2016. *Will the Trans-Pacific Partnership Agreement Reshape the Global Trade and Investment System? What's In and What's New: Issues and Options*. In White Paper. Geneva: Global Agenda Council on Trade & FDI, World Economic Forum.

Wilkinson, Rorden, Erin Hannah, and James Scott. 2016. "The WTO in Nairobi: The Demise of the Doha Development Agenda and the Future of the Multilateral Trading System." *Global Policy* 7 (2): 247–255.

World Bank. 1987. *World Development Report, 1987*. Washington, DC: World Bank.

World Bank. 2016. "Potential Macroeconomic Implications of the Trans-Pacific Partnership." In *Global Economic Prospects*. Washington, DC: World Bank.

WTO. 2011. *The WTO and Preferential Trade Agreements: From Co-Existence to Coherence*. In World Trade Report 2011. Geneva: World Trade Organization.

Zürn, Michael, and Benjamin Faude. 2013. "Commentary: On Fragmentation, Differentiation, and Coordination." *Global Environmental Politics* 13 (3): 119–130.

CHAPTER 8

Strengthening the International Financial Regulation Architecture

Pradumna B. Rana

Introduction

Unlike the other three pillars of the Global Economic Architecture (GEA)[1] which originated at the Bretton Woods Conference of 1944 and have been discussed in earlier chapters of this book, the efforts to build the fourth pillar, namely the International Financial Regulation Architecture (IFRA), began three decades later when capital markets began to integrate across the world and financial globalisation started to increase. Against the backdrop of financial globalisation and integration (Kose et al. 2009), these efforts have led to a highly complex network of international institutions overseeing different parts of the financial markets.

[1] The monetary, international trade and economic development architecture.

P. B. Rana (✉)
S. Rajaratnam School of International Studies, Nanyang Technological University, Singapore, Singapore
e-mail: prana@ntu.edu.sg

P. B. Rana and X. Ji (eds.), *From Centralised to Decentralising Global Economic Architecture*, https://doi.org/10.1007/978-981-19-2041-7_8

The objectives of this chapter are to (i) outline how the IFRA has evolved over time; (ii) identify how the IFRA differs from the other pillars of the GEA; and (iii) looking into the future, present some thoughts on how the IFRA might evolve. The central research question is, will the informal network-based IFRA remain as such or become more decentralised and rules-based like the other pillars of the GEA?

IFRA and Its Evolution

Pre-Asian Financial Crisis IFRA

Under the Bretton Woods monetary system which emerged after World War II and lasted until the early 1970s, governments were to have stable exchange rates and independent monetary policy. The system condoned capital controls and countries were encouraged to actively use these policies to manage their balance-of-payment accounts, in part to ensure "fundamental equilibrium" in international sanctions. Hence during this period, the volume of capital flows across countries was relatively low and financial markets lacked sophistication and comprised mainly conventional banking institutions. Since the mid-1970s, however, Western governments and international economic institutions such as the International Monetary Fund (IMF) and the World Bank began to take a more critical view of capital controls and started to persuade countries to abandon such controls and to promote financial globalisation. With financial globalisation, a number of international institutions with a shared mandate to regulate and supervise financial markets were established (Davies and Green 2008).

In the aftermath of the collapse of Bankhaus Herstatt in West Germany, in 1974, the central bank governors from G10[2] established the Committee on Banking Regulation and Supervisory Practices subsequently renamed the Basel Committee on Banking Supervision (BCBS) and housed it at the Bank of International Settlements (BIS). The latter institution was originally established in 1930 in Switzerland for settling efficiently reparation payments imposed on the Imperial Germany by

[2] The G10 refers to a group of ten countries that agreed to participate in the General Arrangements to Borrow as a supplementary borrowing arrangement to the IMF's resources. G10 countries include Belgium, Canada, France, Germany, Italy, Japan, The Netherlands, Sweden, Switzerland, the United Kingdom and the United States.

the Treaty of Versailles following World War I (Schloss 1958). The collapse of Herstatt had led to a debate on which supervisor, domestic or foreign, should be responsible in the event of problems in bank operations overseas. Hence in 1975, the newly set up BCBS came up with the "Concordat" which for the first time set out some understandings on the respective responsibilities of home and foreign supervisors.

Subsequently, the BCBS has focused on exchanging information on national supervision arrangements, improving effectiveness of techniques for supervising international banking business, and most prominently setting up minimum supervisory standards in areas where they are considered desirable like capital requirements (Davies and Green 2008). The BCBS is now regarded as the primary international standard setter for the prudential regulation of banks and provides a forum for regulatory cooperation on banking supervision matters.

However, as global capital markets integrated and financial markets became more sophisticated, several other international Standard Setting Bodies (SSBs) were also established (Helleiner 2010a, 2010b; Moschella 2016, Baxter 2016). Some of the key SSBs are[3]:

- International Organization of Securities Commissions (IOSCO)—parallel technocratic organisation to the BCBS in the securities market—was established in 1983. Its membership regulates more than 95% of the world's securities markets in more than 130 jurisdictions. The IOSCO develops, implements and promotes adherence to internationally recognised standards for securities regulation. To date, the IOSCO has had a somewhat lower profile than the BCBS. This is in part because cross-border issues faced by securities regulators have been less central and contentious than those in the international banking sector. Nevertheless, the IOSCO members have resolved to (i) cooperate in developing, implementing and promoting adherence to internationally recognised and consistent standards of regulation, oversight and enforcement in order to protect investors, maintain fair, efficient and transparent markets, and seek to address systemic risks; (ii) enhance investor protection and promote investor confidence in the integrity of securities

[3] Other SSBs not shown are: Financial Action Task Force (money laundering) and International Forum of Independent Audit Regulators (audit).

markets, through strengthened information exchange and cooperation in enforcement against misconduct and in supervision of markets and market intermediaries; and (iii) gather and exchange information at both global and regional levels on their respective experiences in order to assist the development of markets, strengthen market infrastructure and implement appropriate regulation.

- Insurance markets remained nation-based for a longer time than the securities markets did. It was only in 1994 that the International Association of Insurance Supervisors (IAIS) was established. The IAIS is a voluntary membership organisation of insurance supervisors and regulators from more than 200 jurisdictions, constituting 97% of the world's insurance premiums. It is the international standard setting body responsible for developing and assisting in the implementation of principles, standards and other supporting materials and guidelines for the supervision of the insurance sector. The IAIS also provides a forum for members to share their experiences and understanding of insurance supervision and insurance markets. In recognition of its collective expertise, the IAIS is routinely called upon by the Group of Twenty (G20) leaders and other international standard setting bodies including the BCBS. The mission of the IAIS is to promote effective and globally consistent supervision of the insurance industry in order to develop and maintain fair, safe and stable insurance markets for the benefit and protection of policyholders and to contribute to global financial stability.
- The International Accounting Standards Committee (IASC) is an independent private-sector organisation that in its own words is a "body working to achieve uniformity in the accounting principles that are used by businesses and other organizations for financial reporting around the world". As stated in its constitution the IASC's goals are to "formulate and publish in the public interest accounting standards to be observed in the presentation of financial statements and to promote their worldwide acceptance", and to "work for the improvement and harmonization of regulations, accounting standards and procedures relating to the presentation of financial statements". The IASC was founded in London in 1973 and by 1998 its membership included 143 accounting organisations representing 2 million accountants in 103 countries. In 2001, the IASC morphed into the International Accounting Standards Board

(IASB). The IASC and the IASB played instrumental roles following the eruptions of the Asian and Global Financial Crises, respectively, in developing international financial reporting standards and global accounting standards (Mattli 2016).

- The Committee on Payments and Settlements System (CPSS) is another international standard setter that promotes, monitors and makes recommendations about the safety and efficiency of payment, clearance, settlement and related arrangements thereby supporting financial stability and economic growth. The CPSS was established in 1990 with the membership of the central banks of G10 countries. The CPSS was upgraded to the Committee on Payments and Market Infrastructure (CPMI) in 2014.

Post-Asian Financial Crisis IFRA

Efforts to build and strengthen the IFRA accelerated considerably after the Asian Financial Crisis (AFC) of 1997–1998 when many believed that the crisis stemmed largely from supervisory and regulatory failures in the financial sectors of the affected countries in rapidly developing Southeast Asian countries and beyond. There was therefore an urgent need for the international SSBs to come up with high quality and globally consistent standards for developing countries to adopt. There were also criticisms that the IMF and the World Bank had not focused much attention on the weaknesses and failures of financial regulation. Instead, their remedial emphasis had been largely on tighter monetary and fiscal policies. It was also pointed out that the IMF contributed to the crisis or worsened it because of the wrong austerity policies that it recommended (Stiglitz 2002; Ito 2007).

Therefore, in October 1998, the finance ministers and central bank governors of the Group of Seven (G7, see Chapter 2) commissioned Han Tietmeyer, former President of Bundesbank, to recommend new structures for enhancing cooperation among the various national and international supervisors, international SSBs and international financial institutions to provide stability in the international financial system.

Tietmeyer consulted widely and in the following year presented a report to the G7 recommending the establishment of the Financial Stability Forum (FSF) to "assess issues and vulnerabilities affecting the global financial system and to identify and oversee the actions needed to address them" (Tietmeyer 1999). The Forum would include the national authorities responsible for financial stability in the G7, namely finance ministries, central banks and supervisory agencies from the major financial centres. It would also include representatives of international SSBs, and international financial institutions (Davies and Green 2008).

In early 1999, the G7 acted on Tietmeyer's recommendation by creating the FSF in part to coordinate the key SSBs that were involved in the emerging international standards regime. The FSF had been meeting on a plenary basis twice a year and since 2001 had also held regional meetings with authorities in the Latin American, Asian, Central and Eastern European and the African regions.

Although not directly involved in developing standards but focusing more on the implementation of standards, at about the same time when the FSF was established, the IMF and the World Bank started regular multilateral regulatory monitoring exercises, by coming out with the Financial Sector Assessment Programme (FSAP) and the Review of Standards and Code (ROSC). As such, the post-AFC IFRA is illustrated in Fig. 8.1 with the G7 as the apex body and the FSF coordinating the activities of the various sectoral international SSBs.

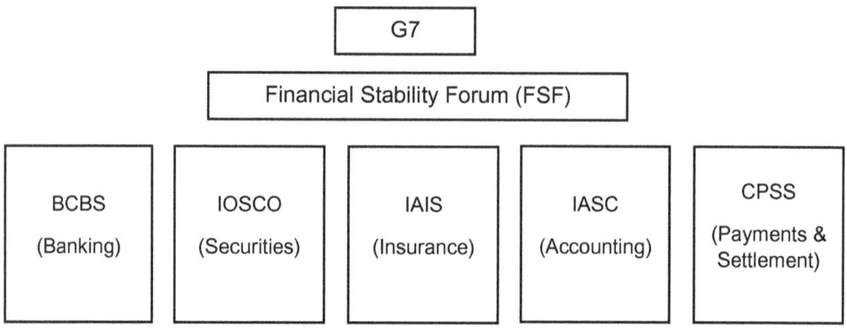

Fig. 8.1 Post-AFC IFRA (*Source* Author) (*Notes* BCBS = Basel Committee on Banking Supervision; IOSCO = International Organization of Securities Commissions; IAIS = International Association of Insurance Supervisors; IASC = International Accounting Standards Committee, IASB = International Accounting Standards Board (since 2001); CPSS = Committee on Payments and Settlements)

Post-GFC IFRA

The Global Financial Crisis (GFC) started in the US with the sub-prime mortgage crisis and exploded with the collapse of Lehman Brother's in the fall of 2008. Regulatory and supervisory failures in the financial sectors of the Western countries were a root cause. The GFC of 2008–2009, therefore, resurrected efforts to reform the IFRA (Dowling and Rana 2010). A number of key actions were taken.

First, the G20 finance ministers and central bank officials' process was upgraded to leaders' forum. The first meeting of the leaders was held in Washington DC in November 2008. At the September 2009 Pittsburgh summit, the leaders labelled the forum as "the premier forum for our international cooperation". The G20, therefore, replaced the G7 as the main oversight body for global economic governance. The G20 is a more legitimate body than the G7, as it includes the membership of dynamic emerging markets. Notably from Asia, the G20 includes Australia, China, India, Indonesia, Korea and Japan (see Chapter 2).

Second, also in the April 2009 summit, the G20 leaders upgraded the FSF into the FSB and made it a peak body responsible for coordinating the activities of international SSBs (Walter 2019). The FSB was given a wider membership that included all G20 countries, Spain, and the European Commission along with the original FSF members. The FSB was also given a slightly larger secretariat and a full-time secretary general (the incumbent secretary general is Dietrich Domanski). The FSB's new mandate was also wider than the FSF's, including tasks such as conducting (jointly with the IMF) early warning exercises, setting guidelines for and supporting the establishment of international supervisory colleges for private institutions, and supporting contingency planning for cross-border crisis management, particularly with respect to systemically important firms. In the regulatory area, the FSB was also given a strong coordinating role vis-a-vis the SSBs.

In addition, the FSB, although it was not given the power to sanction, was assigned a stronger role in promoting compliance with international financial standards. Countries that belong to the FSB must undergo peer reviews which include not only country reviews but also thematic reviews. All FSB members must also undergo FSAP assessments every five years and to publicise the detailed assessments which serve as the basis for the preparation of the ROSCs. The FSB has also committed to taking a more proactive role in providing compliance with international standards among non-members partly by "leading by example" through implementing international standards and disclosing their levels of adherence. See Appendix 8.1 from Helleiner (2010a) for a comparison of the mandates and operations of the FSB and the FSF (Helleiner 2010a; Walter 2019).

Summing up, upgradation has provided opportunities for the FSB, but it has also posed a number of challenges. The FSB's wider mandate has made it a more legitimate institution compared with the FSF which had a narrower membership. The FSB has also been given stronger mechanisms for ensuring compliance including through mandatory participation in regular FSAPs and ROSCs, the new peer review mechanism for FSB members, and mandatory implementation of various standards. The FSB's capacity for micro-prudential and macro-prudential surveillance has also been strengthened.

These changes have also created new challenges for the FSB. First, the FSB is an informal network of SSBs as its legal status and the basis through which it provides oversight has not been given legal consideration. Second, FSB has been given an expanded mandate without the requisite human and physical resources. It is still a relatively small institution hosted and funded by the BIS. Third, FSB's larger and heterogenous membership may make consensus difficult to reach. Finally, the FSB's Charter states that members must implement international standards, but the process of dealing with non-complying members has not been clarified.

Third, since January 2011, the European Union has adopted a region-based European System of Financial Supervision (ESFS) to ensure consistent and appropriate financial supervision throughout the European Single Market. The ESFS comprises the European Systemic Risk Board located at the European Central Bank for macro-prudential supervision, three European Supervisory Authorities (ESAs) (for banking, securities industries and insurance markets) focusing on micro-prudential supervision, and national supervisors (Parenti 2021).

Also in Asia, in order to promote regional financial stability, a group of leading international financial scholars and regulators and international political economists including Plummer (2012), Kawai (2011), Sheng (2009, 2010) and Dowling and Rana (2010) have supported the idea of creating an Asian Financial Stability Board (AFSB). By design, the AFSB would provide a forum for broader information sharing in the areas of macroeconomic and financial stability by including financial regulators, as well as finance ministries and central banks. The AFSB would also discuss regional financial vulnerabilities, regional capital flows, common issues for financial sector supervision and regulation and common efforts at financial integration. The AFSB would also ensure that the views of individual countries are presented to global bodies. The AFSB would focus on capital market rules and regulations (micro-prudential monitoring) and promote the stability of the financial system throughout the region through early warning systems (macro-prudential monitoring). Although currently there is the Asian representative office of the BIS located in Hong Kong, China, advocates of the AFSB make the case for an institution led by Asian countries to which the BIS could be invited to participate. The AFSB is still under discussion and has not been established yet.

Accordingly, the post-GFC IFRA is illustrated in Fig. 8.2.

IFRA vs Other GEA Pillars

In addition to being a latecomer to the scene, the IFRA differs from the other pillars of the GEA discussed in this book in three ways.

First, unlike the other pillars, the IFRA operates on a sectoral basis. This means that the international SSBs focus on and specialise on specific sectors of the financial market. For example, while the BCBS focuses on the banking industry, the IOSCO focuses on the securities market. As financial markets have become increasingly inter-linked, this has led to a coordination problem. In order to partially alleviate this cross-sectoral coordination problem, in 1996, a Joint Forum between the BCBS, IOSCO, and IAIS was established comprising bank, securities and insurance regulators. This Forum meets three times a year (Davies and Green 2008) and was strengthened in the aftermath of the GFC.

Second, the IFRA comprises international institutions and does not have regional counterparts and layers with the exception of the European Union. In other words, the IFRA remains relatively centralised, and it is not decentralising like the monetary, trade, and economic development architectures. This is because membership in the FSF and later the

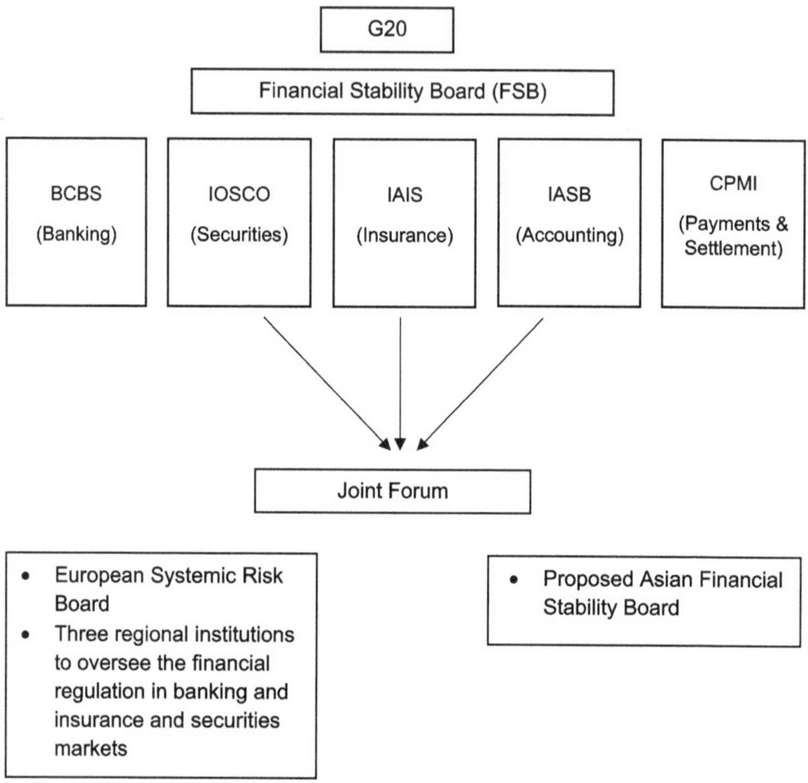

Fig. 8.2 Post-GFC IFRA (*Source* Author) (*Note* BCBS = Basel Committee on Banking Supervision; IOSCO = International Organization of Securities Commissions; IAIS = International Association of Insurance Supervisors; IASB = International Accounting Standards Board; CPMI = Committee on Payments and Market Infrastructure [since 2014])

FSB and other SSBs provides valuable "club goods" type of benefits to both the developed and dynamic emerging markets that are members of the G20 (Walter, 2019). These include learning benefits and status. The learning benefits include privileged access to high quality expertise and knowledge relevant to the emerging policy challenges; forewarning of emerging financial and security risks to domestic banks operating locally; and supplemental surveillance of systemically important countries with financial systems posing spill over risks. Together these have played an important role in sustaining the positive perceptions of the FSB and other SSBs among emerging countries and in diminishing the attractiveness of alternative regional arrangements. China's continued commitment to the FSB and SSBs has been an important reason for the engagement of emerging markets and developing countries. Russia has also recognised the value of the learning opportunities that the membership of the FSB and SSBs provides. Some doubts that India had regarding international financial regulation are also being addressed (Walter 2019). These non-Western economic powerhouses are, therefore, not seeking to establish alternative regional institutions to counter or compete with global ones as is happening on the other pillars of the GEA. Walter (2019) also argues that membership of FSB and other SSBs provides the members with status benefits. These benefits are probably valued most by the officials delegated to those organisations, and by national regulatory agencies that are members.

Despite recent governance reforms in the FSB and SSBs, Jones and Knaack (2019) note that a core-periphery still exists, and more reforms are required. For example, although ten dynamic economy G20 members have been included in the Basel Committee, regulators from emerging markets are less engaged in the proceedings of the Committee. This is for a number of reasons including the lack of institutional capacity in the emerging markets to engage in the discussions. Hence, well-resourced regulators from the industrialised countries dominate the regulatory debate.

Also, the vast majority of developing countries are not members of the Basel Committee and have minimal input to the standard setting processes. Although the Basel Committee has a longstanding Basel Consultative Group to promote dialogue between members and non-members, it is dominated by the developed countries and emerging markets are under-represented.

Third, the key institutions in the IFRA, the FSB and SSBs, are designed to act more as a loose network of national and international officials rather than a rules based inter-governmental institution like the IMF, WTO, and the World Bank. The FSB lacks formal power, has a relatively small complement of staff and has not been ratified by any legislature or treaty. This is because governments are not prepared to accept that they should cede any element of control over their domestic financial system to bodies in which they have only minority interest (Davies 2010). Davies 2010 argues that this is the reason why groupings like the IOSCO and BCBS are sometimes reluctant to accept instructions, or even advice, from the FSB. Central bank governors have also tended to see the BIS as the key forum that they should look up to rather than FSB.

IFRA in the Future

How might the IFRA evolve in the future? Will it continue to be a loose network-based sector-focused complex of international institutions focusing on financial regulation and supervision, or will it be a rules-based international body with sanctions and enforcement capacity similar to the IMF, World Bank, and the World Trade Organisation (WTO)?

In 2008, Eichengreen (2008) had made the case for establishing a rules-based World Finance Organisation (WFO) analogous to the WTO. In the same way that the WTO establishes principles for trade policy without specifying outcomes, the WFO would establish principles for prudential supervision (e.g. capital and liquidity requirements, limits on portfolio concentrations and connected lending, adequacy of risk measurement systems and internal controls) without attempting to prescribe the specific structure of regulation in detail. The WFO would define obligations for its members; the latter would be obliged to meet international standards for supervision and regulation for their financial markets. Membership would be mandatory for all countries seeking access to foreign financial markets. The WFO would appoint independent panel of experts to determine whether countries were in compliance of those obligations failing which the authorities would be able to impose sanctions against the countries that fail to comply. The WFO would, however, not dictate regulatory conditions on countries.

In the post-GEC period, which was initially expected to be the worst crisis since the Great Depression of the 1930s, there were calls for a New Bretton Woods system—a wider and much more comprehensive set of reforms of global economic governance and international institutions (Rana 2014). In those days, the political will for implementing reforms was strong among academics and policymakers alike. Even then, as discussed above, the G20's approach to reform was not bold but incremental.

Presently, because of rising nationalism and populism after the Global Financial Crisis mainly in the West and other parts of the world, it is unlikely that sufficient political will can be garnered to establish such a supranational body with sanctions focusing on finance as the WFO. More specifically, the feasibility of the WFO is questionable for two reasons. First, while there is a global consensus that free trade is beneficial for all, there is no comparable consensus on whether unfettered financial flows have similar beneficial effects (Sheng 2010). Second, despite the interconnected nature of global finance, the costs borne to respond to financial crisis remain concentrated at the national level and at the hands of national financial regulators. This stems from the role of central bank as "the lender of last resort". Nation states are, therefore, unlikely to give up control to a supranational body (Blackmore and Jeapes 2009). Despite these sceptical arguments, pondering on the prospect of establishing the WFO, Wymeersch (2010) notes, that "[o]ver time the idea of creating an equivalent to the WTO may usefully be considered".

Hence, in the foreseeable future, the IFRA will likely continue to function as a loose network of international regulatory institutions focusing on financial regulation and supervision. However, even under this scenario, greater authority should be given to the FSB so that it can effectively coordinate activities of sectoral SSBs. Also as already mentioned above, although emerging market economies are well represented in the FSB and international SSBs, they should be given key leadership positions in these institutions (Walter 2019).

Conclusion

The IFRA is a laggard in the sense that the process of building it started only after the collapse of the Bretton Woods system when global financial markets started to integrate, and financial globalisation took off. During the 1970s to the mid-1990s, a number of international standard setting bodies were established beginning with the Basel Committee on Banking Supervision which is the premier standard setter for the international banking industry.

After the Asian Financial Crisis, based on the recommendations of Hans Tietmeyer, the G7 established the Financial Stability Forum in 1999 to provide oversight over international financial regulations. In the aftermath of the Global Financial Crisis, the G20 upgraded the Financial Stability Forum into the Financial Stability Board (FSB) by expanding membership and jurisdictions to include all G20 countries. This upgradation did not, however, enhance the authority and power of the FSB. Hence, the FSB can be characterised as a loose network of members and jurisdictions overseeing international financial regulations and the work of various SSBs.

The IFRA differs from the other pillars of the GEA in a several ways. First, unlike other pillars, the IFRA operates on a sectoral basis that is with each SSB focusing on particular sub-sectors of finance. Second, the IFRA is centralised comprising the FSB and international SSBs, without regional counterparts and layers except in the case of the European Union and proposals to establish one in East Asia. Third, as loose networks of member countries and jurisdictions, the key institutions in IFRA lack the power to impose sanctions.

How might the IFRA evolve in the future? Will it become a rules-based pillar comprising institutions like the proposed World Finance Organization (WFO) with power to sanction like the other GEA pillars or will it continue to be a loose network-based pillar? The answer is probably no given the rising nationalism and populism in many parts of the world. The spirit of cooperation among countries in the world has damped as was witnessed during the COVID-19 pandemic. In addition, the benefit of globalised finance is not yet established and widely accepted, leading to questions over the necessity of globally regulated financial flows. Also, despite the interconnected nature of global finance, the costs borne to respond to financial crisis remain concentrated at the national level. National financial regulators are, therefore, unlikely to give up their power and policy space to the proposed WFO.

Appendix 8.1

Comparing the FSF and FSB

	Financial Stability Forum (Details from 1999 Tietmeyer report)	*Financial Stability Board (Details from Charter and subsequent statements)*
Mandate	• "assess issues and vulnerabilities affecting the global financial system and identify and oversee the actions needed to address them, including encouraging, where necessary, the development or strengthening of international best practices and standards and defining priorities for addressing and implementing them". (G7 statement) • "ensure that national and international authorities and relevant international supervisory bodies and expert groupings can more effectively foster and coordinate their respective responsibilities to promote international financial stability, improve the functioning of the markets and reduce systemic risk" (G7 statement)	• Assess vulnerabilities affecting the global financial system and identify and review on a timely and ongoing basis the regulatory, supervisory and related actions needed to address them, and their outcomes • Promote coordination and information exchange among authorities responsible for financial stability • Monitor and advice on market developments and their implications for regulatory policy • Advise on and monitor best practice in meeting regulatory standards • Undertake joint strategic reviews of the policy development work of the international standard setting bodies to ensure their work is timely coordinated, focused on priorities and addressing gaps • Set guidelines for and support the establishment of supervisory colleges • Support contingency planning for cross-border crisis management, particularly with respect to systemically important firms • Collaborate with the IMF to conduct Early Warning Exercises • The FSB will promote and help coordinate the alignment of the activities of the SSBs to address any overlaps or gaps and clarify demarcations in the light of changes in national and regional regulatory structures relating to prudential and systemic risk, market integrity and investor and consumer protection, infrastructure, as well as accounting and auditing

(continued)

(continued)

	Financial Stability Forum (Details from 1999 Tietmeyer report)	*Financial Stability Board (Details from Charter and subsequent statements)*
Country Membership (numbers of representatives)	• G7 (3) • Added in 1999: Australia (1), Singapore (1), Hong Kong (1), Netherlands (1) • Added in 2007: Switzerland (1)	G7 (3), Brazil (3), Russia (3), India (3), China (3), Australia (2), Mexico (2), Netherlands (2), Spain (2), South Korea (2), Switzerland (2), Argentina (1), Hong Kong (1), Indonesia (1), Singapore (1), Saudi Arabia (1), South Africa (1), Turkey (1)
Other Members (number of representatives)	IMF (2), WB (2), BIS (1), OECD (1), BCBS (2), IOSCO (2), IAIS (2), CGFS (1), CPSS (1), ECB (1)	Same plus European Commission
Level of Representation	"Representation should be at a high level (that is, Deputy Ministers and Deputy Governors, Deputy Heads of the IFIs, Chairs and appointed members of international groupings)." (Tietmeyer 1999)	"Representation at the Plenary shall be at the level of central bank governor or immediate deputy; head or immediate deputy of the main supervisory/regulatory agency; and deputy finance minister or deputy head of finance ministry. Plenary representatives also include the chairs of the main SSBs and committees of central bank experts, and high-level representatives of the IMF, the World Bank, the Bank for International Settlements (BIS) and the Organisation for Economic Co-operation and Development"
Internal governance	Chairperson Secretary-General Secretariat (in Basel) Plenary (consensus rule) Ad hoc working groups	Chairperson Secretary-General Secretariat (in Basel) Plenary (consensus rule) Ad hoc working Groups Steering Committee Standing Committees
Accountability	Reports to the G7 finance ministers and central bank governors	Reports to the G20 leaders

(continued)

(continued)

	Financial Stability Forum (Details from 1999 Tietmeyer report)	*Financial Stability Board (Details from Charter and subsequent statements)*
Relationship to SSBs	Not specified	• "the standard setting bodies will report to the FSB on their work without prejudice to their existing reporting arrangements or their independence. This process should not undermine the independence of the standard setting process but strengthen support for strong standard setting by providing a broader accountability framework" • FSB will "undertake joint strategic reviews of the policy development work of the international standard setting bodies to ensure their work is timely, coordinated, focused on priorities and addressing gaps" • FSB will "promote and help coordinate the alignment of the activities of the SSBs to address any overlaps or gaps and clarify demarcations in light of changes in national and regional regulatory structures relating to prudential and systemic risk, market integrity and investor and consumer protection, infrastructure, as well as accounting and auditing"
International Standard-setting Compliance Mechanisms	• delegated to SSBs • voluntary IMF/WB surveillance • market pressure • name and shame, and possible sanctions vis-à-vis offshore financial centres	• delegated to SSBs • FSB • IMF/WB surveillance (for members, mandatory FSAPs every five years, and publication of assessments used as a basis for the ROSCs) • market pressure • name and shame, and possible sanctions against all noncooperating jurisdictions • membership requirement to implement international standards • mandatory peer reviews for members

(*Source* Helleiner (2010a) (*Notes* BCBS = Basel Committee on Banking Supervision; BIS = Bank for International Settlements; CGFS = Committee on the Global Financial System; CPSS = Committee on

Payments and Settlements; ECB = European Central Bank; IFIs = international financial institutions; IOSCO = International Organization of Securities Commissions; IAIS = International Association of Insurance Supervisors; IASC = International Accounting Standards Committee; IASB = International Accounting Standards Board (since 2001); OECD = Organisation for Economic Co-operation and Development; ROSCs = Reports on the Observance of Standards and Codes; SSBs = standard setting bodies; WB = World Bank).

References

Baxter, Lawrence G. 2016. "Understanding the Global in Global Finance and Regulation." In *Reconceptualising Global Finance and Its Regulation*, edited by Ross P. Buckley, Emilios Avgouleas and Douglas W. Arner. Cambridge: Cambridge University Press.

Blackmore, Vanessa, and Esther Jeapes. 2009. "The Global Financial Crisis: One Global Financial Regulator or Multiple Regulators?" *Capital Markets Law Journal* 4 (suppl_1): S112–S122.

Davies, Howard, and David Green. 2008. *Global Financial Regulation: The Essential Guide*. Cambridge: Polity Press.

Davies, Howard. 2010. "Global Financial Regulation after the Credit Crisis." *Global Policy* 1 (2): 185–190.

Dowling, J. Malcolm, and Pradumna B. Rana. 2010. *Asia and the Global Economic Crisis: Challenges in a Financially Integrated World*. London: Palgrave Macmillan.

Eichengreen, Barry. 2008. "Not a New Bretton Woods But a New Bretton Woods process." In *What G20 Leaders Must Do to Stabilise Our Economy and Fix the Financial System*, edited by Barry Eichengreen and Richard Baldwin. London: Centre for Economic Policy Research.

Helleiner, Eric. 2010a. The Financial Stability Board and International Standards. In *CIGI G20 Papers*. Waterloo: The Centre for International Governance Innovation.

Helleiner, Eric. 2010b. "What Role for the New Financial Stability Board? The Politics of International Standards After the Crisis." *Global Policy* 1 (3): 282–290.

Ito, Takatoshi. 2007. "Asian Currency Crisis and the International Monetary Fund, 10 Years Later: Overview." *Asian Economic Policy Review* 2 (1): 16–49.

Jones, Emily and Peter Knaack. 2019. "Global Financial Regulation: Shortcomings and Reform Options." *Global Policy* 10 (2): 193–206.

Kawai, Masahiro. 2011. "G-20 Financial Reforms and Emerging Asia's Challenges." In *Asia and Policymaking for the Global Economy*, edited by

Kemal Dervis, Masahiro Kawai and Domenico Lombardi. Washington, DC: Brookings Institution.

Kose, M. Ayhan, Eswar Prasad, Kenneth Rogoff, and Shang-Jin Wei. 2009. Financial Globalization and Economic Policies In *IZA Discussion Paper No. 4037*. Bonn: Institute of Labour Economics.

Mattli, Walter. 2016. "Private Transnational Governance." In *The Oxford Handbook of International Organizations*, edited by Jacob Katz Cogan, Ian Hurd and Ian Johnstone. Oxford: Oxford University Press.

Moschella, Manuela. 2016. "International Finance." In *The Oxford Handbook of International Organizations*, edited by Jacob Katz Cogan, Ian Hurd and Ian Johnstone. Oxford: Oxford University Press.

Parenti, Radostina. 2021. European System of Financial Supervision (ESFS). In *Fact Sheets on the European Union—2021*. Strasbourg: European Parliament.

Plummer, Michael G. 2012. "Regional Monitoring of Capital Flows and Coordination of Financial Regulation: Stakes and Options for Asia." In *Implications of the Global Financial Crisis for Financial Reform and Regulation in Asia*, edited by Masahiro Kawai, David G. Mayes and Peter J. Morgan. Cheltenham & Northampton: Edward Elgar.

Rana, Pradumna B. 2014. "From a Centralized to a Decentralized Global Economic Architecture: An Overview." In *New Global Economic Architecture: The Asian Perspective*, edited by Masahiro Kawai, Peter J. Morgan and Pradumna B. Rana. Cheltenham & Northampton: Edward Elgar.

Schloss, Henry H. 1958. *The Bank for International Settlements: An Experiment in Central Bank Cooperation*. Amsterdam: North-Holland Publishing Co.

Sheng, Andrew. 2009. *From Asian to Global Financial Crisis: An Asian Regulator's View of Unfettered Finance in the 1990s and 2000s*. Cambridge: Cambridge University Press.

Sheng, Andrew. 2010. "The Regulatory Reform of Global Financial Markets: An Asian Regulator's Perspective." *Global Policy* 1 (2): 191–200.

Stiglitz, Joseph E. 2002. *Globalization and Its Discontents*. New York: W.W. Norton & Company.

Tietmeyer, Hans. 1999. "Report to G7 Ministers and Governors by Hans Tietmeyer." Accessed 12 December 2021. https://www.fsb.org/wp-content/uploads/r_9902.pdf.

Walter, Andrew. 2019. Emerging Countries in Global Financial Regulatory Standard Setting: What Is to Be Done? In *CIGI Papers No. 228*. Waterloo: The Centre for International Governance Innovation.

Wymeersch, Eddy. 2010. "Global and Regional Financial Regulation: The Viewpoint of a European Securities Regulator." *Global Policy* 1 (2): 201–208.

Index

A
African Union (AU), 32, 37, 40
America First, 11, 172
ASEAN Economic Community, 102
ASEAN Free Trade Area, 7, 174
ASEAN+3, 10, 11, 15, 20, 57–66, 80, 125, 126
ASEAN+3 Macroeconomic Research Office (AMRO), 9, 11, 14, 15, 20, 51, 56, 57, 59–65, 79, 80, 125
ASEAN Swap Arrangement (ASA), 8, 56, 58
Asia 5+1, 165, 186, 188
Asian Bond Markets Initiative (ABMI), 51
Asian Development Bank (ADB), 6, 12, 14, 16, 51, 67, 68, 73–80, 88, 90, 91, 93, 95–103, 105–109, 162, 168, 169, 178, 181
Asian Development Fund (ADF), 76, 91
Asian Financial Crisis (AFC), 8–10, 12, 18, 31, 43, 51, 56, 62, 63, 65, 66, 124, 132, 169, 201, 210
Asian Financial Stability Board (AFSB), 20, 21, 205
Asian Infrastructure Investment Bank (AIIB), 6, 11, 12, 14–16, 51, 53, 67–71, 74–80, 88, 91–103, 105–109, 147, 162, 181
Asian Monetary Fund (AMF), 12, 59
Asia-Pacific Economic Cooperation (APEC), 14, 178, 181, 182
Asia-Pacific Trade Agreement (APTA), 169
Association of Southeast Asian Nations (ASEAN), 7, 32, 37, 40, 60, 96, 169, 172, 173, 176, 180, 188
asymmetric adjustment, 16, 115, 117, 118, 127, 135

B
balance of payments, 8, 56, 60, 115, 116, 121, 123, 126, 136, 155

P. B. Rana and X. Ji (eds.), *From Centralised to Decentralising Global Economic Architecture*, https://doi.org/10.1007/978-981-19-2041-7

balance sheet, 76, 137, 154, 155
bancor, 115, 117, 118, 126, 127, 135
Bank of International Settlements (BIS), 198, 204, 205, 208, 212, 213
Basel Committee on Banking Supervision (BCBS), 198–200, 202, 205, 206, 208, 209, 212, 213
Belt and Road Initiative (BRI), 18, 20, 101–103, 165, 173, 187, 188
benefit-risk analysis, 4, 13
bicycle theory, 175
Biden, Joe, 66, 143, 149, 152
Bretton Woods, 1–5, 10, 16, 17, 27, 29, 36, 54, 67, 79, 87, 113, 115, 117, 118, 120, 127, 132–137, 140, 154, 161, 165, 179, 181, 197, 198, 209
BRICS, 10, 11, 51, 53, 55, 56, 67–69, 71, 78, 126, 147
Build back better, 149

C

Canada-EU Comprehensive Economic and Trade Agreement (CETA), 172
central bank digital currency (CBDC), 151, 153
Chiang Mai Initiative (CMI), 57, 58, 60. *See also* Chiang Mai Initiative Multilateralisation (CMIM)
Chiang Mai Initiative Multilateralisation (CMIM), 8, 9, 11, 12, 20, 42, 51, 56–66, 79, 80, 125, 126, 162, 180, 182, 186
China-ASEAN Free Trade Area (CAFTA), 169
China International Import Expo, 155
co-financing, 62, 63, 65, 76–78, 89, 93, 98, 104, 105, 108, 162
Cold War, 30, 72, 167, 169, 188
Committee on Payments and Market Infrastructure (CPMI), 201, 206
comparative advantage, 3, 13, 41, 55, 62, 63, 65, 88, 109, 178
Competitive Regionalism, 167
complementary multilateralism, 42
Comprehensive and Progressive Agreement for Trans-Pacific Partnership (CPTPP), 7, 8, 11, 18, 20, 171–173, 175, 178, 180, 181, 183, 187
Congress, 2, 33, 105, 122, 124
contested multilateralism, 11, 12, 52, 53, 164
Contingent Reserve Arrangement (CRA), 51, 56, 57, 79, 126, 147
COVID-19, 9, 19, 33, 59, 91, 98, 105, 120, 125, 133, 147, 210
current account deficit, 114, 138, 139

D

Debt Service Suspension Initiative (DSSI), 34
"debt-trap diplomacy", 188
decoupling, 66, 133, 152, 155
deindustrialisation, 141–143, 145, 154, 155
Democracies Ten (D10), 35
Development Assistance Committee (DAC), 68, 75, 78
Digital Currency/Electronic Payment (DC/EP), 152, 153
division of labour, 3, 13, 41, 43, 53, 63, 78, 80, 97, 100, 142, 162
Doha Development Agenda (DDA), 168, 175, 182
dual circulation, 146, 154

E

Economic Review and Policy Dialogue (ERPD), 64
Eurasian Economic Community, 8
European Bank for Reconstruction and Development (EBRD), 6, 16, 67, 88, 90–93, 95, 97, 98, 100, 101, 104, 105, 108, 109
European Coal and Steel Community, 7, 166
European Commission (EC), 90, 92, 95, 97, 104, 171, 172, 203, 212
European Economic Community (EEC), 7, 8, 166. *See also* European Union (EU)
European Financial Stabilisation Mechanism, 8, 57
European Financial Stability Facility, 8, 57
European Free Trade Association, 7, 166
European Investment Bank (EIB), 6, 16, 67, 88–90, 92–95, 97, 98, 100, 101, 104, 105, 108, 109
European Investment Fund (EIF), 89
European Stability Mechanism (ESM), 8, 57, 59, 63, 65, 125
European System of Financial Supervision (ESFS), 204
European Union (EU), 11, 27, 29, 31, 32, 39, 50, 53, 61, 63, 66, 89, 92–96, 100, 103, 105, 150, 167, 170–172, 177, 182, 184, 185, 204, 205, 210
eurozone, 8, 15, 32, 61, 63, 65, 66, 80, 125, 133
excess returns, 138–140, 155
exchange rate, 2, 8, 29, 35, 114, 117, 119, 132, 135–137, 141, 143, 154, 198

F

Federal Reserve, 66, 137, 142, 143, 148, 153
Financial Stability Board (FSB), 9, 11, 18, 19, 21, 203, 204, 206–213
Financial Stability Forum (FSF), 9, 18, 201–205, 210–213. *See also* Financial Stability Board (FSB)
fiscal policy, 17, 36, 59, 124, 134, 147, 150, 151, 201
Flexible Credit Line, 33, 125
foreign direct investment (FDI), 5, 7, 120, 139, 169, 176
forum shopping, 6, 12, 50, 53, 63, 64, 162, 164
Free Trade Area of the Asia-Pacific, 8, 20
functional complementarity, 3, 17, 43, 50, 54, 65, 75, 79, 162, 164, 175
functional fragmentation, 53, 74

G

G20 fatigue, 19, 33
G8+5, 31, 36
General Agreement on Tariffs and Trade (GATT), 2–4, 165, 166, 168, 176, 177, 180, 185, 186
Generalised System of Preference, 168
global economic architecture (GEA), 1–6, 9, 10, 13, 14, 18, 20, 27, 87, 197, 198, 205, 207, 210
global financial architecture (GFA), 15, 51, 52, 54, 55
Global Financial Crisis (GFC), 8, 9, 16, 18, 31, 32, 34, 43, 56, 58, 66, 114, 119, 120, 127, 131, 133, 140, 173, 182, 203, 205, 209, 210
global financial safety net (GFSN), 2, 12, 16, 42, 50, 51, 55–57, 79, 80, 115, 117, 125, 127, 162,

186. *See also* International Monetary Fund (IMF)
Global Gateway, 103
Global Governance Group (3G), 37, 40
Global Infrastructure Facility, 76
Global Infrastructure Hub, 76
global periphery, 131
Global Reserve Bank, 118, 126
global reserve system (GRS), 3, 16, 17, 113–115, 117, 118, 122, 124–127
global value chain, 7, 170
gold exchange standard, 113, 114, 135
governance trilemma, 183, 184. *See also* impossible trinity
Great Depression, 1, 36, 54, 167, 208
Great Recession, 36
Green Room, 185
Group of Eight (G8), 30, 31, 36–38
Group of Seven (G7), 9, 14, 18, 27–30, 34, 35, 37, 39–43, 55, 165, 166, 173, 201–203, 210–212
Group of 77, 37
Group of Twenty (G20), 9, 11, 14, 15, 17–20, 28, 31–43, 56, 64, 65, 76, 121, 124, 165, 172, 173, 186, 200, 203, 206, 207, 209, 210, 212

H

"healthy" competition, 3, 14, 15, 17, 50–52, 54, 65, 76, 79, 80, 109, 162, 175, 188
hegemony, 3, 17, 115, 127, 133, 134, 137–141, 143–145, 147, 149, 152, 154, 155
Heiligendamm process, 31

I

import substitution industrialization (ISI), 166, 167
impossible trinity, 183
inequity bias, 16, 115, 118, 127, 135
input legitimacy, 14, 34, 36, 37, 39, 41
INSTEX, 133, 150
interest rate, 59, 116, 132, 140, 143, 148, 149, 151, 155
International Accounting Standards Committee (IASC), 200–202, 214
International Association of Insurance Supervisors (IAIS), 200, 202, 205, 206, 212, 214
International Bank for Reconstruction and Development (IBRD), 2, 5, 69, 77, 91. *See also* World Bank (WB)
International Centre for Settlement of Investment Disputes (ICSID), 5. *See also* World Bank (WB)
International Clearing Union (ICU), 16, 117, 126, 127, 135
International Development Association (IDA), 5, 69, 77, 91. *See also* World Bank (WB)
international economic institutions (IEIs), 2, 3, 6, 10, 11, 13, 20, 28, 32, 55, 183, 198
International Financial Corporation (IFC), 5, 96, 97. *See also* World Bank (WB)
international financial regulation architecture (IFRA), 3, 9, 11, 18–20, 197, 198, 201–203, 205–210
International Infrastructure Support System, 100
International Monetary Fund (IMF), 2, 4, 8, 10–12, 14–18, 20,

32–34, 39, 42, 49, 51, 53–56, 58–66, 78–80, 96, 115, 117–127, 134, 135, 144, 147, 162, 164, 165, 180, 181, 186, 198, 201–203, 207, 208, 211–213
international non-governmental organisation (INGO), 5, 6
International Organization of Securities Commissions (IOSCO), 199, 202, 205, 206, 208, 212, 214
International Trade Organisation (ITO), 2, 165. *See also* World Trade Organisation (WTO)

J
Japan-EU Economic Partnership Agreement (JEEPA), 172
Jin, Liqun, 91–93, 108

K
Keynes Plan, 115, 134

L
Latin American Reserve Fund (LARF), 57, 59, 125, 126
Library Group, 14, 28, 29, 35
Li, Keqiang, 102
London Gold Pool, 135, 136

M
mega-free trade agreement (mega-FTA), 7, 11, 18, 20, 180
Memorandum of Understanding (MOU), 15, 65, 76, 77, 92, 96, 98, 104, 162, 180, 181, 188
Mercosur, 7, 40, 172, 177
mission creep, 39, 43, 88
most-favoured-nation (MFN), 176, 182
multilateral development bank (MDB), 6, 67–69, 72, 74–80, 87–92, 96, 105, 109, 124
Multilateral Investment Guarantee Agency (MIGA), 5, 77. *See also* World Bank (WB)
multilateralism-regionalism interface, 179, 180
multiplex world, 12
Mutual Assessment Process (MAP), 39, 40

N
New Bretton Woods (NBW), 9, 208
New Development Bank (NDB), 6, 11, 15, 51, 53, 67, 68, 74–80, 147, 162, 181
New Partnership for Africa's Development (NEPAD), 32, 37
new regionalism, 166–168, 188
Nixon Shock, 29
non-tariff measure (NTM), 176
North American Free Trade Agreement (NAFTA), 7, 177, 178

O
open regionalism, 181
output legitimacy, 14, 28, 34, 38–40, 43

P
People's Bank of China, 114, 132, 137, 151–153
Plurilateral Trade Agreements (PAs), 182, 183
Precautionary Credit Line, 33, 125

public goods, 2, 3, 14–16, 28, 34, 41, 54, 55, 162, 183
Putin, Vladimir, 30, 150

Q

Quad, 165, 166, 185
quota, 32, 33, 120, 122–124

R

regime complex, 12, 41, 164
Regional Comprehensive Economic Partnership (RCEP), 7, 8, 11, 18, 20, 170, 171, 173, 175, 180, 181, 183, 187, 188
regional financial safety net (RFSN), 3, 8, 10, 12, 15–18, 20, 42, 56–59, 61–66, 80, 117, 125–127, 162, 186
regional monetary unit (RMU), 126
regional trade agreement (RTA), 3, 7, 12, 17, 18, 20, 163–165, 167–170, 173, 175–183, 186, 188
renminbi (RMB), 118, 145–147, 149–153, 155
Resilience and Sustainability Trust (RST), 121, 122

S

Safeguard and Accountability Mechanism, 105
sanction, 18, 95, 132, 133, 145, 149, 150, 152, 173, 203, 208–210, 213
secretariat, 9, 29, 33, 178–180, 203, 212
seigniorage, 116, 118, 133, 138, 155
sherpa, 33
Shultz, George, 29
Singapore, 14, 60, 66, 169–172, 179, 212
small and medium sized enterprise (SME), 97, 176, 183
South Asian Association for Regional Cooperation (SAARC), 97
"spaghetti bowl", 12, 177, 178, 181
special drawing rights (SDR), 16, 114, 115, 117–124, 126, 127, 137, 147
standard setting bodies (SSBs), 11, 18, 19, 199–207, 209–214
State Council, 147
state owned enterprises, 176
Stiglitz Commission, 114, 118, 122, 125, 126
substantive legitimacy, 34–36, 39
supranational currency, 115, 117
survey, 126, 177–179
Sustainable Development Goals, 98
SWIFT system, 132, 145, 149, 150

T

tariffs, 2, 3, 166, 170, 171, 176, 177, 187
theory of clubs, 10, 55
Trade and Technology Council (TTC), 172
trade war, 15, 66, 143, 145
Transatlantic Trade and Investment Partnership (TTIP), 7, 92, 170, 171, 183
Trans-Pacific Partnership (TPP), 7, 92, 170, 175, 182. *See also* Comprehensive and Progressive Agreement for Trans-Pacific Partnership (CPTPP)
Triffin Dilemma, 16, 29, 116–118, 127, 135, 136
troika, 40, 65, 95

Trump, Donald, 11, 30, 55, 66, 122, 124, 133, 143, 152, 170–172, 182, 188

U

"unhealthy" competition, 3, 15, 17, 50, 52, 66, 79, 80, 88, 162, 175, 188
United Nations Conference on Trade and Employment, 2
United Nations Monetary and Financial Conference, 1, 27
United Nations Security Council, 40
United States-Mexico-Canada Agreement (USMCA), 167

V

vaccine, 19, 34

W

Warwick Commission, 185
White Plan, 134
whole-process legitimacy, 14, 34, 39, 41, 43
World Bank (WB), 2, 4, 5, 10–12, 14, 15, 32, 34, 42, 49, 52, 54, 55, 67, 68, 72–80, 87–89, 91, 96, 105, 124, 135, 139, 142, 144, 162, 164–166, 175, 181, 198, 201, 202, 207, 208, 212, 214
World Finance Organization (WFO), 18, 19, 208–210
World Trade Organisation (WTO), 3–5, 7, 11, 12, 17, 18, 20, 32, 42, 49, 55, 163–166, 168, 169, 173, 175–188, 207–209
WTO-extra, 176, 183
WTO-plus, 176, 183

X

Xi, Jinping, 145, 173

Z

Zhou, Xiaochuan, 114, 117, 119, 122, 126, 132, 152

Kolibri 360 GmbH
Ferdinand-Jühlke-Straße 7
99095 Erfurt, Deutschland
produktsicherheit@kolibri360.de